THE WILDERNESS FAMILY

www.**booksattransworld**.co.uk

KOBIE KRÜGER

THE WILDERNESS FAMILY

Line drawings by Karin Krüger

BANTAM PRESS

LONDON · NEW YORK · TORONTO · SYDNEY · AUCKLAND

TRANSWORLD PUBLISHERS
61–63 Uxbridge Road, London W5 5SA
a division of The Random House Group Ltd

RANDOM HOUSE AUSTRALIA (PTY) LTD
20 Alfred Street, Milsons Point, Sydney
New South Wales 2061, Australia

RANDOM HOUSE NEW ZEALAND LTD
18 Poland Road, Glenfield, Auckland 10, New Zealand

RANDOM HOUSE SOUTH AFRICA (PTY) LTD
Endulini, 5a Jubilee Road, Parktown 2193, South Africa

Published 2001 by Bantam Press
a division of Transworld Publishers

First published in South Africa as
Mahlangeni (1994) and *All Things Wild and Wonderful* (1996)

Revised version, additional material and photographs © Kobie Krüger 2001
Line drawings © Karin Krüger 2001

The right of Kobie Krüger to be identified as the author of this work has been asserted in
accordance with sections 77 and 78 of the Copyright Designs and Patents Act 1988.

A catalogue record for this book is available from the British Library
ISBN 0593 046765

Set in 11½/13½pt Granjon by Falcon Oast Graphic Art

Printed in Great Britain by
Mackays of Chatham plc, Chatham, Kent

1 3 5 7 9 10 8 6 4 2

For Kobus and our daughters, with love

CONTENTS

Part 2
CROCODILE BRIDGE AND PRETORIUS KOP

KRUGER NATIONAL PARK

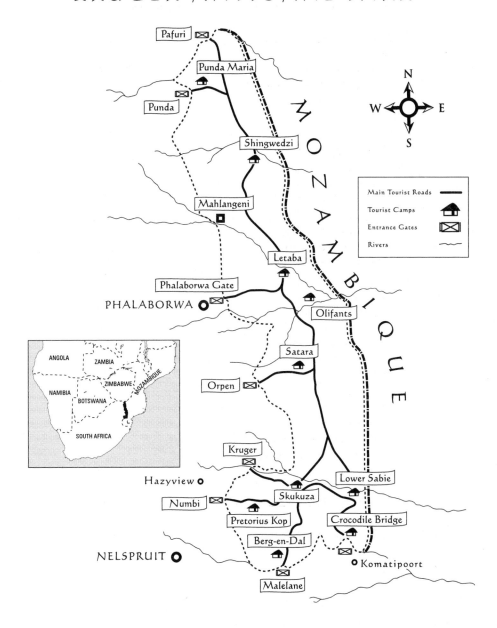

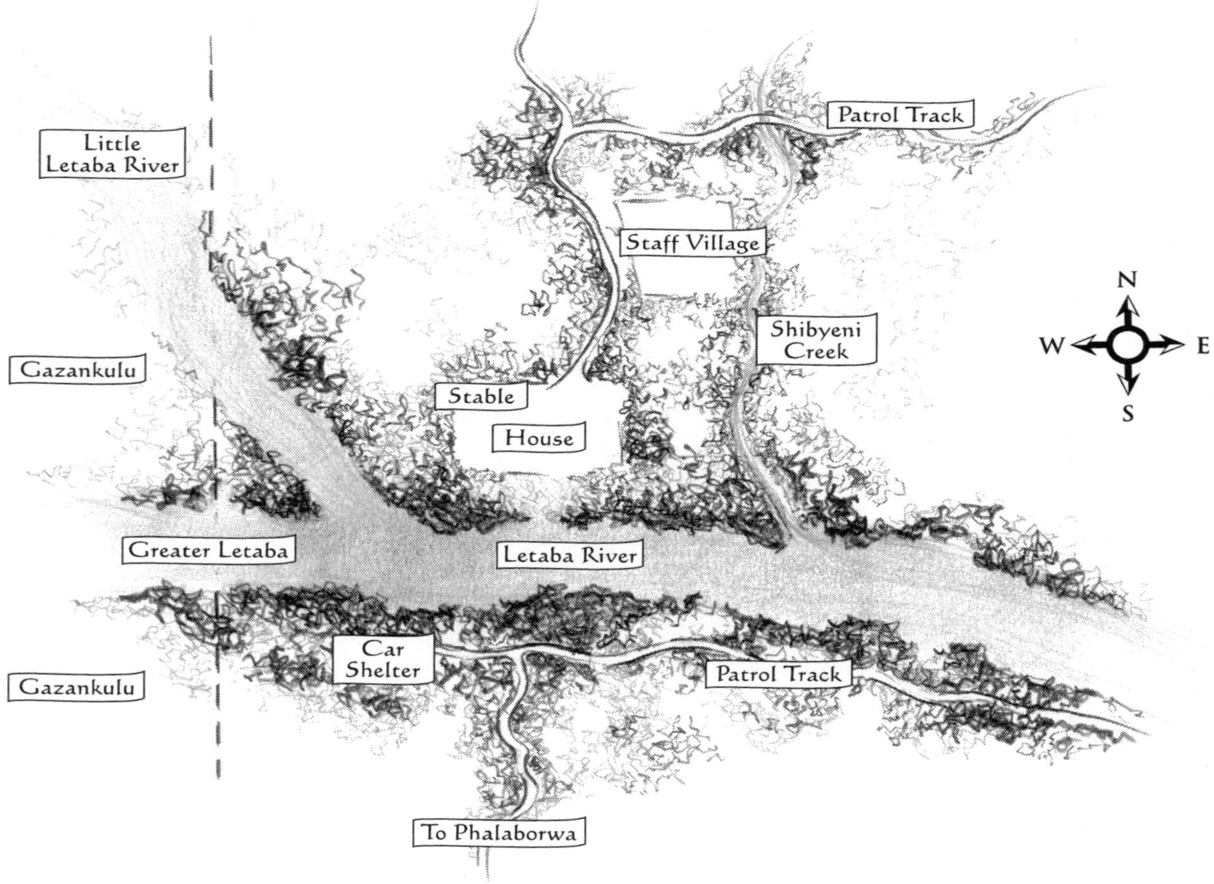

MAHLANGENI

Patrol Track

Shibyeni Creek

Staff Village

Stable

House

Letaba River

Patrol Track

To Phalaborwa

Car Shelter

Little Letaba River

Gazankulu

Greater Letaba

Gazankulu

PART 1

MAHLANGENI

A REMOTE MEETING PLACE

IN A FARAWAY CORNER OF THE NORTH-WEST REGION OF KRUGER
National Park, there is a heart-shaped basin of sand and forest where
two rivers meet. The Little Letaba enters the basin from the north, the
Greater Letaba from the west. They come together in a swirl of froth
and gurgling whirlpools, then settle down to continue sedately onwards
as one waterway, the Letaba River. Its gently moving waters are full of
hippo and crocodile, its sandy shores patterned with game tracks. On all
sides of the river basin, mopani woodlands roll away into a vast landscape of wilderness and solitude.

The area is called Mahlangeni, which is the Tsonga word for 'meeting place'.

One of the most isolated ranger sections in the park, Mahlangeni was
home to my game-ranger husband, our three daughters and me for
eleven years.

Our house on the north bank of the Letaba overlooked the merging
rivers and the forested basin. Squirrels and mongooses played in our garden. Bushbuck and monkeys were daily visitors. A lone leopard patrolled
the neighbourhood at night. Other neighbours included baboons, hippos,
elephants and lions. Throughout the years various strays and orphans
from the animal kingdom were temporary members of our family.

Our days were filled with magical moments and unforgettable
adventures.

HOW WE GOT THERE

KOBUS WAS BORN AND RAISED ON A BUSHVELD FARM IN THE Northern Province of South Africa. Since his early childhood he has loved the African bush and its creatures and wanted to protect them from destruction.

Although I was also born on a farm in the Northern Province, not far from where Kobus was born, we didn't meet until almost twenty years later when we were both studying at the University of Pretoria.

After discovering that we shared not just a first name (mine being the feminine version of his) but also a farm upbringing and a love of wild places, we became good friends. The first time we went out was to see the movie *Born Free* – the story of George and Joy Adamson and Elsa the lioness. It was the most beautiful movie either of us had ever seen, and afterwards Kobus confided to me that his dream was to become a game ranger. It occurred to me that my dream was to become a game ranger's wife.

We got married after we graduated.

Kobus applied for the position of game ranger with South African National Parks but learned there were no vacancies. So we went to live in Windhoek, the capital of Namibia, where Kobus worked as a journalist and I as a translator for three years, then moved to Johannesburg where we lived and worked for another six years before Kobus finally received a letter from the warden of Kruger National

Park, inviting him to Skukuza, the operational headquarters and largest of the park's tourist camps.

We read the letter a hundred times to make sure it wasn't a dream.

The letter also stipulated that 'the applicant's wife be present at the interview'. I wondered why, but lost no time in making arrangements for my mother to look after my three young children for a couple of days.

We arrived at Skukuza in the evening and spent the night in the tourist camp, hardly sleeping but listening to the enthralling sounds of the wilderness night.

In the morning we reported to the chief ranger's office for our interview. It was conducted by the chief ranger and the park warden. They looked stern and official. They asked Kobus why he had applied for the job, and why he would want to leave a good job in the city to work in the bush. Kobus answered simply that the bush made sense to him and that he had wanted to be a game ranger for as long as he could remember.

They seemed satisfied.

They then turned to me and gave me a lecture on the hardships and privations that a game ranger's wife could expect to endure. They warned me of the almost unbearable summer heat, the danger of malaria, the general hazards of the bush, the inconvenience of living far from doctors, schools, shopping centres and other amenities. They reminded me that not even basic services such as telephones and a regular mail delivery were available. They talked at length of the extreme loneliness that one might experience at a remote ranger station, telling me that a game ranger's work often took him away from base for long periods of time, leaving his wife home alone. How would I cope with that? 'Go home and think carefully about this,' they said. 'Give it at least a month. And if you both decide, without reservation, that you are still interested, let us know.'

Kobus and I went back home and talked daily about what life at the Mahlangeni ranger station would mean for us. My main concern was for my children. What if one of them became ill? Or was injured? Where would they go to school?

And yet . . . I so wished for my children to grow up in a time and place where pleasures would be simple, and experiences rich. Wouldn't the advantages of a wilderness childhood far outweigh the disadvantages?

I believed they would.

So Kobus and I confirmed our interest in the posting and, soon after, received the news that Kobus was hired.

Two months later, in the autumn of 1980, we had sold our house in the city, packed up our belongings and, together with our children, were on our way to a new life at this remote meeting place in the land of our dreams.

A DRAMATIC WELCOME

THE WARM AIR WAS THICK WITH THE EARTHY SMELLS OF THE riverine woods and full of the songs of a thousand birds. Splashes of afternoon sunlight played through the traceries of trees on a buttercup-yellow house. Tree squirrels peered down at us from the sprawling branches, twittering enquiringly, bushy tails at full mast. The whisper of small lives was everywhere.

Three blond-haired little girls, Hettie, aged eight, Sandra, seven, and Karin, two, skipped and danced among the trees, babbling and laughing.

'So where is this? Where are we now?' asked Karin.

'Our new home,' explained Sandra.

'. . . the magic faraway land,' sang Hettie, 'where the wee folks dance hand in hand.'

The buttercup-yellow house had an enormous kitchen, a comfortable living room that opened onto a broad veranda, three bedrooms and two bathrooms, all with large windows through which the fresh fragrance of the garden filled the house.

The garden was huge and half wild, a shady oasis of green lawns and indigenous trees and shrubs. The north side of the garden faced the mopani woods, the south side the rivers. Near the west fence, a little thatch-roofed guest cottage nestled among marula and bauhinia trees.

'And what's that?' asked Karin, pointing up at a sausage tree.

'A fruit bat,' replied Sandra.

'A tree fairy,' suggested Hettie. 'Tree fairies come disguised as fruit bats.'

'It's upside down,' remarked Karin.

'That's how fruit bats sleep,' explained Sandra, 'hanging upside down.'

'Tree fairies live in an upside-down world,' offered Hettie.

'Oh, wow!' sighed Karin happily.

In the south fence of the garden I found a gate. It opened onto a stone stairway that ran down the steep bank to the shore of the Letaba River.

I sat down on the top step.

Below me, the wooded bank gave way to a wide, sandy beach. A small rowing boat was moored near the edge of the water. Storks, herons and egrets surveyed the scenery from various perches along the shore. The river was calm and serene, its surface smooth and shiny. Some distance upstream, big rounded rocks showed above the water, the currents forming shimmering ripples around them. Abruptly one of the mounds reared up in a spray of droplets and gave a snort. A hippo head! Further upstream, to the west, the Little Letaba came into view from its northern origins and flowed into the Greater Letaba, the waters meeting and mixing in a foamy swirl. On all sides of the rivers, mopani woodlands rolled away to distant horizons under a crystal-blue sky. The whole riverine landscape seemed half asleep, drugged in the autumn sunshine, lost in a faraway dream . . .

It seemed to me that I was the one dreaming, and the landscape a figment of my imagination.

I got up and went to look for Kobus.

At the back of the house a small, square outbuilding crouched under a huge sycamore fig. I found Kobus inside, studying an array of maps. Some were spread on a desk in the centre of the room, others hung from the walls. Shelves full of books and files took up the rest of the wall space. A few chairs stood around the desk. On a shelf near the desk was a VHF radio transmitter.

'Ah!' I said, taking in the room. 'This must be the game ranger's office.' Then something clicked in my mind, and I added with wonderment, 'And *you* are the game ranger, aren't you?'

'It looks so to me too,' Kobus grinned.

I skipped round the table to get a big hug from my game-ranger husband.

The driver of our furniture truck had been given a detailed hand-drawn map of the area. Fortunately he managed to find the place, arriving just before dusk.

The truck had to be unloaded at top speed to avoid working in the dark. By nightfall the house was in chaos, with boxes, crates and bits of furniture all over the place. We managed, at least, to have our beds in position and found sheets and pillows for everyone in the midst of the confusion.

It had been a long day for us and we were exhausted. So, after a light supper of sandwiches and tea, it was early to bed.

Despite my exhaustion, it took me a while to fall asleep. And when I finally did, I was immediately woken by a strange sound.

'What's that?' I asked my slumbering game-ranger husband.

He slept on, unhearing.

I lay awake for a while, listening and thinking about this strange, dark house, a small haven amid the wilderness. Did I really hear something? Or was it merely my nervous imagination?

I started to doze off, but suddenly heard the sound again. This time I woke Kobus up. 'What's that?' I asked him.

'Hmm?'

'A funny noise. Didn't you hear it?'

'Hmm?'

I lay quietly, waiting for the sound to repeat itself. But it didn't.

Kobus drifted back to sleep.

After a time, I did too.

But again the mysterious sound woke me.

'Kobus! Did you hear that?'

'Huh?'

'That noise . . .'

An owl screeched outside.

Kobus mumbled, 'Owl.'

'No, not that! It was . . . a sort of . . . huffing noise.'

'Probably a leopard,' he muttered sleepily.

'Leopard?' I asked, alarmed. 'But it sounded as though it was right here in the bedroom!'

We remained silent for a while, listening. Down by the river a million frogs were croaking to high heaven. A hippo snorted. Far away, a hyena howled. Other strange sounds drifted through the night. But inside the house all seemed quiet.

Finally Kobus said, 'You're probably imagining things. Try to relax . . . get some sleep.'

'Yes, OK,' I said. It was probably my imagination, I decided. Evidently the peculiar silences of the strange house were troubling me in my sleep.

Finally I drifted off.

Before long, a small, distant voice penetrated the thick fog of my sleep. I woke up. One of the girls was calling me. She couldn't find her way to the bathroom in the dark. The electric generator wasn't running, so we couldn't switch on a light. I reached for the torch on my bedside cabinet and got up.

After helping my daughter, I returned to our room and something – perhaps a movement – caught my attention. I raised my torch towards it, and the slender beam picked out part of a huge, glossy, dark-blotched reptilian body. Wheeling the torch crazily, I illuminated the rest of the scene: the 'thing' had its tail section inside the half-open drawer of my bedside cabinet, its middle part coiled on top of the cabinet and the rest woven into the slats of the bed's headboard.

It was such a bizarre sight that it took me a while to realize what I was looking at.

'Kobus!' I gasped. 'Wake up!'

Prompted by my urgent tone, he woke immediately. 'What's wrong?'

'A huge snake . . . moving onto the bed!' I stammered.

Kobus leaped up like a bolt of lightning, entangled in a bedsheet. 'Stand back!' he ordered.

I didn't need to be told that. I'd already reversed into the opposite wall.

Disengaging himself from the sheet, Kobus groped his way towards me in the darkness. I handed him my torch. He shone it on the snake.

'It's a python,' he told me.

Frightened by the commotion in the room, it was recoiling into the safety of the drawer. As we stood watching it with horrified fascination, the sight of the half-open drawer sparked a memory. Earlier in the day, while furniture had been standing outside waiting to be carried in, I had walked past the bedside cabinet and noticed the drawer half open. I had been in a hurry and was carrying a big box, so I had pushed it shut with my foot with barely a glance. In all likelihood the python had been in the drawer already, and so got carried into the house.

The noises I had heard earlier in the night must have been the snake, huffing and puffing in its battle to push open the drawer and find its way out. My torch had been standing upright on the cabinet, probably right in the middle of the coiled-up body. It was lucky that my hand in the darkness had gone straight to the torch.

Using his rifle-cleaning rod, Kobus 'helped' the snake manoeuvre itself back into the drawer. It was a young python, only some two metres long – which is not very long for a python, but horribly long for a snake. Once the whole snake was finally back inside the drawer, Kobus pushed it shut and carried the cabinet outside into the garden. I accompanied him with my torch. Some distance away from the house Kobus put the cabinet down and carefully reopened the drawer. The python remained shyly inside. We left it alone there and went back to bed, allowing the snake to choose its own time to leave.

I thought this had been a rather dramatic welcome on our first night in our new home. But Kobus said this was the sort of thing that happened if one didn't respect the law of the wilds.

'What law?' I asked.

'Not to bother wild creatures.'

I pointed out to him that I hadn't bothered the snake. It had bothered me.

'You got him carried into the house,' he mumbled in a sleepy voice.

'I did *not*! How can you say that?'

He didn't respond. Probably he was already asleep. How could he fall asleep at the beginning of an important argument?

Poor me. I'd had hardly any sleep at all, and now the night was almost gone. Only through my wakeful vigilance had we escaped an unthinkable battle with a python in our bed. Wasn't I entitled to a little sympathy and gratitude?

We woke at dawn to find the world a glistening, silvery-green place full of exuberant noise. Hippos were bellowing, wild geese trumpeting, baboons barking, squirrels squealing, a thousand birds singing their hearts out.

Kobus brought me a cup of coffee in bed and so I forgave him all his faults.

Sitting up and sipping my coffee, I looked out through the glass sliding doors of our bedroom. And there, in the silvery-green world, was a small herd of elegant bushbuck grazing daintily along the river bank at the edge of the garden. It seemed to me that I was the most privileged person in the world to be greeted by such an exquisite sight early on an ordinary Monday morning.

After breakfast the game guards came over from the staff village to greet us – seven Tsonga-Shangana men, immaculately dressed in khaki uniform.

Kobus and I went outside to meet them.

The men saluted Kobus, but ignored me. (In their culture, to avoid looking at a stranger is a gesture of reverence.)

Kobus returned the salute. After exchanging the customary greetings, Kobus told them that I was his wife.

Still not looking at me, they waited in respectful silence.

I greeted them, saying, '*Awuxeni maphodisa. Minjani?*' 'The sun has risen, guards. How are you?' (In Africa, you always ask people how they are, even if they are strangers.)

Meeting my gaze, the guards replied, '*Eh-heeh! Awuxeni. Hikhona. Minjani?*' 'Indeed! The sun has risen! We are well. How are you?'

'*Hikhona. Ka hisa.*' 'I am well. It is hot today.' (It is good manners to comment on the weather. The accuracy of the comment is unimportant. What matters is to convey that you are keen to talk longer and that you are in no hurry to part company with the person you have just met, because in Africa to be in a hurry is in bad taste.)

'*Ah-heeh! Ka hisa ngopfu.*' 'Oh yes! It is very hot,' they agreed politely. (Actually it was a mild morning, but I didn't know the word for 'mild' in Tsonga.)

'*Inkomu.*' 'Thank you,' I said.

'*Inkomu,*' they replied.

The chief game guard, Corporal Manhique, then welcomed us to Mahlangeni with a cordial speech on behalf of himself and his colleagues. Afterwards we shook hands with the men and learned their names.

Then another man approached us. Dressed in a pair of green overalls, he was stockily built, his short hair greying and his eyes full of the wisdom of his years. He greeted us with a frank stare and a gruff manner. His name, he said, was Filemoni, and his job that of operator – operating the vegetable garden, storeroom, water pumps and electric generator. (Actually Filemoni was Mahlangeni's general caretaker, an efficient, versatile fellow and respected by all.)

Kobus and the game guards spent a while in the office, discussing the day's work, and afterwards left to do a patrol circuit of the area.

I spent the day unpacking.

The girls investigated the rustle and whisper of secret lives in the garden and discovered a whole community of fascinating creatures: thick-toed geckos with large, angelic eyes, tree agamas with Technicolor dreamcoats; coppery toads, ponderous chameleons, fat skinks, and pearly-coloured rain-frogs whose crystal calls sounded like wind-chimes tinkling in a breeze.

At noon we packed a picnic basket and carried it outside to a stone bench under an umbrella tree in the south-west corner of the garden. As we munched our sandwiches, enjoying the view of the rivers, there was a soft rustle in the grass behind us. Turning, we saw an enormous old tortoise, probably a hundred years old, lumbering heavily across the lawn towards us, its club feet stirring the dead autumn leaves. With an air of preoccupied determination it eventually passed within touching distance of us, neck stretched forward, bleary eyes full of ancient thoughts. We wondered where he could be heading, and why his awk-ward gait seemed so full of purpose. Perhaps he was, as Hettie suggested, late for an appointment with a very old friend.

A large herd of beautiful impala came to drink at the river, and we sat and watched them for a long time.

I got up reluctantly to go back indoors and finish my unpacking.

Throughout the warm autumn afternoon a procession of thirsty antelope visited the rivers to drink, and each time newcomers arrived, the girls called me outside to admire them.

In the late afternoon when shadows were lengthening across the shores, a lone elephant bull turned up to graze in the beds of reeds that lined the water. Kobus arrived home, and we sat outside in the garden to admire our majestic visitor. The sun sank into the Greater Letaba River, staining the water ruby red. Red deepened to purple, then paled to silver as the smoky-blue dusk enveloped the landscape. Nightjars started the evening serenade with bubbly songs.

The world of bustling cities was very far away.

From the woodlands beyond the house rose the whooping howl of a lone hyena. We sighed with contentment and went indoors to prepare our evening meal.

*

Later that night, long after we had gone to bed, Kobus woke me, saying, 'Listen! A leopard.'

'Outside?' I asked, alarmed. 'Or next to the bed?'

But then I heard the leopard too. And he was outside. Thank heavens.

PRINCE OF DARKNESS

W E OFTEN HEARD THE LEOPARD IN THE NIGHT. WHEN HE patrolled the neighbourhood we could picture him on his rounds by the rhythmic, rasping sounds approaching from Shibyeni Creek, later drifting down the river bank to the shore, and eventually returning up the bank. Often he would rove around the perimeters of our garden, and I would wonder whether he was looking for a way to get through the fence.

A sturdy three-metre-high fence surrounded our two-acre garden. I knew a leopard couldn't scale a fence that high. But still . . .

We had other nocturnal visitors, mostly harmless creatures who got into the garden by digging holes under the gates. I knew that leopards didn't do that. But still . . .

Kobus said it was romantic to have a leopard for a neighbour, and I agreed, but the idea worried me when I had to go out at night to switch off the generator. Usually Kobus did this, but when he was away from home it was my responsibility.

The generator room was about fifty metres from the house, against the northern fence line. If you know how pitch-black the nights in the bush can be, you'll understand how nervous I felt walking that distance from the house in the dark.

Lions once killed a waterbuck right against that northern fence and spent the whole night there, enjoying their meal. Fortunately Kobus

was home that night, and he went to switch off the generator. If he hadn't been home, I would probably have left the machine running until it ran out of diesel and blew up, or whatever generators do when they are left running.

Often, when I made my way to the generator room at night, I would jump with fright at a tiny movement or a mysterious sound, the distinct crack of a twig or a sinister shadow suddenly springing to life. Usually the sound or shadow would materialize into a honey badger, or a porcupine, and occasionally into an ant-bear or a civet – all of them shy, retiring creatures who wouldn't harm you unless you tried to harm them. Actually I loved having them as visitors, especially the honey badgers who made the sweetest crooning noises when they called out to one another. The porcupines had the irritating habit of digging up our bulbous plants and making a mess of the garden, but they were so delightful to watch when they made off, waddling on short, dumpy legs with pines bristling. My only problem with the nocturnal visitors was that they made my heart slam into my ears when they loomed up too suddenly from the dark while I was thinking of the leopard.

One night, about a month after we had moved in, I had a horrible shock on my way to the generator room.

Kobus was away and I had to go out to switch the machine off. Armed with my torch and mindful of the puff-adder I had found right in front of the generator room the previous evening, I lit the ground carefully as I walked. A puff-adder is a very poisonous snake. It's also a mean and lazy snake. It doesn't try to get out of your way, as other snakes do. It waits for you to step on it so that it has an excuse to bite you.

I picked my way cautiously, playing the slender beam of the torch over the ground and into the shadows of suspicious-looking vegetation. The beam startled a frog, and it leaped up and collided with my leg. Ugh.

Somewhere in the darkness a hyena howled ominously, reminding me that the night belonged to predators, and that primates should be safely up their trees (or in their houses).

In the last twenty-metre stretch the roar of the machine drowned out other sounds and dulled my senses, making it difficult to concentrate on my surroundings. The closer I got to the noise, the more vulnerable I felt. Finally I was only a few paces from the machine room, checking the ground carefully for signs of the puff-adder, my ears ringing with the roar of the machine.

And then it happened.

Something huge leaped on me from behind, almost knocking me to the ground. The torch flew from my hand, rolling some distance into the darkness. Fighting to regain my balance, I turned to try to get my arms between my attacker and myself. It pounced on me again, knocking me off balance once more – and started licking my face.

It was a dog.

Ours.

Another game ranger had given her to us only a few days previously. She was a fully grown ridgeback called Simba who had the habit of knocking people over in boisterous greeting.

I tried to say hello to her, but the chattering of my teeth obliterated my voice.

It took me a while to remember what I was doing outside in the darkness. I retrieved my torch and finally managed to switch off the generator.

As soon as my ears had adapted to the sudden silence, I heard the familiar rhythmic, rasping voice approaching from the direction of Shibyeni Creek.

Simba stiffened, ears straight up in the air, a growl rising in her throat.

'Hush, Simba!' I told her. 'Don't bark!'

She looked at me enquiringly.

'It's our neighbour,' I whispered. 'We haven't met yet, but I think he eats dogs.'

Simba understood, and we hurried quietly back to the house.

PARANOID HIPPOS

OUR NEAREST TOWN WAS PHALABORWA, AN ISOLATED MINING settlement some fifty kilometres to the south of the river.

To get to town we had first to row across the river – much to the annoyance of the hippos – then climb the footpath to the top of the bank where we parked our 'town car' in a shelter under the jackalberry trees.

As soon as we launched the boat the hippos would start grunting, bellowing and swearing at us. And they would plunge and splash about, dive and surface, and raise their gaping jaws in our direction, displaying their huge tusks in a bid to intimidate us.

Hippos are territorial animals and so bull hippos will defend their territories against interlopers. Evidently a bull hippo perceives a boat as an intruder with dubious designs on the resident lady hippos.

Being herbivores, hippos have to leave the water to graze. Since they regard the water as their safety zone they are even more paranoid on land. When a hippo is disturbed while feeding he will charge back to the security of his aquatic haven, demolishing any obstacles, including live ones, on the way. Fortunately hippos prefer to dine at night, and so they seldom leave the water during the day.

At first the local hippos intimidated us with their dramatic threats. But since they never carried out any of the threats, we became so used to their sabre-rattling that we stopped worrying about them. The hippos, in turn, seemed satisfied that their displays adequately cowed the boat and therefore didn't deem it necessary to obliterate it. And so we gradually learned to ignore their threats and became almost nonchalant about them.

But one day, one of the bulls decided sabre-rattling wasn't enough.

The girls and I were rowing across the water when the hippo came right up to our boat and bumped it so hard that we spun around almost full circle. We hadn't even seen him coming. He must have sneaked up on us from behind.

That evening, when I told Kobus about the incident, he insisted that from then on I should always carry a firearm when making the crossing. I wasn't too happy with the idea. I didn't feel comfortable with a gun. But Kobus reminded me that hippos could be dangerous animals and that we shouldn't take their threats too lightly. If that bull hippo became too resentful of our intrusions into his territory, he might attack the boat, or capsize it and then attack us in the water.

Kobus's lecture scared me, and I decided that a gun was something I was going to have to get used to. The trouble with a gun, as Kobus often reminds me, is that most of the time you don't really need it, but when you do need it, you don't need it just a little – you need it desperately.

Kobus also insisted that, whenever he was away, I recruit Filemoni as our oarsman so that I would be free to concentrate on the behaviour of the hippos and to fire the gun if necessary.

Although Filemoni was short and stocky of build, he was amazingly strong, and I discovered that he was able to row us across the water in almost half the time it usually took me. Actually that wasn't as helpful as it may sound. He was a powerful rower, but not a good one. He jerked the oars with short, irregular strokes, causing the boat to leap, plunge, bounce and bump over the water, instead of gliding through it as a boat should. And we got sprayed with water every time he brought the oars up. Usually we were soaked by the time we reached the far bank. But we didn't complain. Filemoni was a fellow whose no-nonsense manner commanded respect. And anyway, he was the most bush-wise person we knew.

At the end of our first autumn at Mahlangeni, we enrolled Hettie and Sandra in school at Phalaborwa. During the week they stayed at the park's private hostel near Phalaborwa Gate, about seven kilometres from town. (This hostel was run by Kruger Park personnel exclusively for the children of Kruger Park families who lived far from town.) Early each Monday morning I drove my daughters to the hostel, and collected them again on Friday afternoons.

After the hippo bull had bumped our boat that first time, the girls and I acquired the habit of scanning the water attentively every time we rowed across. And whenever we spotted a V-shaped ripple coming towards us across the water, we knew it was that mad old bull, on his way to bump our boat again. That was my cue to cock the gun and fire a shot into the water between the boat and the approaching hippo. Luckily, the hippo always retreated and swam back to the herd when I fired.

But there were several times when we didn't sight the approaching ripple and were badly shaken when the hippo bumped the boat. Another unnerving trick of his was to sneak unnoticed right up to the boat, and then suddenly explode from the water alongside us.

After a period of repeated encounters with the bad-tempered hippo, during which I'd fired into the water close to him on several occasions, the hippo backed off for a while, leading me to believe that he'd finally admitted defeat.

But one day, a couple of weeks later, he proved me wrong.

Our whole family was in the boat, chatting away and not taking much notice of the hippos. Karin, who was four years old at the time, was trailing a thin reed alongside the boat as we rowed. Suddenly, with a deafening roar, the mad hippo exploded from the water right next to the boat, his mouth open so wide it seemed he would swallow us all. Karin tumbled backwards off her seat into the bottom of the boat. Trembling with shock, I reached over to help her, but she climbed back onto her seat without any help, looking merely indignant, muttering, 'Heavens! Why can't he behave?'

Meanwhile, the hippo had disappeared. We were still wondering

where he had gone when a sudden, hard thump from underneath the boat caused it to heave and keel dangerously. Fortunately we were all holding on at the moment of impact, and so no-one was thrown overboard.

But Kobus decided that the hippo had sealed his own fate and that deportation papers were in order. He was on his way to Skukuza for the annual aerial census and couldn't arrange the deportation right away, but promised that he'd do so as soon as he returned.

The following day a pair of national servicemen from a military base in Gazankulu were sent to Mahlangeni by their commanding officer to deliver a message to Kobus. Kobus was still at Skukuza, of course, and I was busy inside the house and didn't notice their vehicle arriving on the far bank. Filemoni, however, did and promptly rowed over to collect the young men.

I was not aware of their arrival until they appeared at the front door. I invited them in for coffee, and learned that they were city boys posted to Gazankulu for their military training, feeling quite out of their depth in the wild. As they were preparing to leave, I thought of the mad hippo and suggested that they make their way down to the shore while I fetched a firearm. Neither of them was armed and, besides, they wouldn't know what to do if the hippo attacked.

It took me a while to find the keys to the gun safe, and to open it and select a gun. Remembering the dramatic events of the previous day, I decided to take one of the bigger rifles. Having checked that it was loaded, I went outside – and saw to my dismay that the soldiers were already in the boat and on the water, with Filemoni at the oars. Either they or Filemoni hadn't understood that I'd intended to accompany them in the boat. I hurried through the garden, out the front gate, down the stone stairway and across the shore, all the while scanning the water. By the time I reached the water's edge, the boat was already almost half-way across the river. And then I saw it: that telltale V-shaped ripple on the water, coming downstream and heading directly towards the boat.

I raised the rifle and took aim at a point between the ripple and the boat, but felt too scared to pull the trigger. I had never fired over such a distance – about eighty metres – and was terrified of hitting one of the occupants of the boat. If I moved my aim I would risk hitting the hippo.

Suddenly the hippo surfaced and made a wild lunge for the boat – a thing I had never seen him do before. Filemoni yelled at the hippo and doubled his rowing speed. The hippo followed with grim determination, seemingly intent on annihilating the boat once and for all. I raised the rifle and again took careful aim at a point between the hippo and the boat, but before I could squeeze the trigger, the hippo's head appeared in the sights. I started trembling and couldn't steady my aim. Filemoni rowed furiously, but still the hippo followed. As I moved my aim to keep it ahead of the hippo's nose the bead of the foresight quivered crazily and I wondered how it was possible to steady an aim if you had to keep moving it. The hippo lifted his head to check the distance before hurling himself onto the boat. I stopped breathing, and the bead finally settled into the foresight. There was no time to yell at Filemoni and the soldiers to duck before I squeezed the trigger. As the air exploded, silencing the cicadas and the birds, the recoil punched me so hard in the shoulder that I almost sat down on the ground. A fountain of water erupted right in front of the hippo's open mouth, soaking the occupants of the boat. The hippo reared his massive head, slammed his mouth shut and submerged. I quickly reloaded and scanned the water, trying to find some clue as to where the hippo had gone. A few seconds later I spotted the V-shaped ripple a good distance away from the boat, heading back upstream towards the rest of the herd.

I sat down in the sand. My legs had turned to jelly.

Poor soldiers. They had probably been as scared of me and my rifle as they had been of the warmongering hippo.

They reached the far bank safely and turned to wave at me as they disembarked. I returned the greeting and remained sitting in the sand until their truck had disappeared over the bank.

Then I waited until Filemoni was safely back. We walked across the stretch of sand together and climbed up the stone stairs. We didn't talk. Filemoni was not much of a talker. He was more of a grunter. So he grunted. And I groaned in reply. And we both knew it had been a pretty close shave that day.

A few days later Kobus returned from Skukuza and immediately put the deportation orders into action. He rowed out towards the mad hippo, who was easily recognized by a notch in one of his ears. And while the hippo was still wondering to what he owed the visit, Kobus stood up in the boat and fired several shots from his .375 Magnum into the water close to the animal. As the thunderclaps echoed across the landscape, fountains erupted from the surface of the water on all sides of the hippo.

The mad hippo got the message and lost no time in deciding to emigrate. He made his way north up the Little Letaba River and must have found himself a more peaceful home elsewhere because we never saw him again. The rest of the herd also took note and behaved themselves for quite a while afterwards.

TROUBLES ON A LONELY TRACK

CROSSING THE RIVER WAS NOT THE ONLY DIFFICULT THING ABOUT getting to town. Once across the river, the road itself was a narrow, winding track, leading through steep dongas and dense mopani thickets. No other vehicles used the road because it led nowhere else. It was our own private road, exclusively linking Phalaborwa Gate and Mahlangeni. A lot of things could happen along the way. And if your vehicle broke down en route, you had two choices: fix it yourself or walk the rest of the way.

On Monday mornings when I took the girls to the school hostel we had to leave in the earliest dawn. A private bus collected the Kruger Park children from their hostel and took them to their schools in town. If we were delayed on the road and arrived too late for the bus, I had to drive the girls to school myself and explain to the school principal why we were late.

When the road was dry and in fairly good condition, our journey took just over an hour – unless there were delays, which there often were. Sometimes a herd of buffalo or elephant would take their own sweet time to cross the road, or just stand in the road with no intention of going anywhere. A certain bull elephant would often wait for us near Shimangu Creek, blocking the road and forcing us to reverse several hundred metres down the track, proclaiming his ownership of the road. From time to time elephants would fell a tree across the track. This would mean a really huge delay, as we would have to go home to collect an axe and Kobus – or, if he was not available, Filemoni – to help chop up the tree and get it out of the way.

Impalas running along in front of the car were a regular hazard. Impalas on the road always froze at the very sight of us and remained immobile until we were only metres away from them. Then they took off, straight down the road away from us, leaping zigzag-fashion from one side of the track to the other. To try to squeeze past a herd of high-bouncing impalas on a narrow track in dense bushlands is not a good idea. So we would stop and wait. But when we stopped, they stopped. When we moved on, so did they, doggedly sticking to the track again, completely forgetting about the vast expanses of safe woods on either side of it. Often the only thing for us to do was to stop, switch off the engine and wait . . . and wait, until even the impalas became so bored that they would unthinkingly stroll off into the bush.

Sometimes we got a flat tyre on the road, but with the girls' assistance it usually didn't take long to change a wheel.

Our real troubles came with the wet season. The rains often eroded the surface of the road so badly that, even with my jeep's four-wheel drive engaged, we literally slip-slithered our way along, occasionally skidding off the track into the bush, or spinning around and travelling some distance in the wrong direction. Once when I lost control of my jeep, it almost completed a figure of eight before ending up in a muddy ditch at the side of the track. I was alone, having already dropped the children off at school, and getting out of that ditch without help wasn't easy. I dragged logs, branches and other bush debris into the ditch and packed it all under and in front of the car's wheels until I had more or less built a track leading out of the ditch. The 'track' collapsed several times until I was on the point of giving up in tears and abandoning the car. But contemplation of the fifteen-kilometre walk home added a lot of determination to my efforts.

Seasonal watercourses that remained dry most of the year would suddenly fill up with fast-moving torrents of water after a downpour.

Often we had to stop at flooded creeks and wade barefoot into them to gauge the depth of the water. If driving through didn't seem safe, we would return home and wait for the flow to subside.

When the bush becomes verdant and dense, as happens in the rainy season, you have to drive carefully as you can't see into the thickets on either side of a narrow track. Animals often come dashing out of the bush, right in front of the car. Bends must also be negotiated slowly. If you speed round a curve and find that something huge and grey is suddenly obscuring your view, watch out – that's an elephant, and you're in big trouble.

Once, on a Saturday morning, as Hettie and I were returning from town, a kudu leaped out of the bush at Tsugama Creek where the road wound downhill around a bend. Swerving to avoid the large antelope, I lost control of the jeep and it rolled, landing on its roof. Fortunately neither of us was injured and we climbed out through the shattered windscreen. I was so relieved that we were intact that I decided not even to think about the jeep lying on its roof in the creek until we were safely home and drinking a cup of sweet, strong tea. Tsugama Creek was only about five kilometres from home – a walk of less than forty minutes – but I had forgotten to take my gun along that day and so it was a little daunting walking through the bush, unarmed and without dogs. Luckily, the only animals we encountered along the way were warthogs, monkeys and a trio of giraffe who stood in a clump of trees alongside the road and peered down at us with puzzled expressions. Hettie said that walking home was a wonderful experience and that we should do it more often.

Early the following morning, Kobus and the game guards went to retrieve my jeep from the creek and found that hyenas had chewed up two of the tyres in the night.

For many years I used to think that, since I was making the ninety-kilometre round trip to the hostel and back almost every Monday and Friday, I would eventually learn to do it with skill and confidence. But my confidence never grew. The more I travelled on that lonely track, the more I became aware of all the disasters that could occur.

During our fourth autumn at Mahlangeni, on a Friday afternoon as we were returning from the hostel, the jeep's engine suddenly died on us and no amount of trying would get it going again. I peered under the bonnet and tried to remember the things Kobus had taught me about a car's engine. But nothing came to mind. Then I remembered my sister's philosophy: 'If all else fails, read the instructions.' I got out the instruction manual and started reading. (Actually I think her philosophy refers only to household appliances.) Anyway, I read the instruction manual from cover to cover but it didn't tell me what was wrong with my car. I gave up. We were well and truly stranded, twenty kilometres from home.

Kobus was away in the eastern border area and wasn't expected back for at least another week. Filemoni had taken a few days' leave to visit his wives at his tribal village in Gazankulu. No-one else would know to come looking for us. We would have to walk.

I looked at my watch. It was almost four o'clock – we wouldn't finish the journey before dark. At dusk the predators would start their nocturnal activities, and all good primates would return to the safety of their trees. I didn't want to spend the night up a tree, so I suggested that we should stay where we were, spend the night in the jeep, and tackle the walk first thing in the morning. Hettie and Sandra (then aged eleven and ten) reckoned that we would be able to make it home before dark if we jogged all the way. I reminded them that Karin was only five years old and couldn't be expected to jog twenty kilometres. (Well, neither could I.)

It was settled. We would spend the night in the car and walk home the next morning.

It was hot in the car, so we made ourselves comfortable under a mopani tree next to the road and drew pictures in the sand. Our water bottle was already half drained, but luckily we had some oranges in the car. The girls told me that we could also chew mopani leaves if the thirst got too bad.

We drew and played pebble games in the sand, and I tried not to worry too much about our long walk the next morning. I thought of the lone rhino bull that we often saw grazing in the marshy area of Nhlarweni, and of the leopard we had recently spotted at Shimangu Creek. I thought of the lions that frequented the area, and of the elephant herds that could be anywhere, any time. Well, I had a power-ful 9mm-parabellum pistol with me. But you don't shoot at a rhino or an elephant with a pistol. Actually you don't shoot at a buffalo or a lion with a pistol either. The best thing to do is to make sure they don't notice you. If they do, you must take care not to bother them. If they think you're bothering them anyway, well, then you're in trouble. Depending on what kind of animal thinks you're bothering him, you either stand your ground or run away. You don't run away from big cats, for instance. They are faster than you. You stand your ground, look confident and try to communicate your friendly intentions to them with your body language. If they don't believe you, then you will have to put on a really ferocious act – a fierce, unflinching look straight in the eyes, a slowly raised chunk of wood and a blood-curdling yell. The trouble is that your body language has to be sincere, because if it isn't, the animal will know. What I don't understand is how you get your body language to express sincere friendliness or ferociousness while you're frightened to death. Probably it takes a lot of practice.

You don't stand your ground against angry rhino or buffalo, of course. Once they're in the act of charging you, they don't stop to read body language. So you run. But since they are much faster than you are, your only chance of survival is to outwit them. Fortunately both buffalo and rhino are myopic and will run right past you if they lose sight of you. So, while running as fast as you can, get ready for a disappearing act. Dive into a thicket, a donga (gully) or a burrow, or scramble up the nearest climbable tree – but don't waste any time about it.

While I was reviewing my bush wisdom and playing pebble games in the sand with the girls, a faint sound suddenly caught our attention. We looked up, straining our ears to identify and locate it.

It was the low, distant rumble of a heavy vehicle approaching from the north. But it wasn't on our road; it was on the firebreak that ran alongside the boundary fence in Gazankulu. I told Karin to sound the jeep's hooter, and the two older girls and I took off through the dense tangles of mopani scrub, sprinting four hundred metres to the fence as fast as we could. By the time we reached it, we were out of breath, badly scratched and, worst of all, too late. The truck was well past us.

I told myself that if one vehicle had come along the firebreak, another could. So I accompanied Hettie and Sandra back to Karin and collected my pistol. Cautioning the girls to stay close to the jeep, I hurried back to the fence and sat down under a bushwillow tree to wait.

A flock of red-billed hoopoes in the branches above startled me with an outburst of hysterical cackling. When they finally shut up, the only sound that came from the silent bush was the repetitive, monotonous calling of a bush shrike.

After about half an hour I was as bored and lonely as the bush shrike and longed for the company of my daughters. I no longer felt so sure that another vehicle would appear, and decided to go back to the jeep. But as I got up, a brilliant idea suddenly came to me: I would build an obstacle across the road.

I climbed through the high fence into Gazankulu, ripping my clothes in the process. Then I started hauling logs and branches out of the bush and piling them on the road. It's surprising how many logs and branches are needed to construct a barricade large enough to stop a big truck, even on a narrow track. My exertions left me saturated with perspiration and covered in a fine red dust, and my shadow on the ground showed that my hair was looking wild. On either side of the barrier I scraped the word HELP with big arrows pointing towards the fence.

I stood back to admire my handiwork before making my way back into the park to my daughters. And then, to my surprise, I heard a distant hum approaching from the north. I waited and listened, hardly breathing in case I missed some important clue. It was definitely another vehicle, coming my way along the firebreak. But it didn't sound like an army truck. The drone wasn't deep enough. That baffled me a bit, because the only vehicles that ever used this track were army vehicles.

The drone increased steadily, and eventually a dilapidated old pick-up truck came into view. When the driver saw me, he abruptly slammed on his brakes. He looked as though he was going to turn round and drive away. I frantically waved my arms, called out and beckoned him to please come back. Apparently the sight of me had scared him out of his wits. I guess you couldn't blame him. He wouldn't have expected to find a woman out alone in the bush with wild hair, torn clothes and wearing a pistol.

Hesitantly, he drove to where I was standing. The driver was a youngish man who looked alarmed and spoke only Portuguese. His passenger, a Shangaan man, looked just as alarmed as the driver and spoke only Tsonga. In a mixture of Afrikaans, English and Tsonga I explained that my car had broken down inside the park. I could see in their eyes that they understood what I was saying, but didn't want to be troubled.

I told the driver I would be really grateful if he would take a message to Phalaborwa Gate for me; after all, he was heading in that direction and would pass quite close to the gate before turning onto the tarred road. He looked worried and definitely annoyed. I was puzzled, but explained that I had my children in the car, and that we were thirsty and far from home. Eventually he agreed to help. I asked if he had something for me to write on. He found a blunt pencil and a scrap of dirty paper in the truck. I wrote a short message to the gate official, Desmond Wilcox: *'Please help. Stranded approximately 25 kilometres north of gate on Mahlangeni road. Kobie and kids.'*

I handed the note to the driver. He stuffed it into his shirt pocket and stared suspiciously at the barricade in front of him. I walked over and began dismantling the structure, heaving logs and branches out of the way and hoping the two men would lend a hand. But they didn't.

Once I'd cleared sufficient space for them to get through, they drove on without another word. It was only then, as the pick-up moved past me, that I noticed the large, bloodstained tarpaulin across the back. The men were poachers. No wonder they had seemed so wary of me – and my pistol and my roadblock.

I went through the fence again and back to my daughters. When I told them about the two poachers, they doubted as much as I did that my note would be delivered. If the park officials at the gate spotted the bloodstained tarpaulin on the back of the pick-up, they would investigate further, and if there was an antelope beneath the tarpaulin, as I believed there was, the poachers would be apprehended.

We resigned ourselves to a night in the jeep.

It was by then late afternoon, and splashes of silver light streaked the savannah grass as the sky turned a deeper, darker blue. We sat under our mopani tree and talked about past adventures and special memories. A family of warthogs and a herd of impala crossed the road only a few metres from us. We sat very still, hoping that our presence wouldn't alarm them. They remained unaware of us, and it was delightful to watch them ambling by so peacefully.

From the distant hills to the east came the eerie, hooting calls of wild dogs. A pair of red-eyed doves in a nearby tree gurgled a sweet song, and occasionally zebras barked from the far bank of the gully behind us.

Sandra suggested that we build a small fire in the road as soon as dusk settled in, just for the fun of it. A fire always looked so cosy in the bush. I agreed that it was a great idea.

A lone elephant bull startled us when he silently emerged from the mopani bush a short distance away. We rose quickly and made our way quietly back to the car and got inside. The elephant tore a branch off a mopani tree and loaded some foliage into his mouth. Then he stood chewing and thinking for a while before moving on.

When we got out of the car again, we decided to begin gathering twigs and wood for our campfire.

I had just started breaking some small dead branches from a fallen tree when a distant sound attracted my attention, and I looked up.

Immediately the girls also halted their activities and looked up with alert expressions.

It was a faint hum, far away to the south. Was it only the wind?

Gradually the hum became a rumble. It wasn't the wind. We waited and listened.

Occasionally the drone grew fainter and disappeared for a while. But we knew it was because of the dips in the landscape, coupled with the direction of the wind. Finally, the pitch changed completely as the vehicle turned into the nearby gully. A few seconds later it climbed out of the gully, and then we saw it: a Parks Board Land-Rover, approaching us on the winding track. It was a wonderful sight.

The driver was Robert van Lente, a Parks Board road engineer who lived near Phalaborwa Gate. The gate official had sent him a message: *'Kobie and kids in trouble, 25 kilometres on Mahlangeni road. Need help! URGENT!'*

Poor Robert. He had actually been worried that he might not find us alive.

We untied the girls' hostel luggage from the jeep's roof-carrier and loaded it into Robert's Land-Rover. And then we were, at last, on our way home.

When we arrived at the river, dusk had already settled, but the magenta sky above the western horizon still shimmered on the water, enabling us to keep an eye on the hippos as we rowed over. As soon as we'd beached, we looked across the water and saw Robert's silhouette on the far bank where he had waited to see us safely home. We waved before he disappeared into his car and drove off.

Later, while the girls and I were preparing our evening meal – a mixed salad of home-grown vegetables, with home-baked bread; fried, home-caught fish, and home-grown strawberries with tinned cream for dessert – we agreed that it was really good to be home again, and that we owed a debt of gratitude to the poachers who had, after all, been good enough to deliver my note to the gate official.

*

For many years I had this recurring dream: my car breaks down and I have to walk home. I encounter a pride of lions on the way and try to sneak past them without being noticed. But they always notice me. So I have to stand my ground and rely on my body language to communicate my sincere friendliness to them.

It was really a nightmare.

BEWARE OF ELEPHANTS

A LONE ELEPHANT BULL OFTEN USED TO GRAZE ON THE SHORE IN front of the house. Every once in a while, when we wanted to row across the river, we would have to wait patiently for him to graze his way past the spot where the boat was moored.

One Saturday morning, when Kobus and the girls wanted to go to town to attend a school athletics meeting, the elephant was grazing in the reeds right next to the boat again, and it was obvious that he was in no hurry to leave. So my family sat down on the top step of the stone stairway and waited.

And waited . . .

Finally the elephant started moving on, ambling off along the shore in a westerly direction. Kobus and the girls made their way down to the boat while I waited at the top of the stairs to wave them goodbye.

From the bottom of the stairway to the boat's mooring place was a walk of about sixty metres. As my family moved on across the sand, the elephant continued quietly on his way, seemingly unaware of the small party of humans approaching the boat behind his back. The whole scene was utterly tranquil. A family of Egyptian geese grazed along the water's edge. Herons, darters and egrets calmly surveyed the river from their various perches along the shore. The hippos were peaceful and lazy. By the time Kobus and the girls reached the boat, the elephant was quite far away.

Then, suddenly, the quiet scene exploded.

For no apparent reason, the elephant had spun around, trumpeting and screaming with fury. Now he came thundering across the shore like a runaway train – heading straight for Kobus and the girls.

Kobus unslung his rifle, released the safety catch and took aim. The two older girls, Hettie and Sandra, started to run but immediately remembered a rule of the wilds: when there is danger, stay with the person who is armed. They skidded to a halt, turned and stood courageously, facing the charging elephant.

But Karin panicked – she was only five years old – and though she knew the rules as well as her sisters did, the sight of the screaming giant must have filled her with such terror that her instincts commanded her to flee. And so she fled.

I looked on helplessly as she sprinted across the sixty-metre stretch of open sand towards the stairway. My instincts told me to run to her, but I dared not for fear of drawing the elephant's attention to a vulnerable little girl, separated from the protection of her father's rifle.

Kobus, Hettie and Sandra stood dead still as the mad beast bore down on them. Kobus had his finger on the trigger. Having waited until the last possible moment before firing, he was about to squeeze the trigger when, suddenly and surprisingly, the elephant came to a dramatic stop, a fountain of sand and pebbles flying up from the ground at his feet as he slammed on the brakes. He stood for a moment, staring at them disdainfully with myopic eyes. Then he tossed his massive head and, with one last ear-splitting trumpet, turned and walked away.

By this time Karin had reached the stairway and was sprinting up the stairs towards me. I met her halfway down and hugged her to me. She was shaking and panting for breath, but said only, 'He ... he almost gave me a fright!'

Together we walked across the shore to meet up with her father and sisters. And as we all stood and watched the elephant walking away into the distance, we wondered what had caused his frightful tantrum. Perhaps he didn't like people sneaking to their boat behind his back. Or perhaps he was, as Hettie suggested, a little batty.

Unfortunately, this was not to be our last encounter with the batty old elephant.

In the late afternoon of the following day, we saw him grazing on the bank of the Little Letaba River. Unlike the Greater Letaba, which is a perennial river, the Little Letaba is essentially a seasonal river in which only a few stream-linked pools remain in the dry season. We often saw buffalo, elephant and other game cross the Little Letaba in the dry season to graze on the far bank. Sometimes, when the animals got the idea that the grass was greener on the other side of the boundary fence, they would try to break through it to dine in Gazankulu.

Whenever Kobus saw animals heading towards the fence, he went after them to herd them back to our side of the river. As game ranger, he had to do this to prevent them from becoming trophies for hunters in the unprotected areas outside the reserve.

The batty elephant continued to graze on the bank of the Little Letaba for a while and then walked across the dry riverbed to the opposite bank. Kobus kept a watchful eye on him, and when it became apparent that the elephant was on his way to the boundary fence, Kobus went after him.

Generally a ranger persuades an elephant to turn away from the fence by clapping his hands and shouting until the animal gets the message. In the case of an obstinate animal, the ranger might fire a number of shots into the air.

But when Kobus walked up to the elephant that day, the grumpy old giant was in no mood for discussion and promptly charged. Kobus ran and hid behind a tree, but the elephant came looking for him. As the massive grey beast crashed through the bush towards him, Kobus abandoned his cover and sprinted towards the bank of the Little Letaba. The elephant followed at great speed, ears flat against his skull, trunk tucked under his chest, silent and deadly serious. The only sound following Kobus was that of big clumps of earth and bush debris exploding underneath the elephant's feet.

Kobus reached the bank of the Little Letaba and rushed headlong down it through the tangled vegetation, reasoning that the elephant wouldn't follow him down the steep slope. But to his surprise, the elephant came crashing down the bank after him. When Kobus's feet hit the soft, thick sand of the dry riverbed, he realized that he could never outpace the elephant.

Turning, he fired a warning shot into the ground just to the right of the elephant's feet. The riverbed seemed to explode as the thunderclap reverberated through the air, but the elephant didn't miss a step. He was now less than fifteen metres away. Time was up. Kobus aimed for a frontal brain shot and fired. But the massive head tossed, the bullet missed, and the elephant kept coming. Kobus had only one bullet left. His reflexes took over and he fired again. He neither heard the whiplash of the shot nor felt the slamming recoil; his eyes were riveted on the enormous forehead, now almost upon him. The elephant stopped suddenly. His hind legs buckled and he went down in slow motion. His huge bulk struck the earth with a hollow sound.

Kobus stood motionless for a while. Then he walked up to the elephant. Nine paces separated them. Nine human paces equal about two steps for an elephant.

Hettie, who had been sitting in the garden reading at the time, had jumped up at the crack of the first shot and run to the fence. She saw her father standing on the riverbed of the Little Letaba with the elephant bearing down on him, and she saw him fire the second shot, and then the third and fatal shot. When she saw the elephant go down only a few paces from her father she fled indoors.

I was busy inside the house when I heard the shots. I ran outside and met Hettie on her way in. I stopped to ask her what had happened, but she was too shocked to talk and could only point towards the western fence of the garden.

Reaching the fence I looked down and saw the elephant lying in the sand of the Little Letaba, with Kobus standing quietly next to him. I knew how terrible he felt, and my heart went out to him. Only fear for his own life would allow him to slay one of the wild creatures he loved so much.

Elephants are wonderful beings. Intelligent, sensitive and gentle, they can also be playful and imaginative. The calves are tenderly nursed, protected, instructed and reared to maturity by the breeding herd. The elephant herd is a complex family group characterized by a highly developed social structure and the deep bond that links its members.

Although elephants are generally known to be easygoing and tolerant, there are of course exceptions to the rule, and a grumpy elephant is certainly something to be avoided – that is, if you can get away fast enough. If he's determined to get you, you're really in trouble.

Another good rule to remember on finding yourself in the company of elephants is to stay well away from the calves. If a cow suspects you of bothering her calf she will throw a tantrum that might frighten you to death.

Some elephants don't like cars. I have often, on rounding a bend, found myself nose to nose with an elephant in the road. And even though I am always very quick at backing away humbly, the elephant will almost invariably force me to reverse several hundred metres down the road before he is satisfied that my car and I have acknowledged his superiority.

Our chief ranger, Dirk Ackerman, says that when an elephant stops a vehicle by blocking its path and forcing it to reverse, he's only looking for company and someone to play with.

I'm not so sure about that.

And even if it's true, I don't want to play with an elephant.

I'm too small.

FOSTERING A HONEY BADGER

ONE DAY, WHEN KOBUS WAS PATROLLING THE NORTHERN REGION OF his section, he came across a pathetic little bundle huddled underneath a sickle-bush. It was an abandoned, injured honey badger cub, only a few weeks old and weak from hunger and deprivation. His mother had evidently been killed while defending him from a predator. Kobus picked up the cub, wrapped him in his jacket and brought him home.

After bathing the cub in warm water, we disinfected and dressed a bad wound in his neck. He was very docile and seemed to have no fear of us. I fed him a fortified milk-and-honey solution through a baby's bottle, and he loved it. The gluttonous little fellow then demanded his feed every three or four hours, day and night. I soon suffered from lack of sleep, but the sight of the cuddly little fellow lying snugly in my arms, his forepaws hugging the bottle, and his face a study in total contentment, never ceased to delight me.

Though his neck wound responded well to treatment, he remained lame in his hind legs. We worried that he had suffered damage to his nervous system and might never be able to walk. Fortunately we were wrong. It was only through lack of nourishment that he was lame, and the milk-and-honey solution soon proved to be the perfect remedy. After a few days he started stumbling about, then walking and finally running around.

*

A honey badger is a mighty little bundle of energy and the bravest of all carnivores. Utterly fearless and powerfully built, it is capable of attacking an intruder many times its own size. Yet honey badgers are normally not aggressive. When encountered in the veld, they are usually seen going about their private business at a very purposeful trot. Only when cornered and threatened will they attack – and when they charge at an 'enemy' their ferocity is awe-inspiring, they say. It's probably true, but I myself have never encountered a ferocious honey badger. I have often stopped to say hello to wild ones in the veld, or in our garden at night, and they seemed shy and retiring to me, and not in the least aggressive. Kobus once even sweet-talked a young, wild honey badger into allowing him to tickle its head. Though honey badgers are nocturnal, they are also quite often seen in daylight. Omnivorous, they feed on a variety of insects and small animals, bulbs, roots, honey and the pupae of wild bees.

We named our foundling cub Buksie, which means 'little tough guy'. By this time our Mahlangeni family had grown to include two dogs, two horses and a dozen bantams, and the girls were utterly delighted with the addition of a honey badger cub.

Karin, not yet at school, became Buksie's constant companion, and before long Buksie was a very spoilt little honey badger. He expected Karin to roughhouse with him from morning till night and he refused to go to sleep unless he had a human finger to suck on, preferably Karin's. Karin had to sit patiently, her finger in his mouth, until he nodded off.

Buksie never tired of playing and sometimes, when his boisterousness became too much for Karin, she would try to run away from him and hide in her bedroom, but he'd catch up with her long before she reached it. Often I would catch and hold him, giving her the chance to get away. But as soon as she locked herself in, Buksie would rush up to her door and bang and scratch on it, begging her with his sweet cooing noises to come out please and play some more, and eventually she relented. She looked forward to weekends when her sisters would be home to help her play with the lively cub.

Though Buksie was boisterous, he played gently and never left a scratch or a tooth mark on us. He loved to chew our toes, but did so with tenderness, and so the chews were merely ticklish. We found his gentleness both endearing and surprising, for we had raised a banded mongoose the previous year, and though Mufi was an affectionate little fellow, he was careless with his teeth and we often got nipped rather severely. Mufi also gave the dogs a hard time. Stalking up to them unnoticed, he would pounce on them and attack their tails. The dogs were rather relieved when, at the age of about nine months, Mufi left us to join up with a local colony of banded mongoose.

Buksie loved to hug and cuddle everybody, including the dogs and the horses. The dogs didn't mind but the horses studiously ignored him, or tried to. Buksie would charge at a horse, grab a hind leg and try to clamber up it. The horse would lift its leg in an attempt to get rid of the pestering cub, but Buksie still hung on. So the poor horse would be stuck with one leg in the air, pretending to be oblivious to the honey badger dangling from it.

At first Buksie slept inside the house, but eventually he became too destructive and we had to teach him to sleep outdoors. Kobus built him a little tent-shaped reed shelter at the edge of the patio outside our bedroom. Buksie found it to his liking and moved right in. Often he

would curl up in his reed shelter in the heat of the day so that he could stay up longer at night to chase after frogs in the garden. He was slowly turning into a nocturnal creature and a predator. By the age of six months he was sleeping only in the daytime and spending his nights roaming the riverine bush where he soon discovered a host of delicious dishes – lizards, frogs, snakes and other small reptiles. On a few occasions he turned up carrying a dead snake in his jaws, proudly parading his trophy before us.

At about this time, Buksie acquired a passion for changing the natural geography of a place, and before long our garden was full of holes and craters. Whenever Kobus and the girls went fishing in the evenings, Buksie loved to go along and dig up the shore. Once, when we all accompanied Kobus on a camping trip to Byashishi Creek, Buksie spent the night digging holes in the ground underneath our camp beds, smothering us with dust clouds.

As he grew older, he abandoned his reed shelter to sleep in the burrows he dug for himself. Never content to sleep in the same burrow twice, he dug himself a new one every day, first in our garden and later, thank heavens, in the surrounding riverine bush. Snoozing there during the day, he would turn up every evening at sunset to play with us before setting off on his nocturnal hunting trips.

We would be sitting outside, watching the sun sink into the river. From somewhere in the bush, Buksie would come running along and clamber his way up the high fence. He knew there was an open gate he could use, but honey badgers don't need gates. Once he reached the top of the fence, he would let go and plummet to the ground on the inside. Then he would charge over to where we sat, purring and crooning with happiness, jump onto our laps and greet us with fond hugs, gurgles and kisses.

Buksie knew full well that he was no longer allowed in the house, but he never stopped looking for a way to sneak indoors. Once inside, he needed only a few moments to turn the whole house into a battle zone. With a few fast sweeps of his paws, he'd clear the bookshelves, upend the pot plants, open cupboards and drawers and send their contents flying. Even as we chased Buksie frantically from room to room he would, without missing a step, strip the beds and bat the cushions off the chairs. And anything on a shelf or table would also end up on the floor. He really enjoyed himself.

We quickly learned our lesson. As soon as dusk approached, every door and window was properly secured and would be opened again only after Buksie had departed on his nocturnal hunting expedition.

One night when Kobus wasn't at home Buksie decided to pay me a surprise visit. It was around midnight and the sliding glass doors to our bedroom were open, with only a screen door blocking Buksie's access to the house. Lying on his side, Buksie hooked his long, curved talons into the mesh and heaved the screen door wide open.

With one scramble he was on the bed.

It's quite a shock to have a heavy animal land on you in the deep of the night. Buksie was almost a year old by then, and weighed in at about 12 kilograms (26 pounds). After greeting me with a big hug and a fond

gurgle, he started bounding all over the bed, landing on top of me with every second bound. Telling him to stop didn't help – he was having a great time. At the end of a lengthy battle I finally managed to wrestle him to the floor, shove him outside and secure the glass doors. By this time I was drenched in perspiration. It was a sweltering night, and with the glass doors now closed the cooler air from the river could no longer be felt in the room. I lay glowing on the sticky sheets, feeling sorry for myself for having to choose between melting in a hot, airless room and wrestling with a honey badger.

A few weeks later Dirk Ackerman paid us a visit. We were sitting outside, enjoying drinks with him and catching up on park news, when Buksie turned up for his evening visit. After greeting each of us (the chief ranger included) with a boisterous hug, he knocked the garden table over and dashed off with a six-pack of beer in his teeth.

Kobus bolted after the honey badger – out through the front gate and off along the river bank. Buksie couldn't see too well where he was going as the pack of beer was in the way, and for a while this slowed him down a bit, enabling Kobus to catch up. In the ensuing battle, the badger and the beers rolled down the steep bank and disappeared into the riverine bush. That was the last we saw of the beers that night, but not of Buksie.

Before long, he rejoined us. This time he latched onto Dirk's wallet and made off with it. Again Kobus gave chase. When he finally caught Buksie, he pinned him down firmly and managed to retrieve the wallet.

Buksie charged right back to us with intent, mischievous eyes. But Kobus was ready for him. As Buksie leaped through the air to pounce on a pair of binoculars, Kobus caught him in mid-pounce and gave him a good smack on the bottom. Indignantly, Buksie made his way off into the darkness . . . or so we thought.

We enjoyed a relaxed meal before Dirk retired to the guest cottage in the garden. No sooner had he put his foot inside than we heard his yell of surprise. We dashed over. Evidently the door had not been properly closed and Buksie had managed to push it open. The interior was a scene of utter devastation. Dirk's suitcase had been opened and his clothing lay scattered all over the room. The bedding was a heap on the floor and the bedside table and lamp were upended. And worst of all, an important geomorphological map that Dirk had brought along had been shredded to bits.

Acutely embarrassed, we apologized profusely to Dirk and tried to explain that Buksie – who was now nowhere to be seen – wasn't usually so destructive. (Perhaps he'd only wanted to show the chief ranger who was really boss at Mahlangeni?)

A few months later, twin sets of honey badger spoor in the surrounding veld indicated that Buksie had met and made friends with a wild badger, presumably a female. During his nightly visits to us, he often seemed preoccupied, as though he was waiting for someone to join him. Perhaps the girl badger was hiding nearby, too scared to come inside the garden.

Buksie's visits to us became less frequent, and we imagined that he was roaming the night with his wild friend. At first he disappeared for only a few days at a time. But later on, weeks and even months would go by without us seeing him.

We missed him very much, but cherished each surprise visit. And we took comfort in knowing that our sweet friend had successfully returned to the wild.

CHILDREN OF THE WILD

DURING MY INTERVIEW IN THE CHIEF RANGER'S OFFICE AT
Skukuza, when I was warned about the hardships that a game
ranger's wife could expect to endure, they forgot to tell me that the
greatest hardship of all would be to send my children away to boarding
school.

Well, it wasn't really a boarding school. It was a private hostel and a
very nice one, but still . . . I needed to have my daughters home every
day of the week, to see their smiles, hear their laughter, share their
exuberance. I wanted to be the one to answer their questions and
nourish the natural curiosity of their fertile minds; to comfort them if
they were sad; to tuck them in at bedtime and read them a story.

Definitely the sending away of one's children to school should be at
the top of the list of hardships.

Fortunately my daughters didn't seem to think so. For them, the
hostel meant having lots of friends. And perhaps it also meant learning
about surviving in the strange world outside the protection of our
isolated home.

The Kruger Park hostel had none of the strict rules and regulations
of a public boarding school, for which I was grateful. It was a homely,
friendly place, nestling in a large garden surrounded by mopani woods
and overlooking a pond where wild animals often came to drink.
Altogether there were about twenty residents in the hostel, some of

them brothers and sisters, all of them delightful, sunny-natured children, as children of the wilds usually are.

The first time Karin went away to school, I could hardly sleep all week. I knew Hettie and Sandra would take good care of her at the hostel, but still . . . She seemed so young. Wouldn't she miss me terribly? I could hardly wait for Friday.

Finally Friday came round. I drove early to the hostel and had to wait for the school bus to bring the children. At last, there was Karin getting off the bus. I ran to her. 'How was your week?' I asked anxiously.

'Nice,' she said, and climbing into the car she fell asleep. Her sisters had to fetch and carry her hostel luggage for her.

'What's wrong with Karin?' I asked them.

'Nothing,' they told me. 'She's spent all week playing herself into a state of exhaustion.'

After that, every Friday afternoon when I fetched the girls, Karin fell asleep as soon as she got into the car.

On the last Friday of every month, Kobus and his game guards made a trip to town to replenish our stocks of diesel, maize meal and other provisions for the staff village and us. On their way back they stopped to pick up the girls, saving me the trip. Usually the truck was loaded to capacity when they arrived at the hostel. Hettie and Sandra rode in the cab with their father, but Karin climbed onto the back with the game guards where she could curl up atop the sacks of maize meal. The game guards kept a protective eye on her lest she got thrown from her lofty bed by sudden bumps or curves in the road. When they arrived home, I was often moved almost to tears to find my exhausted little girl sound asleep atop the sacks of meal.

Hettie once wrote an essay about life at the hostel which, to me, shed some light on Karin's end-of-the-week fatigue.

Children who grow up in the wild don't really know what it's like to have friends until they start school. Growing up alone isn't that bad though, as long as you have a sister or brother, or even a pet to play with. In any case, it doesn't occur to you that life could be different.

When children who've grown up alone arrive at the hostel for the first time, they are astonished to find that they have such an abundance of playmates, and they become wild with joy. They chase each other around, shouting and laughing with excitement, and they dance and shriek and cavort about, generally behaving like clowning baboons, as if trying to compensate for all the lost opportunities of their pre-school years.

But by nightfall they suddenly remember that they miss their mothers. And the nostalgia is profound, because in their pre-school years Mommy was always there. She never went anywhere without them. The nearest town was too far away, neighbours were too distant, and baby-sitters non-existent. So wherever Mom went, they went, and it never occurred to them that there could come a time when Mom would be out of reach for a comforting hug at bedtime.

When the tears start flowing here at night, the older children step in and offer comfort where they can, remembering only too well how they felt themselves, not that long ago.

When we first came to live in the reserve, Karin was only two years old. By the time she was five, she could name almost every wild creature in the park, including many of the bird species. We were very proud of our clever child. But we also sometimes forgot what an unusual education she was getting.

One day, when we were travelling to Johannesburg to visit my parents, we drove past a cow grazing in a field alongside the road. Karin yelled for Kobus to stop the car and, after taking a good look, asked, 'What's that? A donkey or something?'

Later, at a filling station, we noticed an ordinary black cat in a nearby tree. Karin was fascinated.

'Oh wow!' she exclaimed. 'Look at that strange animal!'

I felt very guilty, and immediately bought her some picture books about domestic animals so that she wouldn't appear too ignorant when she started school.

From a tender age, Karin loved to draw. During her first year at school, two of her drawings were chosen for the school's annual art exhibition.

The girls and I attended the exhibition. There were various groups of pictures, each depicting a different theme. One of these was 'Water', and most of the pictures in this group were of peaceful ponds surrounded by flowers and trees. But there was one drawing of an underwater scene in which half the space was taken up by a hippo with its enormous mouth wide open, and the rest of the space by a crocodile, also with a wide-open mouth and displaying a fearsome array of teeth. I had no doubt who the artist was. Karin was the only Kruger Park child in her class, and she knew that water spelt trouble.

Among another group of pictures, of which the theme was 'Road Safety', there was a drawing of two men on bicycles riding along a winding track through the bush, rifles slung over their shoulders. The two cyclists were, of course, two of our game guards out on patrol. And the rifles slung over their shoulders portrayed my daughter's only understanding of road safety.

Their teachers sometimes mentioned to me that my children wrote unusual essays. Instructed to write about the peace and harmony of nature, Hettie described a weekend we had spent camping on the banks of the Tsendze Stream when a hyena had stolen one of our blankets and a cooking pot in the night, and baboons had ransacked our camp the next day. She concluded that there was beauty and perhaps harmony in nature, but not much peace, and certainly no law and order.

Asked to describe an impending rainstorm, Sandra wrote that the first sign of one was that hippos got out of the water – they knew the rivers would soon be in spate, and they didn't want to drown in the floods. (Her teacher didn't believe her. But I did. We often saw our resident hippos leaving the water prior to heavy rains.)

In an essay titled 'My Most Cherished Possession', Karin wrote that this would have been her new pair of shoes, but a hyena ate them one night when she'd forgotten them outside.

Strangely my daughters were never able to write essays of a dramatic nature. Whenever they were asked to describe a frightening incident, they claimed they could not do so, due to lack of experience. Scary things happened only where lots of people lived together, when you could expect to encounter hijacks, robberies, traffic accidents, muggings and murders.

So they would come to me at the weekend, asking for my help with the writing of a dramatic essay. I would remind them of the various close encounters we'd had with wild animals. But, to my dismay, they wouldn't agree that those were scary incidents.

My bush-wise daughters have a deep love of the wilderness and of all its creatures, great and small. They understand the behaviour of wild animals; they can read spoor and decipher the smells and sounds of the bush. Their senses are constantly attuned to their surroundings and they know how to avoid dangerous situations.

One day when Kobus was away from home, Hettie and Sandra (then aged fourteen and thirteen) saw a large herd of buffalo crossing the dry bed of the Little Letaba and heading for the boundary fence. There were numerous calves among the herd. Saddling their horses, the two girls called the dogs and set out after the buffalo. They drove them back across the river and herded them deep into the mopani bush to the north. (Herding wild buffalo is, surprisingly, almost as easy as herding domestic cattle.) As I stood watching the cloud of billowing red dust followed by two young girls on horseback, my heart filled with admiration for my bush-wise, compassionate children. I knew that they weren't doing this out of bravado or a sense of adventure, but out of concern for the buffalo. Only a few days previously, hunters in Gazankulu had shot two of our elephants. The girls hated the sound of gunshots coming from Gazankulu and they wanted the buffalo and their calves to be safe from the guns of hunters.

Perhaps there is logic, after all, in my daughters' reluctance to regard close encounters with wild animals as frightening experiences. Animals have no malice, they attack only in self-defence, they hunt only when they must eat. It is man, the most successful predator on earth, who is the most dangerous of all creatures.

SOLITUDE

GETTING USED TO THE ISOLATION IN THE EARLY YEARS AT
Mahlangeni was really nothing compared to adapting to the
searing summer heat, the crazy whims of the electric generator,
the paranoid hippos, the unpredictable river, the perils of the lonely
track, snakes, mosquitoes, malaria, tick fever ... The solitude simply
did not get much of a chance to feature as a problem.

By the time I actually got down to thinking about it, it seemed to me
that solitude was a thing that settled on you in gentle ways. Perhaps
initially it takes some getting used to, but once you begin to enjoy
the company of plants and animals you are no longer lonely. In fact, the
feeling of freedom and space can get quite addictive. There is something
about solitude, you see, that lets you discover the simple goodness of
being.

Although I missed Kobus and my daughters when they were away
from home, I rarely had time to feel lonely. My two faithful dogs, Simba
and Janna, guarded me with loyalty and devotion and followed me
around wherever I went. Our three horses and twenty bantams also
kept me company, as did the family of squirrels and the many wild birds
who lived in our garden. A small family of bushbuck – usually four or
five females with their young – often grazed along the river bank at the
edge of the garden. They were so tame that they looked me straight in
the eye when I talked to them.

Naturally I was also well acquainted with the resident hippos. When the dogs and I took our daily stroll along the shore we always stopped to say hello to them. They would swim closer and stare enquiringly at us. But when I talked to them, they remained mute. Only when we turned away and walked on did they find their voices again and would discuss the dogs and me noisily behind our backs.

And then there was old Filemoni, always around somewhere, either pottering in the vegetable garden or fishing down by the river. He didn't talk much, but always greeted me with a friendly grunt.

When household chores didn't take up all of my time, I liked to garden, read and listen to music. And like all good solitary people, I kept a diary and talked to myself. My days were full and far too short, and often it would be midnight when I went to bed. Though I would have liked to sleep later in the mornings, the whole neighbourhood woke up at dawn and made sure that I did too. It was nice to hear them all applauding the sunrise so exuberantly, but sometimes I wished they would do it a little later, especially the Egyptian geese whose trumpeting screeches always startled me awake rather rudely.

My favourite hour at Mahlangeni was that time before sunset when the rivers reflected the crimson sky, and the woodlands were filled with sprinkles of golden light. It was the hour when the birds sang with liquid voices and when the dogs and I took our daily walk.

In the early years at Mahlangeni, I walked only on the shores near the house where it was easier for me to read the tracks of animals in the sand, where I could see far ahead and where I knew the landscape by heart. Once you know a particular area well, it is easier to spot a dark shape that wasn't there the previous time, or to pick up a feeling that all is not as it should be.

Later, when my dogs and I became more confident of our bush wisdom, we started to venture inland along the patrol tracks and the game paths. The dogs were well trained and stayed close to me, usually leading by a few paces, ears pricked and noses to the ground, constantly vigilant, always ready to tell me if there was reason for us to turn back.

Often we came within close range of magnificent animals – eland, kudu, buffalo, waterbuck – who remained unaware of our presence as we took care to keep downwind and to make no noise at all. Other times we made the acquaintance of weird and wonderful creatures such as leguaans, turtles, tortoises and, once, the longest python in the world. It took the python so long to sail across our path that we eventually got bored waiting for its tail end to emerge from the bushes at one side of the path and disappear into the bushes at the other side.

It was only at night that the vastness of the wilderness sometimes struck home. But the dogs had their sleeping mats on the covered patio outside the sliding doors to the bedroom, and I needed only to call their names softly to hear the swishing of their wagging tails as they acknowledged my call.

Nights at Mahlangeni were never silent, of course. Nocturnal creatures have busy agendas, and often an entire orchestra of diverse sounds would animate the night. Frog choirs and cricket concerts droned and quivered the backing for the songs of owls and nightjars, for the whining calls of bushbabies, the whooping howls of hyena, the rasping cough of our neighbour the leopard, the roar of a lion. Often the dogs would wake, alerted by a strange noise that seemed too near, or a wild smell brought by the wind. And when they barked at the shadows and the gusts of wind, I felt protected and at peace with my wilderness home.

MEMORIES OF A SYMPHONY

ONE OF THE NICE THINGS ABOUT SOLITUDE WAS THAT I COULD PLAY my music at full volume. If it bothered my wild neighbours I wouldn't know it and couldn't care. It served them right for waking me at dawn when I needed to sleep longer.

One morning, while I was gardening and listening to the beautiful strains of a Mozart symphony that filled the whole garden, the dogs barked, announcing a visitor. I looked up and saw a vehicle turning in through our back gates. It stopped, and a young man got out. He looked lost and confused. As I approached him he was taking in the dogs, the horses, the garden, the house, the music . . . Then he saw me and said, 'Oh. Hi! Good morning. It seems, uh . . . it's a house. Someone lives here.'

In the spirit of the moment I turned and, looking at the house, replied with a smile: 'Why, yes, it looks so to me too.'

Looking sheepish but laughing now, the young man introduced himself and explained that he was doing research for a thesis on ecological engineering. He'd been granted a permit to travel to the Shimuwini Dam on the Letaba River. He frowned, adding, 'But I guess I got lost.'

'Yes,' I said. 'You have. Would you come into my husband's office? He keeps a large map of the area there. I can show you how to get to Shimuwini.'

But the young man remained rooted to the spot, apparently hypnotized by the music.

'Mozart,' he informed me. 'Fortieth Symphony.'

I smiled, because naturally I knew what was playing. He stood listening attentively to the last strains of the symphony's haunting finale, then, when the music had ended, asked shyly, 'What other Mozart recordings do you have?'

At that stage we didn't have a large Mozart collection but we had works by many other composers, and I invited him inside to look at them. He became totally absorbed in the record and tape collection, so I left him to it and went to make coffee.

He chose Mozart's Coronation Concerto, put it on the turntable, then wandered out into the front garden.

When I carried the coffee out, I found him sitting on our swing – a half-cut tyre suspended from a beam between two mopani trees. Swaying gently to the rhythm of the music, he was watching the hippos playing in the river below. He was so lost in his reverie that he didn't hear me approaching. I put the tray down on the grass and sat down next to it to pour the coffee. He got off the swing and joined me on the grass.

We drank our coffee and listened to the concerto. The warm and rich melody filled the garden and soared out over the river where even the hippos seemed entranced by its beauty. A fish eagle dived from the sky and sailed the air above the water, its wild, piercing cries resounding in the music-filled landscape.

We didn't talk as we sipped our coffee and listened to the music. During the solo part of the larghetto movement, my guest poured himself a second cup of coffee and stirred it absent-mindedly, although he'd forgotten to put sugar in it.

When the last strains of the finale had faded, leaving their dulcet echoes in our minds, he told me that back home in Pretoria the concerto didn't sound the same.

He got up and carried the tray back into the house for me. Then I showed him the map and explained to him how to get to Shimuwini. Before he left, he asked, 'Isn't it lonely for you out here?'

I told him no, that loneliness didn't bother me.

About a month later, a Mozart tape turned up in the post. And after that, every other month or so, a new Mozart tape arrived with the mail. The postmark indicated that they came from Pretoria. It wasn't difficult to guess who the sender was.

Perhaps he cherished the memory of that day when he lost his way and unexpectedly came upon a Mozart symphony in the wilderness. And perhaps he sent the tapes to ensure that Mozart would always play at Mahlangeni. Or perhaps he believed that it must, after all, sometimes have been lonely for me, and that Mozart would relieve the loneliness.

I was never lonely.

But as long as we lived there, Mozart often played at Mahlangeni.

ENCOUNTER ON THE KOPPIE

SOME TEN KILOMETRES FROM OUR HOUSE A LONE, BOULDER-STREWN koppie (hilly outcrop) rose from a vast, flat stretch of mopani bushveld. A baobab tree, more than a hundred years old, graced the eastern slope of the koppie, its tapering branches reaching up towards the large boulders of the higher slopes. From the summit there was a wonderful view of the surrounding plains and of a large pan (lake) some distance to the south. We loved to spend a lazy Sunday afternoon on the flat boulders of the summit, armed with binoculars for spotting animals as they trekked across the wooded plains to drink at the pan.

During our seventh year at Mahlangeni, some good friends of ours from the city, Louis Roodt, his wife Joan and their three children, came to visit for the Easter weekend. We decided to take them on our favourite Sunday-afternoon outing.

We drove in our pick-up to the foot of the koppie. Hettie, then aged fourteen, Sandra, thirteen, Karin, eight, and our friends' daughter Thelma, aged six, all leaped from the back of the truck and scurried up the slope. I was about to caution the girls to wait for us, but my voice couldn't compete with their energetic enthusiasm, so I let them go.

Together with Louis and Joan and their two younger boys, Kobus and I followed at a more sedate pace. Our progress was slow as Louis was leading both small boys by the hand, their young legs struggling with the climb. Kobus had not brought his rifle along that day. This didn't really worry me as we had climbed the koppie on numerous occasions and had never seen anything other than dassies (hyrax) on the slopes.

We were still a long way below the girls when they reached the top. Joan and I were deep in conversation when Kobus suddenly held up his hand. I knew that signal. It meant: shut up and pay attention.

I stopped in mid-sentence.

And then we all heard it: a deep, rumbling noise coming from the slopes above. It sounded like a rock-slide to me. But when the rumbling stopped, Sandra's voice reached us from the summit. The single word she screamed was 'Leopard!'

Kobus, who was already running up the slope towards the girls, yelled at them to come down. I sprinted after Kobus, my only thought being to get to the girls before the leopard did.

The deep rumbling noise rose again, and even in the heat of the moment it dawned on me that the noise wasn't that of a rock-slide or of a leopard, but the growl of an angry lion.

And then we saw her: a lioness bursting from a cover of boulders and shrubs. She stopped short of the children and crouched, gathering her hind legs beneath her flattened body and uttering a deep warning growl that rose in volume until it rumbled like thunder over the landscape.

The girls fled headlong down the slope, crashing through shrubs and over rocks – all except little Thelma. She stopped and turned, looked right into the face of the crouching lioness less than ten metres away, and immediately froze with shock. She stood, rigid with fright, unable to do anything but stare at the snarling animal.

Hettie, who had glanced over her shoulder and witnessed the scene, turned round and clambered back up towards her friend. The lioness saw Hettie approaching and warned her with a crescendo growl not to come any closer.

But Hettie never hesitated.

Rushing forward, she grabbed the paralysed little girl firmly in her arms and propelled her headlong down the slope.

Meanwhile, Sandra had also glanced over her shoulder and, seeing Hettie scrambling away from the lioness with Thelma in tow, turned immediately and rushed back up the slope to help her sister. Ignoring the furious growls of the lioness, Sandra joined the other two girls and grabbed one of Thelma's arms. Together the two sisters and their shocked little friend then fled pell-mell down the koppie.

Kobus and I were still sprinting up the slope towards them, oblivious of the shrubs and rocks that scratched and cut us as we ran, our eyes on the lioness and the children. Karin came tearing past us, her legs scratched and bleeding, but the only thing that mattered was that she was safe – we were between her and the lioness. Then Hettie and Sandra came running past us with the ashen-faced little girl between them. And a few seconds later Kobus stood facing the lioness – unarmed.

With an angry warning snarl she charged, drawing up very close to Kobus. Slowly she lowered her body into a crouch and gathered her hind legs beneath her. She was coiled for attack.

Snatching up a rock about the size of a rugby ball, I rushed towards them and took up a position some two or three metres behind Kobus.

Kobus stood his ground as the cat communicated her intentions to him in the thundering language of lions.

I was shaking like a leaf, my heart pounding in my ears. With my adrenaline-heightened senses, I experienced every moment and every tiny detail of what was happening in vivid slow motion.

Kobus was talking calmly to the crouching, snarling lioness: 'Easy now, old girl . . . easy now . . . calm down.'

It's strange, but I always forget how big lions really are until I see one up close. As I stood gaping at the huge cat, I tried to ignore her size and concentrate on her face. Her blazing yellow eyes didn't seem a good feature to focus on, so I chose instead the funny-looking crinkles on her puckered nose.

She roared again, making me jump, and the earth seemed to shudder.

Kobus was still talking to her in his calm, soothing voice. 'Easy now . . . don't worry . . . we won't harm you.'

(We won't? Then why was I standing there clutching an enormous rock?)

Slowly, Kobus looked over his shoulder and signalled quietly but firmly that I should retreat. It dawned on me at last that his safety, as well as mine, depended on whether he succeeded in placating the lioness. If I left, she'd feel less threatened. Feeling slightly embarrassed, and being careful not to annoy her with any sudden movements, I put the rock down carefully and turned away.

As I made my way down the slope, I held my breath and listened. The lioness was still growling but less aggressively now, and Kobus was still talking calmly, soothingly, pacifying her with his voice: 'Easy, old girl, easy now. Calm down . . .'

Her growls became softer and softer . . .

Once I was safely away, Kobus followed.

The crisis was over.

When we reached the foot of the koppie, we looked back and saw the lioness on the summit, standing in magnificent silhouette against the paling sky. She roared once more – a warning to us not to intrude again into her territory.

Kobus told us that he'd noticed that she was in lactation, and he believed that she had chosen the koppie as a nursery for her cubs. That, of course, accounted for her aggressive behaviour. She was a mother protecting her young.

Later Sandra explained that when she'd reached the summit, she'd heard a deep rumbling sound, and turning towards it, looked straight into the eyes of a big cat. In her hurry to get away and to warn the others, she had no time for a second glance, and so called out what she expected to see – a leopard – which is far more likely to be seen on a koppie than a lion.

The girls were still pale with fright and Karin, sobbing softly, said that her legs were hurting. On closer examination we saw with relief that the wounds were superficial. Her tears were those of shock rather than pain.

There was a lump in my throat as I hugged her to me. I hugged my other two girls too, as Louis and Joan comforted Thelma. I couldn't find the words to tell Hettie and Sandra how proud I was of them for not having hesitated to turn back to help their young friend – and each other.

CAMPING UNDER THE STARS

DURING THE LONG DRY MONTHS OF WINTER, WHEN THE CREEKS and seasonal rivers run dry, the animals gather close to the perennial rivers and waterholes. In Kruger, many of the waterholes are actually artificial drinking places filled from boreholes. Located in areas where natural waters occur only during the rainy seasons, they provide an alternative source in winter for thirsty herds no longer able to migrate to pastures outside the park. These artificial water sources also prevent overcrowding of the natural ones, and so help to preserve the surrounding pastures which would otherwise be stripped bare and eroded by thousands of hooves.

Kobus regularly patrolled his whole section during the dry months to monitor pasture conditions and water availability. During winter school holidays the girls and I often accompanied him on these patrol trips.

On one of these trips we spent the first night camping at Shipikana Creek. We arrived in the late afternoon and pitched our tent under apple-leaf trees on the bank of the dry watercourse. There was about an hour left before sunset, so we went for a walk along the creek.

Some three hundred metres from our camp, a pride of lions burst from the dry bed of the creek and streaked past us like lightning, fleeing as if they'd seen ghosts. It happened so suddenly and so close to us that I initially mistook them for a herd of eland – they looked so huge and had almost the same colouring.

I had once again forgotten how big lions really are.

Later we came to a rocky ridge overlooking a valley in which a herd of elephant grazed. We settled ourselves comfortably on the grass between the rocks to enjoy the magic hour of sunset. Bathed in the golden light of the winter afternoon, the savannah below us was a perfect backdrop for the dark shapes of the elephants, their tusks glinting as the last rays of sunlight played on the ivory. We counted forty cows and eighteen calves, of whom four were infants. We might have missed a couple of infants, though, because baby elephants walk underneath their mothers' bellies between their legs most of the time and are not easy to spot.

The herd grazed quietly. If they made any sound at all, it would have been the low rumbling noises periodically emitted by the cows to keep contact and communicate their positions to one another. But we were too far from them to pick this up.

Soon the western horizon was aflame with reds and purples, and the evening shadows settled over the valley floor. Only the plaintive laments of plovers interrupted the vast silence, and later, the noisy swearing of a distant troop of quarrelsome baboons heading for the safety of their trees.

When the dusk began to settle too heavily on my shoulders and down my spine, I suggested to my family that we follow the example of the baboons and head for camp.

In southern Africa, twilight is brief and darkness falls fast. We reached our camp just in time to avoid the plummeting of the blackout. For a while it was so dark that the only sources of light in the universe seemed to be our little campfire and the stars. But while we were preparing our evening meal at the fire, a pearly luminescence touched the rim of a dark horizon, and then a full moon rose to bathe the trees and the veld in a bluish glow. The sweet, melodic call of a pearl-spotted owl rang out from the apple-leaf trees across the creek and was answered by the purring trill of a scops owl. From somewhere, the haunting howls of a lone hyena soared out into the night and drifted across the veld in rising and falling echoes.

As we sat around our campfire, waiting for our stew of venison and vegetables to cook, we remembered previous times we had camped under the stars. There was the night at Pambi Creek when we were woken by a huge scraping sound that seemed to be shaking the earth around us. Peering carefully out through the open tent flaps, we saw a dark shape the size of a mountain. It was an elephant rubbing his backside against the trunk of the tree under which our tent was pitched. After a minute or so, when the tremor had begun to reach Richter scale proportions, it stopped suddenly. And the elephant – satisfied that the itch on his rump had been taken care of – left, disappearing into the night as silently as he had come, thank heavens.

And there was the night at Timatora Pool when two adult lions paid us a visit and made themselves at home within metres of our tent. They spent the whole night there, playing, rolling in the grass and lazing about. We shone a torch at them, but they merely lifted their heads to

stare nonchalantly back at us. When Kobus checked on them in the early dawn, they were dozing, stretched out on their backs, paws dangling in the air. As soon as the first glints of sunlight touched their bellies, they sat up suddenly, ears pricked, noses to the wind, and stared out across the savannah. Something in the air was calling them. In the next moment they rose and were gone, swallowed by the silent veld. The dogs emerged from our tent where they had been forced to stay the night, and spent the next two hours sniffing each and every blade of grass and grain of sand around the camp.

Another unforgettable night was the one at Shambali Springs when two hippo bulls decided to have a territorial quarrel some ten metres from our camp. At first we heard only the crashing rattle of something big moving in the dark. Kobus got up and shone a torch in the direction of the sound, and there they were, two angry-looking hippo bulls spoiling for a fight. In the beam of the torch they looked bigger than steamrollers. Soon they were hurling abuse at each other with voices like the strangled roaring of aircraft in trouble. Before long, the noise got too much even for Kobus. He loaded his rifle and fired a couple of shots into the air to let the two warring bulls know there were other places they could go to sort each other out. Fortunately they got the message and left.

As we sat talking around our campfire at Shipikana Creek, remembering the hippos at Shambali Springs, lions started grunting and roaring to the west of us. Soon afterwards another pride, probably the one we had come across earlier, started up to the east of us. This soon became a competition, with each pride endeavouring to outroar the other.

I was reminded of a frightening thing that had once happened to Hugo van Niekerk, one of our Kruger Park pilots, when he had to camp out in the bush one night with a group of visiting scientists. Hugo is a man who needs some solitude and personal space when resting, so he had pitched his tent some distance away from the other campers. As soon as he'd gone to bed, the local lion population commenced a roaring competition close by. It gradually gained in volume until it resembled an ongoing earthquake. Lying on his camp bed inside his tent, Hugo wished that the lions would shut up and go away so that he could get some sleep.

Instead, the two contesting prides declared war and charged at each other, ignoring the fact that Hugo's tent occupied the space between them – the battle zone, as it were. The cats let fly, attacking tooth and claw, raising vocal hell, and in the process breaking the guy ropes and more or less taking Hugo's tent with them. Hugo, wanting no part in the dispute, hastily abandoned his demolished quarters, leaving the frenzied animals to sort out their problems on their own. Luckily the lions were too absorbed in their territorial quarrel to pay any attention to Hugo, and he escaped unharmed.

I tried not to think of Hugo's story while we enjoyed our evening meal around the campfire. The two prides were still roaring at each other, but I consoled myself that the vocal exchange appeared to have an andante quality about it. Perhaps the lions were only trading ideas and not actually threatening one another. They didn't let up though, and we went to bed that night with the thundering stereophonic rumble in our ears.

At the time we had only one tent, so Kobus and I slept in it while the girls slept in the truck, Karin inside the cab and the two older girls in the back. Kobus had spread and tied a heavy tarpaulin across the rails over the open back so that they would be safe, but Hettie and Sandra insisted on folding it back so they could enjoy the view of the moon on the veld. (While sleeping? I wondered.)

I placed our washbasin on its three-legged stand against the rear of the truck, reasoning that if a lion intended to jump into the back it would first collide with the basin and so create enough noise to waken us.

As usual, we slept with the flaps of our tent open. Kobus had his rifle next to his bed, and the dogs slept across the entrance to raise an alarm.

I didn't sleep much. The trouble with lions is that if you come across them during the daylight hours they usually flee, but at night they suddenly remember they are the kings of the bush and revert to being supremely confident predators.

The lions continued their roaring all night, sometimes very close, sometimes further away.

Some time between three and four in the morning, the space in the back of the truck became too narrow for the two older girls. Sandra clambered out of the truck and, dragging her camping mattress and sleeping bag with her, went and made her bed on the ground next to the campfire, which by this time had died down to a few glowing embers. I called out and invited her to share the tent, but she declined.

I was too tense to go back to sleep. I called out to Sandra again, insisting that she come and sleep in the tent. But she answered that the dogs had joined her by the fire and that she was perfectly safe.

Soon afterwards, a lion suddenly roared so close to us that we could hear the intake of his breath just before he sounded off. I flew out of bed, but then saw that Kobus was already up. He took his rifle and told me not to worry. He was going to sit at the fire and watch over Sandra.

I could finally relax and go to sleep.

At sunrise, Kobus came into the tent and woke me with a cup of coffee. He was smiling. He said one of the dogs had had a good night's rest. He had gradually encroached on Sandra's mattress – first his head, then his paws, and finally the rest of his body. Sandra had meekly rolled over each time he'd nudged her, and had ended up sleeping on the hard ground.

My poor daughter. First she had given up her sleeping place to her sister, and then to the dog.

After breakfast we packed up and travelled on. It was a beautiful winter's day, the sky a crisp, cool blue, the mopani leaves coppery red, bronze and ochre, the savannah grasses golden-blond. We stopped at various waterholes along the way, and while Kobus inspected the boreholes, pumps and reservoirs, the girls and I peered at game tracks in the sand or sat about quietly, enjoying the evocative music of the savannahs.

In summer the mopani veld rang with the strident call of cicadas, but in winter there was often an exquisite silence, broken only by the gentle rhythm of a breeze or, perhaps, by the distant bark of a zebra or the plaintive call of a goshawk in flight. But sometimes, quite suddenly, there would be a faint rustle, the crack of a twig, a sigh in the air and a pungent, musty smell brought by the wind. Then, as if by magic, the enormous dark shapes of an entire elephant herd would materialize from nowhere to fill the apparent emptiness of the silent veld.

In the late afternoon we arrived at Shambali Springs and pitched our camp under marula trees at the foot of an enormous boulder overlooking a reed-lined pool. This was the same spot where the two warring bull hippos had once disturbed our sleep, and we hoped the two had since settled their differences and would allow us a peaceful night.

At sunset a klipspringer appeared for a moment in silhouette on top of the large boulder behind our tent. Poised like a ballet dancer, the dainty little antelope surveyed our camp briefly, then launched itself into a perfect pinpoint leap to disappear from view.

Later came a herd of eland, their approach announced by the rhythmic clicking of their kneecaps. As we sat talking at our campfire, they grazed peacefully near us, until the wind changed suddenly and something – perhaps a strange smell – alarmed them and they fled into the night. For a while the bush seemed oddly silent, and we wondered if there were lion in the area. When lions are out hunting, the night knows and becomes eerily quiet. The dogs sat up abruptly, ears pricked, and Hettie drew our attention to a dark shape moving silently towards the water. It was a lone buffalo bull. We watched as he drank at the pool in the moonlight.

Having finished our supper, we were all yawning, and so it was early to bed to make up for the previous night's disturbed sleep.

But once again, the wilderness night allowed us no peace.

About an hour after we had gone to bed, we were woken by the snarling grunts of feeding lions. Had they caught and killed the lone buffalo we had seen drinking at the pool? As we listened to the eerie noises, we knew all too well that this was merely the beginning and that the rest were soon to follow.

And so they did. As soon as the local scavenger folks – the jackal and hyena – got news via the wind that there was a kill in the area, they were on their way. And before long, another peaceful night under the stars turned into an arena for an insane concert – this time of lions snarling and growling, jackals wailing and yapping, hyenas whooping, cackling, chortling, giggling and howling.

TO HAVE AND TO KEEP

'To have and to keep for all to enjoy, and to preserve and protect for future generations.'

President Paul Kruger (1898)

ENCOMPASSING TWELVE THOUSAND SQUARE MILES OF AFRICAN savannah, Kruger National Park is a great swath of grassland, thicket, woodland and riverine forest; a wildlife sanctuary larger than Wales.

The park has many faces, many moods. In summer temperatures soar above 40 degrees Celsius, and humidity mounts as cumulo-nimbus clouds build up and brood above the horizon. Day after day the air thickens, and the antelope grow still, tense, ears twitching, nostrils flared. Waiting. When the swirling clouds finally dissolve into sheets of rain, the rivers and watercourses churn into muddy torrents. After the rains, the savannahs stand in soggy silence, drinking the life-giving moisture. It is a season of birth and new growth. The newborn cavort under the watchful eyes of their mothers and the animals are sleek and content as they crop the new season's grasses or nibble on the tender shoots of trees and shrubs.

In the winter months of June, July and August, the earth is dry, the skies clear and cool. Many of the trees lose their leaves, the tangles of summer vegetation thin out and the grasses fade to a brittle gold. Game herds gather in large numbers near the perennial waters, grazing on the pale-gold savannahs under an azure sky.

From the Crocodile River in the south to the Sabie River near

Skukuza, thickets of acacia and bushwillow woodlands dominate the landscapes. Extending east towards the Lebombo Mountains are vast tracts of marula and knobthorn savannah, while to the west are the rolling landscapes of the Malelane-mountain bushveld. North of the Sabie River, extending towards the Olifants River, the thickets give way to open savannah – oceans of grass dotted with knobthorn and marula-tree islands. North of the Olifants begins the mopani country, the trees growing in unbroken stands that seem to stretch for ever. Further to the north and north-east, massive baobabs stand sentinel over a landscape of rugged hills and ridges. In the northernmost reaches of the park is the sandveld region with its forests of ghostly fever trees and unique flowering plants. Occurring throughout the park are the riverine forests that run along the six major rivers and their various tributaries.

Maintained by one of the world's most sophisticated conservation management systems, Kruger Park is a sanctuary for a spectacular array of wildlife, as well as a haven of peace and inspiration for its visitors. The tourist camps are neatly laid out, fenced in, with beautifully thatched cottages and bungalows set among green lawns and indigenous trees. All the major camps have a first-aid centre, a shop and a restaurant.

The park is divided into twenty-two ranger sections, each of which is manned by a game ranger and a team of usually about ten game guards. Some of the ranger stations, such as Mahlangeni, are in remote areas of the park, while others are situated near rest camps or entrance gates.

Visitors to the park are inclined to believe that anyone wearing the familiar khaki uniform with the green shoulder flashes is a game ranger. Most people in uniform, however, are tourism officials, administrative staff and maintenance staff. Others in uniform are the research staff, the veterinarians, the two helicopter pilots and the eight trail rangers who conduct walking tours in certain areas.

The game rangers also wear the khaki uniform and green epaulettes, but if you look closer you will see a little gold-plated badge pinned to their shirt with the legend 'Game Ranger'. That is, if you ever get the chance to look that closely at a game ranger. They are a rare species and are seldom seen, preferring the solitude of the wilderness to the company of human beings.

Their daily and intimate involvement with the ways of the wild shapes them into a breed apart. They acquire a sixth sense that enables them to tune in to the mysterious frequencies of nature that transmit information about the whereabouts and state of mind of all wild creatures. Or so I suspect.

The game rangers are responsible for protecting the reserve from both man-made and natural disasters. Coping with drought, disease, fire, flood and poachers are just some of their responsibilities, and there are many others. Together with their teams of game guards, they are on call twenty-four hours a day, and nature doesn't give her wardens much time off duty.

They patrol the far reaches of their sections, often on foot in the blazing African sun, to track a sick or wounded animal or to free it from a poacher's snare. They spend long nights hiding without shelter in the inhospitable Lebombo Mountains, waiting for the armed poachers from Mozambique who hunt our elephants and rhino for their ivory. They fight raging bush fires, work in torrential downpours, battle in times of drought to provide water for thirsty animals or to rescue them from the mud of drying rivers and pans where they become trapped in their search for water. Close encounters with fangs, claws and tusks are part of their daily lives, yet only a very few of them have ever had to use a firearm in self-defence – a testimony to that sixth sense of theirs.

The game guards are used primarily in an anti-poaching role, but they also assist with many of the other duties of the game ranger. Most of the game guards in Kruger are members of the Tsonga-Shangana tribe. Their language is Tsonga, and they call themselves Shangaan people. Being native to the lowveld bushlands, they have the necessary bush knowledge to make them supreme trackers. Brave, bush-wise and trained in the use of firearms and combat strategies, they make up a formidable battalion in the war against poachers. They are men of mettle who will never hesitate to perform their duty, no matter how harsh or dangerous the circumstances may be.

Together with the game rangers, the game guards constitute the front-line troops of conservation – the keepers of this precious Eden.

OUR INTREPID GAME GUARDS

OUR GAME GUARDS AT MAHLANGENI OCCASIONALLY HAD THEIR wives and young children staying with them at the staff village, but for the most part the families lived in neighbouring Gazankulu where they tended their farms and other family businesses. Every year at Christmas a party was arranged for the staff in the village, and the families in Gazankulu were invited. Kobus shot a buffalo for them for the occasion, and lots of jabula (African beer) was ordered from Skukuza. The families from Gazankulu arrived several days before the party to help with the preparations, the women striking in their traditional costumes with lengths of coloured cloth knotted over one shoulder and the children adorned in beads and trinkets. At night they sang to the accompaniment of their tribal drums, and when the howl of hyenas or the roar of lions echoed their music, the magic of Africa was alive at Mahlangeni.

Because the Mahlangeni section was so large, our game guards were often away for days on end, camping in tents in the bush wherever they were working. When Kobus was also away from home, he usually arranged that one or two of the game guards remained at base to keep an eye on the homestead. They were brave, loyal men who often and unhesitatingly helped me out when things went awry. I could not imagine life at Mahlangeni without my gallant neighbours.

Naturally, they also had their fair share of hair-raising encounters with wild animals.

Late one Sunday afternoon, game guard Makasani Maluleke was returning from a jabula party in Gazankulu, cycling back home to Mahlangeni in a happy if somewhat too relaxed mood. Cruising downhill at a fair speed he saw, rather too late, an elephant standing at the bottom of the slope, right in the middle of the track. Luckily the elephant had its back to the oncoming bicycle and was either asleep or deep in thought. Makasani braked hard but the bicycle skidded, overbalanced and ended up – together with Makasani – right underneath the elephant's belly.

The elephant screamed '*Whazat?*' and spun around. Seeing nothing untoward in the landscape ahead it concluded that something was amiss in the landscape down under, and stuck its trunk under its belly to investigate. Makasani, crawling on all fours, made a hasty exit between the elephant's hind legs and took off at top speed. He looked back only when he got to the top of the rise. The elephant had discovered the bicycle under its belly and had pulled it out with its trunk. Holding it at eye level, it examined the bicycle with a puzzled expression. After a long, hard look, the elephant put the bicycle down and, according to Makasani, walked off into the bush shaking its head.

Game guard Samuel Nkuna almost got killed one day when he and his colleagues were tracking an injured waterbuck along the southern bank of the river, not far from the house. While he was following the spoor, something in the undergrowth at the foot of a mkuhlu tree caught Samuel's attention and he went off to investigate. As he approached the tree, his eyes glued to a suspicious-looking shadow in the tangled vegetation, a flash of movement revealed an enormous leopard. Without any warning, it charged. Samuel saw only a yellow blur hurtling at him. As Samuel hit the earth, his rifle flew from his hands. The leopard sank its fangs into Samuel's shoulder, but let go and disappeared into the bush as the other game guards shouted and came running to Samuel's aid. They helped their colleague to his feet and brought him home.

Kobus and I cleaned and dressed the two deep fang marks in his

shoulder as well as some claw marks on his chest. Samuel explained to us that he'd had no time to cock and raise his rifle before the leopard was upon him. He didn't want to go to hospital, reasoning that Kobus and I had done a good enough job of doctoring his wounds. But Kobus explained to him that septicaemia caused by carnivore bites could be fatal if not treated effectively, and so he drove Samuel to the hospital at Phalaborwa. Fortunately Samuel's injuries weren't extensive, and after a few days in hospital he was discharged.

Million Mabunda, a young trainee game guard, once had a terrible experience with an elephant cow. After Million and the other game guards had been to repair a stretch of boundary fence between the park and Gazankulu, they were cycling home in the late afternoon. Eventually Million fell somewhat behind, pedalling peacefully along at his own pace. Dusk had already settled and visibility in the mopani woods wasn't too good. All of a sudden Million found himself in the middle of an elephant herd. Braking furiously, he accidentally pulled up right between a cow and her calf.

Naturally, no elephant mother in the world will tolerate such inconsiderate behaviour towards her calf. The cow wrapped her trunk around Million, plucked him from his bicycle and tossed him high into the air. Million landed many metres away in a thicket of mopani scrub. Then the furious cow tackled the bicycle, tearing it apart and stamping the pieces into the ground.

Million didn't wait around to find out what the cow was planning to do next. He crawled through the mopani scrub in the opposite direction as fast as he could until he reached a clearing. Leaping to his feet, he took off at lightning speed. The elephant didn't follow him and he made it safely to the staff village. When he got there, he was so shaken that he couldn't remember what had happened.

One of the Shangaan women came to the house to call me (Kobus wasn't home). She couldn't tell me what had happened to Million except that, whatever it was, it must have been something really terrible. I grabbed the first-aid kit and ran over to the staff village.

Million was sitting up, and although he appeared to be in shock, he showed no signs of physical injury, apart from an impressive collection of scratches and bruises.

I asked him what had happened.

He wasn't sure, he said, but he suspected that a whirlwind had blown him off his bicycle.

Since it had been a clear, windless day, I expressed my doubts about his explanation.

He thought it over and agreed that it couldn't have been a whirlwind. In fact, he said, it had just occurred to him that it had been a buffalo that had knocked him over.

I asked if the buffalo had hurt him. He shook his head, saying he couldn't tell; his body was numb.

But then he suddenly remembered that it hadn't been a buffalo: it had been a lion. The lion, he explained, had jumped out of a tree and flattened him.

Although I didn't think this likely, I once again expressed my concern, adding that he was fortunate that the lion had not injured him seriously.

He agreed. But after a few moments he decided the lion story wasn't the correct one either. Two rhinos, he told me, had stormed out of the bush and slammed into his bicycle, knocking him off it.

I felt clueless. By then it was dark, and too late to investigate the incident for myself, so I decided to go home. I asked the other game guards to keep a watchful eye on Million and to call me if his condition got worse.

Early the next morning I went back to see Million. The poor man looked a wreck. He had been unable to sleep, he told me, and his body was aching from his head to his toes. Fortunately, though, his memory had returned and he told me about the elephant.

I asked two of the game guards to accompany me, and we went off to investigate the 'scene of the crime'.

It was a shocking sight. Judging from the disturbed ground and broken vegetation, as well as the spoor and the pieces of bicycle lying around, the elephant cow had thrown a spectacular tantrum. Some eight metres from the wrecked cycle we found the spot where Million had landed and flattened the mopani scrub.

I ran home and radioed a message to Letaba Camp, requesting an ambulance for Million. (The park has its own ambulances.) Then I hurried back to the village. Feeling terrible about having doubted Million's latest explanation, I took him some strong, sweet tea and tried to make him as comfortable as possible until the ambulance arrived.

A thorough examination at the hospital revealed that he had no serious injuries but was suffering from severe shock. Fortunately he responded well to treatment, and after a few days of rest was allowed to come home.

We hope Million will one day enjoy telling his story to his grand-children and great-grandchildren.

THE WHIMS OF THE GENERATOR

O N THE DAY THAT WE MOVED INTO MAHLANGENI I FOUND A letter waiting for me in the kitchen. It was from my predecessor, Marcia – wife of game ranger Cobus Botha. (The couple had been transferred from Mahlangeni to Satara in the central district of the park.)

Dear Kobie

Before starting the generator in the mornings, make sure that both the refrigerator and the freezer are switched off, else their engines might blow. Ten seconds after the generator is running smoothly, you can switch on the freezer. This will cause a change in the pitch of the generator's drone. Wait until the pitch is back to normal again before switching on the refrigerator.

If you have an automatic washing machine you will have to disconnect or remove its water heating elements. They will draw too much power and trip the generator.

Don't use an electric kettle or coffee-maker or anything that boils water. They will also trip the generator.

Before using an iron, switch off the freezer as well as the refrigerator. Don't let your iron get too hot. If you hear a change in the pitch of the generator's drone, switch off the iron.

If you want to use an electric toaster, don't do so while the iron, vacuum cleaner or washing machine is running. If you hear the generator straining, switch off the refrigerator and freezer immediately.

When using a hairdryer, observe the same rules as for the toaster.

A sewing machine doesn't use much power, but at night, when your electric lights are switched on, take care not to have more than two other appliances running at the same time as your sewing machine.

On the other hand, the generator doesn't like to run when no power is being drawn. As you know, the engines of a refrigerator and a freezer run only periodically. (As soon as a certain temperature is reached, they automatically shut down for a period of time.) When it happens that the engines of both the fridge and the freezer are resting at the same time, and no other electric appliances in the house are in use, the generator overheats. So it's best to keep at least some of the lights in the house burning during the day to make sure power is being used.

Call me on the radio if you have troubles.

Good luck!

Your predecessor, Marcia

As you can see, advanced qualifications in mathematics, engineering and philosophy are required to cope with the neuroses of an electricity generator.

I was very grateful that I had a gas stove and didn't have to run through the checklist before cooking. Unfortunately gas freezers and refrigerators don't work very well in a climate as hot and humid as ours, so we had an electric freezer and refrigerator. And they gave me a lot of headaches.

In the summer months we had to put virtually anything edible – even maize meal, oats, flour, powdered milk and the like – into cold storage. In the winter months I froze as many vegetables from our garden as possible, to see us through the long summer months when vegetable gardens didn't survive the onslaught of insects and heat. Whenever we managed to catch fish in the river, I froze some of those as well. When the generator was off, the freezer maintained its freezing temperature for about twelve hours, as long as you didn't open it and let hot air rush in. But the refrigerator defrosted each time and had to be towel-dried before the generator was switched on again.

We could use the generator for only about ten to twelve hours out of every twenty-four, or it would overheat and also use up huge quantities of diesel. (And getting diesel to Mahlangeni wasn't easy. Kobus said it was only a miracle that he managed to balance the heavy drums in the boat without overturning the flimsy vessel.)

It took me a long time to come to terms with the quirks of the generator. In the beginning I often got confused and accidentally caused the machine to fade, sputter and die. This frightened me, as I lived in constant fear that my mistakes might cause the generator to blow up or break down. And it annoyed Filemoni, because to crank up the engine again was no picnic. When the generator was in a foul mood, no amount of cranking would get it going again – it needed to cool off first. And I always felt terrible when I saw Filemoni storming out of the generator room with his hands in the air, cursing the gods who'd created the machine.

Luckily it was quite simple to switch the generator off – merely a flick of a switch – except when the switch failed to disconnect (which happened fairly often) and you then had to disconnect the battery terminals to shut the machine down. This was not too difficult a thing to do, but very nerve-racking.

I liked to read in bed before going to sleep, especially when Kobus was away. Reading relaxed me. But just when I was feeling nice and drowsy and was about to put my book down before drifting into dreamland, I would remember with a horrible start that I had to go out into the dark and fearsome night to switch off the darned machine.

By the time I reached the engine room I was wide awake and decidedly tensed up. I particularly loathed the moment when, on opening the door to the room, the full volume of the engine's roar hit me. I would rush in and flick off the switch as quickly as possible to avoid being paralysed by the noise. When the switch failed, forcing me to spend some time in the company of that roaring machine while groping for its battery terminals in the dark, my heart rate increased to about four hundred beats per minute. Sometimes I did something wrong and the terminals gave me an electric shock, stopping my racing heart in its tracks.

By the time I was safely back inside the house, my heartbeat was scrambled, my nerves were jangled, and I couldn't sleep. I couldn't read either, or do anything else, as the electricity was off and the house as dark as the night outside.

One evening, while Kobus was hospitalized with malaria, I was sitting quietly in the house doing some sewing. Suddenly a reverberating bang frightened the fruit bats out of the sausage tree outside my window, and the house was instantly plunged into darkness. Feeling panicky and disorientated, I groped my way towards the bedroom to find my torch and pistol. I heard one of my daughters moaning softly in her sleep, but mercifully none of them woke up. The 'gunshot' had come from the other side of the house, furthest from their bedroom. I thought of the Mozambican refugees who were sometimes found carrying AK 47 rifles or other firearms. When I finally had both pistol and torch, I hurried through the house to the kitchen and peered outside. The dogs were barking without feeling sure what they were barking at. The quiet, moonlit night revealed nothing. Then, to my relief, I saw two game guards, armed with torches and rifles, running towards me from the staff village. As they reached the gate they started calling out to me. I answered to let them know I was unharmed. A few seconds later they were standing in front of me with puzzled expressions. Neither they nor I could think of a plausible explanation for the loud bang and subsequent loss of power. The game guards took the dogs and walked along the perimeters of the garden to inspect the fences, but returned after a while to report that all was well.

We went over to the generator room to see if we could determine why the machine had died. As we opened the door, there was a strong smell of burning. The generator itself looked undamaged. But as I shone the torch over the walls, we saw that the distribution board had exploded and burnt out. Evidently a short circuit had been responsible for the explosion.

I thanked the game guards for their concern and help, and made my way back to the dark house.

Early the next morning I radioed Louw, the technician at Letaba Camp, requesting help. On his arrival at Mahlangeni, he was appalled at the extent of the damage. I apologized profusely, thinking that I might have been responsible in some way. (Perhaps too many, or perhaps not enough, lights had been burning while I was using my electric sewing machine.) But Louw kindly reassured me that it wasn't my fault that the distribution board had exploded. The bad news, however, was that it would take a number of days to put together a new distribution board. Parts would have to be ordered from Skukuza. We would have to do without power for several days.

But the story has a happy ending. When the new distribution board was finally ready to be installed, Louw brought us a new and more powerful generator to replace the old one. And with the demise of that temperamental old machine that had terrified me and exasperated Filemoni for so many years, most of Marcia's complicated rules mercifully became redundant. The new generator even had a switch that didn't fail.

MALARIA AND A MONTH OF MISHAPS

DURING THE LATE SUMMER OF 1984, I AWOKE ONE NIGHT TO FIND Kobus rummaging in the cupboard for blankets. This was odd since it was a particularly warm March night. When he was back in bed and well covered, he shivered so violently that his teeth were chattering. I got up and fetched another blanket.

Within minutes he wanted to go to the bathroom but was feeling too cold to get out of bed. Once he had motivated himself sufficiently to make the short trip, he dashed from the bed to the bathroom, almost freezing in the process. His teeth were chattering as he dived back under the covers and, idiots that we were, we both laughed at the scene.

Even under three blankets, Kobus was still cold, so I fetched yet another quilt. Only then did it dawn on us that he could have malaria, and we resolved to visit the hospital for blood tests the next day.

In the morning, though, Kobus felt better and, dismissing the ailment as flu, he went off to work. I didn't think it was flu. I was recovering from a bout of tick fever at the time, and I thought it likely that Kobus was coming down with the same thing.

Late that afternoon he came home feeling tired and dizzy and he went to lie down. Soon he began to shiver violently. His face turned blue and his teeth chattered. He complained that he couldn't get warm, even under the many blankets I piled on top of him. I had no doubt then that it was malaria. Remembering the things I had read about the disease, I knew that Kobus had to get to hospital without delay. I thought of radioing Letaba Camp and asking for an ambulance, but Shibyeni Creek was flooding its banks and the ambulance would not be able to get through. The only way to get Kobus to Phalaborwa would be to row him across the river and get him to my jeep. But he was too ill that evening to get up and walk down to the river.

After several exhausting hours the rigor finally passed, only to be followed by a burning fever. He had a severe headache, felt nauseous and complained of thirst, but couldn't swallow the water I offered him.

In the early hours of the next morning, the hot stage passed and was followed by a stage of drenching perspiration. Although Kobus was sweating freely he felt much better. At dawn we made our way down to the river, rowed across and headed for the hospital at Phalaborwa.

A blood smear was taken, and *Plasmodium falciparum* (pernicious malaria) was diagnosed.

Malaria is caused by protozoal parasites of the genus *Plasmodium* which are transmitted by female anopheline mosquitoes. Four species of *Plasmodium* are known to infect humans, not all of them equally dangerous. Three of the species cause repeated periodic attacks of fever, but although patients may become severely ill, these cases don't always end fatally if left untreated.

The fourth species, *Plasmodium falciparum*, causes the severe form of the disease known as pernicious (or malignant) malaria. Unless treated promptly and energetically, pernicious malaria is fatal.

Kobus was now critically ill, so treatment commenced immediately.

The fever attacks raged on constantly and violently. After twenty-four hours he still hadn't responded to treatment and so the doctors began administering chloroquine intravenously. Because of a staff shortage the ward sister allowed me to nurse my husband. I was grateful, since it enabled me to stay at his bedside day and night.

During the cold stage of a fever attack, I piled as many blankets as I could onto Kobus, sometimes rushing into other wards to steal blankets from unoccupied beds. Even so, he shivered so violently that I had to hold him down to keep him from falling off the bed. Often his face would turn blue and he would have difficulty breathing. The ward sister showed me how to administer oxygen when this happened. The cold stage sometimes lasted as long as two or three hours.

As soon as the cold stage passed, he developed a severe headache and became delirious while his temperature rocketed to 40 degrees and above. The hot stage is the worst part of each attack as it is severe and long-lasting (three to six hours), and sometimes the patient starts to fear that he can't keep on fighting for his life – the exhaustion is overwhelming. During the hot stage I put an oxygen tent over Kobus's entire bed, then sat down next to him, sometimes reaching under the tent to touch his hand so that he knew I was still there.

During the third stage he perspired freely and his bedclothes became sodden, but he felt much better. In these brief periods, I took down the oxygen tent and helped Kobus to take a few sips of water. Then in a short while the whole exhausting, frightening cycle would be repeated.

There was no time for sleep. Sometimes, during the sweating stages, I dozed fitfully in the chair next to Kobus's bed, but never for longer than a few minutes at a time.

When, after forty-eight hours, he was still not responding to the chloroquine, I began to feel sick with fear. During one brief break between attacks, I rushed to the nearest telephone and called the Institute for Tropical Diseases in Tzaneen. I asked what treatment was available for a patient with pernicious malaria who was not responding to chloroquine. The director informed me that quinine, given intravenously, would be the next step. (While quinine works faster than chloroquine and other derivatives, it has more serious side-effects.)

I talked to the ward sister and when she found out that the hospital had no quinine, she agreed to order some immediately.

A while later, as the doctor was making his rounds and studying Kobus's fever charts, I heard him telling the sister to order quinine immediately. She answered that she had already done so and that it was on its way.

Fortunately, that same evening, before the medicine arrived, Kobus seemed to improve. He was finally responding to treatment. As relief swept over me, I discovered that I was completely exhausted. I could hardly keep my eyes open and my thoughts were becoming so scrambled that I had trouble deciphering them. I cornered the sister on duty and asked her to keep watch over my husband while I allowed myself my first few hours of sleep in three days.

Barely awake, I drove myself the ten or so kilometres to my daughters' hostel inside the park. Not wanting to wake anyone, I slipped inside and quietly collapsed on an unoccupied bed.

I saw the girls early the next morning and told them about their father's illness. I was relieved that I could reassure them that Kobus was on the road to recovery. I wouldn't have wanted them to know all the fears that had been filling my mind over the past few days.

Since the schools were closing for the autumn holidays and Kobus seemed to be a little better, I took the girls home two days later. For the next week or so, I drove to Phalaborwa every morning, spent the day at the hospital, and returned home in the evening. The game guards kept a watchful eye on the girls in my absence, and the girls also knew how to use the radio in case of an emergency. Hettie took care of the cooking, and there was always a plate of delicious food waiting for me when I got home.

Ranger Ben Lamprecht of Letaba called on the radio every evening, both to enquire about Kobus and to make sure that I had arrived home safely.

As if things weren't bad enough with Kobus being so ill and in hospital, just about everything else that could go wrong at Mahlangeni did so during this period.

First, the gas ran out, so we couldn't use the gas stove. Luckily we had a little coal stove tucked into a niche beneath the hot-water tank behind the house. Filemoni lit a fire in it every morning to supply hot water to the household. While we were without gas, the girls used the little coal stove for cooking.

This was also the week when the generator's distribution board exploded, which meant that the electric fridge and freezer were out of action, and the time when a paranoid hippo was making life very difficult. Not wanting to row across the river again after a particularly nasty incident one morning, I told Filemoni I would use the longer route via Shimuwini to get home.

Little did I know then that even more trouble awaited me at Shimuwini. Well, not that same day, but on the following day.

Shimuwini was a large dam in the Letaba River, some thirty-five kilometres south-east of our house. A huge weir made up the eastern wall of the dam. The water spilled over the weir onto a concrete strip several metres below the top, and then into the lower reaches of the river itself. The concrete strip was about two metres wide and crossed the whole width of the river under the weir.

If you drove carefully and looked where you were going, you could drive across the river on the concrete strip in comparative safety, except of course when the river was in spate.

On my way home from the hospital that afternoon, I found only a thin trickle of water dribbling over the weir. Driving slowly and carefully, I managed to get safely across.

When Ben called from Letaba that evening, he reminded me that the following day was pay day, and that Mahlangeni's game guards needed to report to Phalaborwa Gate to receive their salaries, and then to go into town for their monthly shopping.

I walked over to the village and told the staff I would drive them to Phalaborwa the next morning.

As I stepped out onto the veranda early the next morning to enjoy a cup of coffee, I was shocked to see that the Little Letaba was in spate, forcing a deluge of foamy brown water into the Letaba. We would need to leave immediately to get to Shimuwini before the flood reached the dam and started spilling over the weir.

I quickly said goodbye to the girls and drove over to the village in Kobus's Land-Rover to pick up my passengers.

When we arrived at Shimuwini some fifty minutes later, we found to our dismay that a thick sheet of water was already spilling over the weir. We got out of the truck and walked down to the bank to assess the situation.

The water running over the concrete strip was only a few inches deep, not too deep to drive through but deep enough to obscure the strip.

The only other way to get to Phalaborwa would be via the high-water bridge near Letaba Camp – a journey that would take between three and four hours. I consulted my passengers. They agreed that the water didn't seem too high yet, and that it would be a lot nicer if we could manage to cross the river right here, at Shimuwini, which was only one hour's drive from Phalaborwa. I took a deep breath and convinced myself that if I drove carefully, keeping close to the wall, everything would be fine.

Engaging the four-wheel drive, I cautiously drove down the rocky path onto the concrete strip. And then I got really scared: the sheet of water spilling over the weir cascaded onto the truck in a solid torrent. It was like driving into a waterfall. I turned the windscreen wipers on full blast, but they didn't really help much.

Once you're on the concrete strip, you cannot go back. It's too tricky to reverse on that narrow strip. And even if you managed to stay on it while you reversed, you would hardly be able to continue back up the rocky slope without missing the winding track and crashing into the river below. I had no choice but to press on, even though things were getting worse every second. If I kept too close to the wall, the water cascading over it pounded the car relentlessly, and if I moved too far from the wall, I risked being swept off the concrete strip and into the deluge below.

We were about halfway across the strip when, with a horrible thump, the two left wheels of the Land-Rover slid over the edge and we were balancing precariously over the swirling waters below.

Before I had time to recover from the shock and to start thinking coherently, the man next to me opened his door and got out, letting himself down onto some large rocks in the water below us. The other men immediately followed suit, clambering over the front seat to get out. (The rear door of the Land-Rover was stuck and couldn't be opened from the inside.)

Soon all six men were standing on the uneven rock formation, up to their waists in the water. Leaning into the current to keep their balance, they were straining to lift and push the Land-Rover back onto the concrete strip. I called out to them, begging them to come out of the water before they got taken by crocodiles or were swept away in the deluge. But they either couldn't hear me or were ignoring me.

I had to get out of the car and persuade them to get back onto the strip. We would abandon the vehicle and walk – or crawl – along the strip to the opposite bank. First I took my identity document and stuffed it into my blouse pocket. (I don't quite remember why I did this, except that it seemed like a good idea at the time.) Then I kicked off my sandals, opened my door, and was immediately drenched by the torrent of water cascading over the weir. I got out and stepped carefully onto the concrete. Clinging to the sides of the truck I made my way slowly around it to the edge of the strip. Before I could talk to the men, they saw me and cried out angrily, commanding me to get back into the truck. I tried arguing with them, shouting above the noise of the water, but they wouldn't listen and insisted that I get back into the truck immediately. Somewhat cowed by their authoritative manner, I obeyed.

I sat and watched nervously as they battled in the water, keeping my eyes wide open for crocodiles. Finally they managed to heave the truck until the two wheels came level with the concrete, and then, with a huge shove, pushed the Land-Rover safely back onto the strip.

I switched on the engine again, feeling both very relieved that all had gone well and terrified that I might drive over the edge again. Two of the men apparently shared my fear, and decided to walk ahead of the car to show the way.

They moved carefully along the strip, shuffling sideways like crabs for better balance against the current. I followed slowly, grateful to find that this way it was a lot easier to stay on the strip.

We reached the far bank safely, and I felt deeply indebted to my gallant companions.

By the end of the week, Kobus was begging the doctor to let him go home. He said the hospital room was giving him claustrophobia. I don't know if the doctor believed him, but I did. Game rangers are very prone to claustrophobia since they spend most of their lives outdoors. Eventually the doctor agreed to discharge him.

Kobus had lost a lot of weight and was a frightfully frail and pallid version of the strong man he used to be. But once he was back home at his beloved Mahlangeni, he soon started to regain his strength.

And so a difficult month of malaria and other mishaps finally came to an end.

COPING WITH SNAKES

URING THAT INTERVIEW IN THE CHIEF RANGER'S OFFICE AT Skukuza, when I was warned about the hardships that a game ranger's wife could expect to endure, they forgot to mention snakes.

In the early days at Mahlangeni, it didn't occur to me that snakes had the right to be in our garden and I declared war on them. I had such a deep mistrust especially of the mambas and cobras that I wouldn't even negotiate with them. If they came anywhere near the house I reached for the shotgun. I hated this warfare with all my heart, but the trouble was I believed it to be my duty, as the mother of three young children, to keep poisonous snakes out.

I also felt responsible for the safety of my brood of bantams. When a snake finds its way into a poultry run, it creates mayhem. My bantams roamed free during the day but were locked up at night to protect them from predators.

One night when Kobus was away, I was woken by a hysterical commotion in the hen house and I knew right away that a snake was in there. Grabbing a torch and my pistol (a shotgun would have killed most of the bantams as well), I rushed outside.

When I reached the hen house I found to my horror that there was a Mozambique cobra inside and that it had already bitten one of the hens and devoured all but one of her chicks. The snake was still busy swallowing a chick when, startled by the gleam of my torch, it reared its head, immediately offering a good angle for an accurate shot.

Unfortunately I got confused. I had the pistol in my left hand and the torch in my right, and so I shot at the snake with the torch while lighting the scene with the pistol. Of course this didn't work, and the cobra escaped into the darkness.

I rushed over to aid the bitten hen but found she was already dead. I picked up her orphaned chick and took him inside with me. Feeling sorry for the chick, I let him sleep on the bed with me in an empty shoebox lined with cotton wool. Having shared my bed for just one night, the chick woke up believing I was his mother.

He followed me around like a puppy, cheeping pathetically whenever he lost sight of me. So I carried him about in my shirt pocket, which he loved, until he became too big for the pocket and had to learn to run fast enough to keep up with me. As he grew older and became more confident he ventured into the garden during the day but, come sundown, he trotted back into the house where he took up nocturnal residence on my bedside cabinet.

I tried to introduce him to his kin, but he refused to believe that he was a chicken. He wanted only to be with me. Whenever he saw me reading in the garden, he would rush straight to me and perch contentedly on my lap. Even though he eventually accepted his fate and learned to spend his nights in the hen house with the other bantams, by day he would have nothing to do with them. He passed his time scratching around in the garden on his own.

I felt sorry for my loner, and so I was very grateful when another ranger's wife sent me a beautiful young bantam hen. She was red, not white like my other hens, and just the right age to be a companion for my lone rooster. I promptly introduced them, but the silly rooster refused to take any notice of the cute red hen and went about his business as if she didn't exist.

Feeling very disappointed about this, I carried the hen over to the other bantams and introduced her to them. But she, in turn, would have nothing to do with them and ran off, back to the loner. He continued to ignore her, but she followed him around like a shadow. After a few days her perseverance paid off. The lone rooster began to notice how attractive she was, and it finally dawned on him that he was a chicken.

After the episode with the Mozambique cobra we enclosed the hen house in a second layer of wire mesh to make it doubly snake-proof.

It took me the better part of a year to realize that snakes were as scared of humans as we of them, and that they would only strike out in self-defence. So I came to the conclusion that the thing to do was to avoid snakes, not kill them. In any case, I couldn't go on with the warfare – it was too upsetting.

I devised a set of ground rules on how to avoid snakes and taught them to my daughters. For instance, don't climb trees with dense foliage. Never poke your hands into places where you can't see what's going on inside (such as rock crevices, dense vegetation, holes in the ground). Always watch where you place your feet. Don't walk through flowerbeds, dense scrub or long grass. Don't walk under low branches without first looking up for snakes. Never leave the house at night without a torch. Light the way directly in front of your feet. Keep the gauze screens on windows and doors closed at all times to prevent snakes from entering the house. And if you encounter a snake at close quarters unexpectedly, don't make any sudden movements. Retreat carefully and quietly.

My rules have proved very successful. Throughout the years neither my daughters nor I have been bitten by a snake. Only Kobus has, but we'll come to that later.

Shortly after I had resolved to avoid snakes rather than kill them, an unfortunate episode marred my good intentions. I was alone at home and had just had a shower before going to bed. As I opened the bathroom door I was greeted by the sight of a huge Mozambique spitting cobra lying on the floor right in front of me. I leaped backwards and slammed the bathroom door. Standing behind the closed door I couldn't decide what to do next. My clothes were in the bedroom, and the cobra was blocking my only way to get to them.

According to my textbook on snakes, the Mozambique spitting cobra is one of the most lethal snakes in Africa, second only to the mamba. It is nervous and highly strung and can move with considerable speed. It can also 'spit' its venom and reach its target (usually the eyes) at a distance of two to three metres with remarkable accuracy.

Despite the snake's reputation, I didn't feel like spending the night in the bathroom. Climbing out through the window in a state of undress didn't seem a good idea either. So I gritted my teeth and opened the door again – just a crack. The cobra was still there, but had moved slightly. Its head was some distance down the passage now, and only its tail section remained between the bedroom and me. Performing my very best high-cum-long jump, I reached the bedroom safely. After throwing on some clothes, I grabbed my torch and ran to the village to ask for help.

Three game guards answered my call, and when I told them about the snake they quickly armed themselves with sticks, whips and an assegai (a sharp, light spear).

I led them back to the house to show them where the snake was. It had now moved into my bedroom, and when it saw us it disappeared behind a bookcase. I offered to help, but was promptly ordered out of the house. Not ungratefully, I complied and stepped outside onto the veranda.

I could hear furniture being moved about, plans of action discussed and commands exchanged, then the sharp cracking of whips, accompanied by some colourful language. A sudden silence indicated that the battle might be over. Sighs of relief and some self-congratulatory remarks confirmed that the battle had indeed been won.

The game guards came out of the bedroom with the dead snake impaled on the assegai. I shuddered at the sight and felt sorry for the snake, but was immensely grateful that I hadn't had to kill it myself.

As our gauze screens remained shut day and night, we were never able to explain how snakes got indoors.

Karin charged into our bedroom one evening, announcing that she had discovered a snake in the most dreadful place of all: right inside the toilet bowl. We rushed to the bathroom and found a cobra with its head raised over the side of the toilet seat. On seeing us, it dived back inside and disappeared into the plumbing. We racked our brains, but couldn't think of any way to get the snake out of there. In the end we decided to leave the toilet seat up (in case the snake wanted to get out) but keep the bathroom door closed (so that we would find the snake there in the morning if it decided to come out). It didn't emerge though, and we never saw it again. We were decidedly skittish about using the toilet for quite a while afterwards, and didn't dally when we did.

Kobus said there was enough oxygen above the water levels in the plumbing for a snake to make its way safely along the pipes. Was that the answer to our question as to how snakes found their way into the house? If so, I didn't like it.

In the winter of 1988 Kobus and his colleagues were capturing zebras for relocation to another park. As they were herding the zebra into a catching enclosure, Kobus spotted a purple-glossed snake lying right in the path of the approaching zebras. Wanting to save the snake, he grabbed it by the tail and neck but, before he could toss it out of the way, the snake bit him on the hand. The attending vet, Dr Cobus Raath, who was running directly behind Kobus, reached out to assist him and, in doing so, was also bitten on the hand.

The purple-glossed snake is a seemingly harmless burrowing snake, and since it doesn't usually bite people, the properties of its venom are unknown.

Neither Kobus nor the vet had the time just then to worry about their bites as they wanted to complete the difficult capture exercise first. Once this was over, they decided the snake probably wasn't poisonous but swallowed some antihistamine tablets just in case.

When Kobus came home that afternoon, his hand and forearm were hideously swollen, the skin so tight it looked almost translucent. The girls and I were horrified and asked what the heck the zebras had done to him. He explained about the snakebite.

I rushed to the bedroom to fetch a sterile needle from the first-aid kit, and then to the refrigerator to find a vial of antivenom, but discovered to my dismay that the expiry date printed on the label was almost three months back. The trouble with antivenom is that it usually expires before anyone has reason to use it. Once it has expired, it does more harm than good.

I hurried back to Kobus and found him sitting in front of the television, watching a game of rugby.

'We'd better drive to the hospital right away,' I told him. 'The antivenom has expired.'

'Not now,' he said. 'I have to watch the game.'

'You can't!' I exclaimed. '*You* might expire in the meantime.'

'I'll go afterwards,' he offered. 'It's the cup final.'

'What if you're comatose by then?' I asked. 'How do I get you to the hospital?'

'You'll manage,' he said. 'Now please get out of the way so I can see the screen.'

Rugby is almost a religion in our country, so I knew Kobus would not miss a game if he could help it. But wasn't a snakebite more important than rugby?

I went to ask the girls their opinion. Hettie suggested we switch off the electric generator, letting her father believe it broke down. Sandra didn't think this was a good idea. She said he might get a heart attack if the TV went dead while the match was on, and if he didn't, he would certainly storm out of the house and go straight to the generator to see why it had stopped. Karin agreed with Sandra.

I gave up.

While Kobus enjoyed the rugby, I tried to find information on the venom of the purple-glossed snake. According to the textbook, it was a shy snake, seldom seen and not known to be aggressive. No records existed on the effects of its venom. Apparently Kobus and the vet were the first human beings in recorded history to be bitten by the purple-glossed snake.

It occurred to me that the least I could do for mankind was to record my husband's reactions to the venom.

I rushed to the lounge to check how he was doing. His breathing was irregular and I could see that he was in pain, but this might have been because his team was doing badly in the match.

I remembered another book that might be helpful and went off to find it: *Let's Get Well* by Adelle Davis, an American nutritionist. I looked up the text on snakebite and found some valuable advice. The author recommended that the victim immediately be given massive doses of vitamin C, at least 4000 milligrams, followed by further frequent doses. According to the author, vitamin C inhibits the penetration of toxins into cells and also reduces the toxic effects of poisons entering the system.

I fetched the bottle of vitamin C tablets from the refrigerator and shook out eight 500 mg tablets. Bracing myself for the task of feeding them to the victim, I returned to the lounge. Fortunately Kobus was so involved in his rugby game that he swallowed the pills just to get me out of his hair.

When the game finally came to an end, I tried to put my foot down and insist that we drive to Phalaborwa right away. Kobus protested, saying that he was feeling much better, and offered to go the following day.

It's no use arguing with a game ranger.

It wasn't even dark yet, but when I looked for him again Kobus was fast asleep on our bed. The glands in his neck were swollen and his face had lost some colour. He certainly didn't look well. As I touched his swollen arm lightly he woke, groaned and went back to sleep. Obviously his arm and hand were painful. Not knowing how to man-handle a sleeping husband, I distracted myself by preparing supper for our daughters.

Before going to bed, I woke Kobus to give him another 500 mg dose of vitamin C. He had a good night's sleep, while I hardly slept at all. I lay awake, listening for changes in the rhythm of his breathing. I also shone my torch on his hand and arm at regular intervals to check for signs of subcutaneous bleeding. And I woke him several times to feed him further doses of vitamin C.

In the morning Kobus looked and felt much better. (Only I looked and felt terrible from lack of sleep.) His hand and arm were less swollen than they had been the previous day and were apparently also less painful. Three days later, both hand and arm were back to their normal size and the puncture marks were healing nicely.

We learned later that the vet, Dr Raath, had suffered from severe headaches and nausea for several days. His hand and arm had remained swollen and painful for more than a week, and the puncture wounds on his hand had turned septic. He had taken only antihistamine tablets.

It seemed to me that Adelle Davis had a point about vitamin C.

A few weeks later, ranger Johan Oelofse came across a Shangaan woman in the bush who had been bitten by a puff-adder. She was one of a group of Mozambican refugees passing through the park on their way to Gazankulu. After she had been bitten she couldn't keep up with the rest of the group, and so they went on without her. Johan helped her into his vehicle and brought her to Mahlangeni, the closest ranger station.

The woman's leg was painfully swollen by then and I doubted whether the vitamin C treatment would do any good at such a late stage. But wanting desperately to help her, I gave her 5000 mg of vitamin C together with some calcium tablets to alleviate the pain. Before Johan drove her to the hospital at Phalaborwa, I gave her another handful of vitamin C tablets, explaining that she should take a couple of tablets every half hour or so. The poor woman was exhausted but managed to communicate her gratitude with a nod and the shadow of a smile.

Two days later, when Kobus came home, I told him of the incident. He radioed the official at Phalaborwa Gate, asking him to contact the hospital and enquire about the condition of the Shangaan woman who had been admitted for snakebite two days previously.

The reply from the hospital was that she must have been feeling much better: she had discharged herself the previous day. I was so relieved to hear that. I hoped she had found her family in Gazankulu and was doing OK.

Anyway, it seemed that I had acquired another living testimonial for Adelle Davis's vitamin C theory. Although I wouldn't rely solely on vitamin C to save someone's life in cases of mamba or even cobra bites, it is comforting to know that the vitamin appears at least to some extent to inhibit the progress of the poison.

Once I came to terms with the fact that snakes had the right to live, I felt a lot better about myself. I still don't particularly like snakes, but at least I know how to cope with them. First we must aim to avoid them, and secondly we should take care never to be without a substantial supply of vitamin C.

THE REIGN OF THE RIVER

THE LETABA RIVER HAD MORNING COLOURS, NOON COLOURS AND evening colours. In winter it was placid, enigmatic, lazy, its surface as smooth and shiny as a mirror. In summer it became turbulent and restless, its water level rising and receding continuously according to the amount and frequency of rainfall in the catchment areas.

For us, the river with its ever-changing moods and the hippos with their booming voices constituted the most romantic features of Mahlangeni.

But they also gave us a lot of trouble.

Each time the river was in spate and we had to go to town, we were faced with the difficult choice of either braving the current in our flimsy boat, or taking the vast detour via the high-water bridge near Letaba Camp. And every so often we would choose braving the waters rather than spending all those extra hours on the road. But more often than not, we regretted the decision as soon as we got swept into the nightmare of a raging torrent. Fortunately we survived our mistakes. But after each hair-raising crossing we promised ourselves that we would never, ever again risk rowing across in a flood.

But then some day (usually a Friday when the children had to be fetched) the river would suddenly be in spate again, and the road via Letaba Camp would seem so very, very long . . .

If I was home alone, I would sigh deeply and opt for the endless detour. But if Kobus was home, I relied on him to decide what was to be done. Being a man, he usually decided that it was safe enough to row across and would offer to fetch the children. At this stage of the negoti-ations, it would occur to me that it was in fact *not* safe to row across. So invariably an argument ensued. Kobus always won, but by then I would be so convinced that it was definitely not safe to row across that I always went along, because when the children arrived home, I would need to be in the boat with them to make sure . . . well, I don't know of what. I would just need to be with them.

So we would go down to the shore and drag the boat a couple of hundred metres upstream along the sand. The stronger the current, the further upstream we had to launch the boat to compensate for the distance that the current would sweep us downstream.

And as usual, the moment we launched the boat and felt the power of the roaring torrent as it gripped our little vessel and began to hurl us downstream, I knew beyond any doubt that the four-hour journey via the high-water bridge would have been bliss compared to this. And as I watched Kobus straining every muscle as he battled to row against the current, I knew that we were crazy to do what we were doing.

By the time we finally reached the far bank – usually beaching in an almost impenetrable thicket of reeds and many metres downstream from our usual anchoring spot – I would be so badly shaken that I could

hardly talk. And then, having made our way through the dense reeds to the car shelter at the top of the bank, we would agree, while rubbing bruises inflicted by the reeds, not to bring the children back across the river but instead to drive them home via the high-water bridge. Because really there is just no comparison between the inconvenience of a few extra hours on the road and the terrible rage of a crazy river.

And yet, despite the countless occasions when I felt angry at the river for all the troubles it caused us, I got immensely upset when, in times of protracted drought, the river dwindled to an inferior muddy stream. At such times, we longed to see the river in all its dramatic splendour again. There is something about a massive roaring body of water, rolling on relentlessly to its distant destination, that is exhilarating beyond words.

Another problem that came with floods was that the hippos left the water. Since a hippo on land is far more dangerous than a hippo in water, we had to be especially careful to avoid meeting them on the river shores. Often they would quietly leave the water many hours prior to a flood, and we – unaware of the approaching deluge – would have no idea that they had done so.

My closest encounter with a hippo on land happened on a Friday morning when Filemoni was away on leave and I had to row across on my own. After securing the boat, I started up the winding footpath through the thickets of croton bushes to the car shelter at the top of the bank. About halfway up the path the sound of something big stepping on a twig stopped me in my tracks. A short distance ahead, to the right of the footpath, the croton thickets gave a shudder and out peeked a hippo, its eyes locked on me, its face the biggest I had ever seen up close. Instinct commanded me to turn and bolt for the safety of the boat, but my mind screamed, 'Wait! Never get between a hippo and the water.' At that moment I was right between the hippo and his aquatic haven. For two terrible seconds we stood facing each other, and I felt certain that if we both opted to dash for the safety of the river, the hippo would overtake me and probably annihilate me in the process. So I put my head down and ran straight into the dense tangle of croton bushes to my left, creating an impressive tunnel through the almost impenetrable thickets, stopping only when I'd reached the top of the bank. Then I turned to see where the hippo had gone.

Surprisingly, he hadn't fled into the water. He had chosen a direction opposite to mine and had steamrollered a highway through the croton jungle to the west of the footpath. Apparently the sight of me had given him such a fright that he'd forgotten that a hippo felt safe in the water. I guess I hadn't looked too good that morning.

After this incident Kobus and the game guards went across the river and chopped a wider clearance through the croton thickets on either side of the footpath to reduce the chances of another close encounter of the same kind.

Apart from the risks involved in crossing the river, the exercise itself was an exhausting one.

The river had a wide bed flanked on either side by high banks. A narrow stone stairway led from our front gate down the bank to the riverbed. In winter, when the water level was low, the dry shore between the stairway and the water's edge usually covered about sixty metres. In summer, when the waters rose, the dry shore shrank and sometimes disappeared for a while under the swollen river.

On the far side of the river there was no sandy shore between the water and the bank. The bank rose directly out of the water at a fairly steep angle and then undulated in even and uneven slopes until it flattened out at the top into mopani savannah. Hauling the girls' hostel luggage down the steep stairway every Monday morning, then across the sandy beach to the boat and finally up the opposite bank to the car was a major operation.

One Monday morning, as the girls and I were making our way up the opposite bank, I slipped on the dew-covered grass and went crashing down, losing my grip on the suitcase I was carrying. It slid down the bank and plunged into the river. (It was Sandra's suitcase, containing all her school clothes for the week.) Rushing down the slope I jumped back into the boat and rowed furiously after the drifting suitcase. Fortunately

I managed to retrieve it before it sank or emigrated to Mozambique.

On Friday afternoons the whole luggage-hauling routine was, of course, repeated in the opposite direction. And whenever I combined a trip to the hostel with a trip into town to buy groceries, the latter added considerable weight to the load that had to be ferried over. Sometimes the groceries didn't all fit into the boat and a second trip had to be made to get everybody and everything across.

Whenever Kobus replenished our supplies of diesel, petrol and gas, these also had to be conveyed by boat. Rowing the heavy, awkward containers across wasn't easy.

Then there were times when frequent rainfalls in the catchment areas caused continuous rising and ebbing of the water level of the river, and each time it ebbed it left a broad strip of muddy sludge behind. It also left the boat stranded in the mud, usually some distance from the ebbing water. It's not too difficult to drag a boat across dry sand, but dragging it through sludge is a messy and exasperating business. On Monday mornings, at times such as these, we carried our decent shoes in a bag and wore old canvas shoes on the trek through the muddy morass. We also took a container of water and some towels along so that, on reaching the far bank, we could wash the mud from our feet and legs before putting on our respectable shoes.

One Saturday morning, while the river was ebbing after a flood, our new chief ranger, Bruce Bryden, turned up at Mahlangeni to pay us a visit. Bruce had brought along a new rifle that he wanted to show to Kobus, and the two men made their way down to the shore to test the weapon.

Karin was feeding titbits to a tame tortoise in the front garden, while some distance away from her Hettie was stroking the head of one of our horses who was grazing on the lawn.

As Bruce fired the first shot down by the river, the echoing thunderclap startled the horse. It reared with fright and its head smashed into Hettie's jaw, knocking her unconscious. She collapsed onto the grass. As the bewildered horse turned to flee, one of its hooves came down on the side of Hettie's head, opening a deep gash in her temple.

Karin, who had turned towards the river when she heard the shot, swung round as she heard the horse whinnying. First she saw the horse taking off in fright, then her sister lying slumped on the grass. She ran to Hettie as fast as she could. Extremely shocked to find her lying with her head in a pool of blood, Karin thought that the shot had hit her sister. Shouting to her father for help, she sprinted towards the front gate and the river shore. The men heard her calls and, within seconds, came rushing up the stone stairway. I was busy inside the house when I heard Karin shouting for help. I ran outside.

When I reached the scene, Kobus and Bruce were already kneeling at Hettie's side, feeling her pulse and lifting her eyelids to check her pupils. She was still unconscious and her long blond hair was soaked in blood. Shaking with fright, I rushed back into the house to fetch bandages. After we had bandaged the wound, Kobus lifted Hettie gently and carried her down the stone stairway to the boat.

There was no time for canvas shoes, towels or water. We hurried through the mud to the boat, sinking up to our ankles in the sludge. Bruce helped us drag the boat through the deep mud to the water. I got into the boat and sat down so that Kobus could hand Hettie to me. While Kobus took the oars and Bruce helped launch the boat, I turned to look at my other two daughters who were standing on the shore, ashen-faced but bravely waving us goodbye.

Bruce volunteered to stay with them until we returned.

At the far side of the river, Kobus carried Hettie up the steep bank to the car. I sat in the back of the car with Hettie, cradling her head in my lap. She had in the meantime regained consciousness but was as white as a sheet and lay very still. The wound was bleeding through the bandages and I noted vaguely that my clothes, arms and legs were covered in mud and blood.

Kobus drove as fast as he safely could, and we arrived at the hospital just over an hour later. Bruce had meanwhile radioed ahead to Phalaborwa Gate, and the official on duty there had in turn contacted the hospital to let them know we were bringing in an injured girl.

On our arrival at the hospital the staff were waiting for us with a gurney in place to rush Hettie inside. When they saw that Kobus and I were also covered in blood and mud they concluded that we, too, had been injured. It took some explaining to convince them that they needn't bring gurneys for us as well. While Hettie was wheeled to the operating theatre, Kobus and I located a tap in the garden where we quickly rinsed off the worst of the dirt before going back inside.

When Hettie came out of the theatre some thirty minutes later, she looked a lot better. The deep gash in her head had been stitched and dressed, her hair had been washed, and she had regained some colour in her face. She was even smiling at us. At least, it was a brave smile if not a very successful one. Her jaw was severely swollen where the horse's head had struck her, and most of her front teeth were broken.

A series of tests was carried out to determine whether there had been any brain damage, but thankfully the results were negative. She'd suffered only a mild concussion. After a couple of days in hospital she was allowed to come home. I took her to a dentist, and when the repair work to her teeth had been completed, she looked as good as new and as beautiful as ever.

After this incident, the Parks Board generously decided to construct a causeway across the river at Mahlangeni.

We first heard the news on the VHF radio one morning when the park warden called and quite casually told Kobus to start looking for a place to build a causeway. We went wild with excitement. After five and a half years of crossing the river by boat, we could hardly imagine how it would feel to travel across it in luxury.

Some five hundred metres downstream from the boat's usual mooring, near the mouth of Shibyeni Creek, there was a place where the river ran wide and shallow over a rocky shelf. It was the ideal place to build the causeway.

As soon as the construction of the causeway was under way, Kobus borrowed a bulldozer and cleared a road from our main gate, rounding the north-east corner of the premises to run down the bank to the site of the causeway. On the far side of the river he cleared a road slanting up the bank to meet the patrol track at the top.

When, after three months, the causeway was finally completed and the construction workers had left, we had to wait a couple of days for the cement to dry.

And then, at last, the big day dawned.

It was 12 August 1985. For the first time in the earth's history as we know it, human beings would cross the Letaba River at Mahlangeni via a causeway. We all got into the car and drove down to the river along the new road that Kobus had cleared. Then we drove slowly across the river, waving like royalty to the watching hippos. At the far side of the river we got out and walked the full length of the causeway to see how that felt. It felt just great. The hippos swam up close and looked at us with quizzical expressions. I explained to them that, through the technological and engineering achievements of mankind, the river had now been tamed. Never again would its unpredictable moods, or the paranoia of its inhabitants, cause us grief.

Not only did the causeway bring a great deal of change to our own lives, it also brought new dimensions to the lifestyle of the entire neighbourhood.

A herd of elephants were the first to discover it. But let me explain about the 'no entry' sign.

Kobus had, some years previously, found an official 'no entry' sign lying in the bush in the middle of nowhere. It is known that elephants have the habit of pulling out official signs and then abandoning them somewhere deep in the bush. As Kobus did not know where the sign had originally belonged, he brought it home and deposited it in our storeroom. On the day of the opening of the causeway, he remembered the sign and planted it on the far bank at the entrance to the crossing. It made our causeway look more official, he said. (Personally, I believed Kobus was feeling so possessive of the causeway that he'd become a little deranged.)

That night the herd of elephants visited the south bank. Apparently they took offence at this intrusion of officialdom into their territory. They pulled the sign out and discarded it some distance away in the riverine bush. Then they all filed across the causeway.

The next morning we found our brand-new causeway covered in elephant droppings. We could see by the spoor that the elephants had not really wanted to come and graze on our side of the river. After they'd walked the full length of the crossing, they had made a U-turn and returned to the south bank. Apparently they had merely wanted to satisfy themselves as to the purpose and user-friendliness of the causeway. Or perhaps they had wanted to show us what they thought of the 'no entry' sign.

Many other species of game, such as waterbuck, kudu, impala, bushbuck and warthog soon discovered the benefits of the causeway and began to use it regularly to get to whichever side of the river they wished to be. The traffic tended to be particularly heavy early on Monday mornings when we were in a hurry to get to school.

The baboons who slept in the jackalberry trees on the far bank of the river were especially delighted with the causeway and used it daily to get to our vegetable garden and pawpaw trees. When they saw us watching them on their way across, they promptly struck up a relaxed pose and made themselves comfortable, pretending that they merely wished to sit on the causeway and admire the view from that particular vantage point. But we knew baboons. The only kind of view they appreciated was one with food in it.

Although life became a great deal easier with the causeway, I was wrong when I thought that the river had been tamed.

It hadn't.

In February 1988, two and a half years after our crossing was built, I woke up in the early dawn one morning, wondering what had disturbed my sleep. The Egyptian geese hadn't arrived yet to startle me awake with their raucous trumpeting, and it was unusual for me to wake up before they did. I then realized it was the sound of helicopters directly above the house that had woken me. They seemed to be hovering there somewhere, and it bothered me a great deal as I couldn't think of any reason why they should do so, or why they should be there in the first place. But then it suddenly dawned on me that I wasn't listening to the sound of helicopters but to the thundering roar of a raging river. I rolled over in bed to look out of the glass doors: the river had flooded its banks and the torrent had risen to the level of the garden. Uprooted trees and huge logs were being tossed about like matchsticks in the spuming surf. I leaped out of bed, dressed in half a second and ran outside.

As I stood gaping at the thundering waterscape, the dogs and horses were doing the same, with ears pricked and noses to the wind.

Fortunately the water level wasn't quite as high as it had seemed from the bedroom. It was still a few metres below the top of the bank, which meant that at least the garden and the house would not be flooded within the next few minutes or so. There was still time for me to make myself a cup of good, strong coffee from which to derive support. But first I opened the front gate and walked down four steps to the edge of the torrent. Forty-two out of the forty-six steps were submerged. Only the crest of the opposite bank still showed, and it appeared to be out of reach for ever. The whole landscape was alien. Every familiar landmark had disappeared under the stupendous waterscape. Naturally there was no sign of the causeway. I hoped it hadn't disintegrated under the weight of the deluge. And where was our boat?

I looked along the bank for the iron pole that held the long anchoring chain. Ah, there it was – or at least the top few inches of it that still showed above the water. But why was the chain dangling loosely in the current? Because . . . oh heavens, yes . . . because our boat had slipped its anchor! It was probably speeding headlong towards the far-off ocean! I could hardly bear the thought of never seeing our boat again.

But there wasn't time to stand there and agonize. If I didn't hurry up and do something I could end up in the ocean myself, and I hadn't even had a cup of coffee yet. I quickly found a stick and stuck it into the bank to mark the water level.

After two cups of strong coffee I felt brave enough to start thinking of some emergency plans. First I made a list of all the humans and animals that would have to be evacuated: the people in the staff village, the dogs, horses, bantams, the little scrub hare that I was fostering at the time, and me. What an exodus it would be! How would we go about it?

I decided to go outside and check on my marker before losing my calm unnecessarily.

Fortunately the marker was still dry.

Perhaps evacuation wouldn't be necessary after all.

Twenty minutes later I checked my marker again and found the stick still standing safe and dry just above the water level. Evidently the flood had reached its zenith and had stabilized.

Kobus had spent the night at Olifants Camp where he had attended a meeting the previous day. When I called him on the radio to tell him about the flood, he said he could hardly wait to get home to see it for himself. As it was a Friday he told me that he would drive to Phalaborwa to pick up the girls and bring them home via the high-water bridge.

After talking to Kobus I rushed outside again to check whether things still looked the same out there (just in case I had been hallucinating a little). If anything, the scene appeared even more dramatic than I had remembered it.

I hurried to the site of my marker. It was still as it had been. Feeling a lot more relaxed now, I walked along the crest of the bank to appreciate the awesome beauty of the river in spate. As I approached the mouth of Shibyeni Creek, I saw a torrent of water cascading from the Shibyeni into the Letaba.

Worried that Kobus and the girls would be cut off from home by the flooded creek, I went to check the depth of the water where the road dipped through it a little distance beyond the staff village. There was a lot of water in the creek, but a strip of mud on either side indicated that it might be ebbing. I placed a marker at the water's edge so that I could check on it later in the day. As soon as I had done this, a movement on

the opposite bank caught my attention. A magnificent nyala bull stepped from the thickets and walked down to the water's edge. Not wanting to startle the animal, I immediately froze. He caught sight of me, but because I remained as still as a statue he couldn't decide what I was. I had never before had the privilege of looking a nyala straight in the eye. Enjoying every second of our unique encounter, I held my breath as the animal studied me thoughtfully. Satisfied eventually that I was nothing in particular, he lost interest and contemplated the flooded creek for a while before sauntering off into the bush.

I went back home to divide the rest of my day between gaping at the river and checking on my markers.

Meanwhile Kobus and the girls were having a tough time trying to get home. Kobus had collected the girls at their schools several hours early, explaining to their headmasters that they faced an enormous detour and wanted to get home before nightfall.

They crossed the high-water bridge in the early afternoon, but when they reached the Tsendze Stream an hour later they found it in spate. Unable to get through it, they had to alter course and drive many kilometres along firebreaks and patrol tracks to circumvent the Tsendze. More than once the vehicle was bogged down in muddy watercourses and they had to dig their way out. Luckily Shibyeni Creek had ebbed sufficiently to let them through.

They finally arrived home at dusk, covered in mud. Although the earlier ferocity of the flood had abated somewhat, I was happy at last to be able to share the spectacular scene with my family.

For many weeks after the flood the causeway remained submerged and, since our boat had disappeared, the only way to get the girls to school was via the vast detour over the high-water bridge.

One day, when the water had finally ebbed to a level where we could almost see, or rather guess, where the causeway was, we parked our car on the opposite bank again and walked across. The water came up to our knees and the current was still so strong that we had to shuffle sideways like crabs to avoid being swept off. Kobus carried Karin, who was then ten years old, on his shoulders, while I carried the rifle for protection against hippos and crocodiles. The older girls – Hettie was then sixteen, and Sandra fifteen – walked between us, and we all held hands to help steady one another in the current.

Walking across the river was certainly not a very safe thing to do, but it was so much quicker than making the 160-kilometre detour. We did this for another three weeks until the water level had ebbed sufficiently to allow a vehicle across.

And so we learned that the river could not be tamed.

I was willing to forgive it for flooding the causeway for all those weeks, but not for abducting our boat. It had been such a faithful little vessel, and had conveyed so many supplies, groceries and humans – sometimes sick or injured ones – for so many years.

WILDFIRE

KOBUS CAME HOME LATE ONE AFTERNOON AND, HAVING NOTHING of immediate urgency to attend to, agreed to accompany me on my daily walk. I was elated as he had been very busy for several weeks and we had spent little time together.

It was a beautiful afternoon. Winter had almost gone and the first hints of spring were in the air. We walked along the dry bed of Shibyeni Creek for some distance and then climbed its eastern bank. As soon as we reached the top of the bank, Kobus stopped and, looking at some distant point in the sky, announced: 'There's a fire.'

I looked up at the sky and asked, 'Where? In heaven?'

Kobus was already turning and starting down the bank. 'I'd better get there fast. Sorry to cut our walk short.'

'Don't they have their own firefighters in heaven?' I asked hopefully.

My little joke wasn't appreciated. Probably it wasn't even heard. I stood gazing at some white clouds above the eastern horizon for a while, wondering which one of them was the culprit. They all looked pretty much alike to me. It always amazed me how a game ranger could spot a telltale cloud, sometimes almost on the other side of the world. And even if the whole sky was overcast, he would point out one ordinary-looking cloud among the many and tell you there was a fire.

I'd never before accompanied Kobus on a fire-fighting exercise and I suddenly decided that for once I'd like to do so.

I hurried home. Kobus and the game guards had already collected their fire beaters (flat squares of perforated rubber attached to long sticks) and other fire-fighting equipment and were boarding the pick-up truck.

I jumped into the passenger seat, announcing that I was going along to help.

After some fifteen minutes on the road we could see the distant, orange-red glow of the fire. Soon grey smoke began to fill the air. When we arrived at the edge of the fire it looked to me like a veritable inferno, but Kobus assured me that it was a relatively small fire. Burning to the north of the road and driven by a strong wind, it was advancing rapidly.

Using grass torches, Kobus and the game guards started setting a backburn – a smaller fire which, set against the wind, burns slowly and can be controlled while it eliminates the flammable material in the path of the larger fire.

I looked up at the veil of white smoke that boiled skyward and felt small and threatened. So I climbed onto the back of the pick-up in order to feel a little bigger. Up there I also had a better view of the activities around me.

Driven by the wind, the advancing fire had a lot more momentum than the backburn, and I worried that the backburn wouldn't spread fast enough to stop the advancing blaze from jumping right over it. I watched as a large flame from the major fire licked at the undergrowth and lower branches of a tree and then leaped suddenly to the top, turning the tree into a twenty-metre-high torch.

While some of the men hurried along the track setting the backburn, the others collected their fire beaters and began extinguishing the backburn's rearmost flames to prevent them from leaping across the track into the grass and bush behind us.

Ash rained down on me and swirled in the churning air as the roar of the advancing fire grew louder. The flames of the backburn danced leisurely on through grass and scrub, advancing slowly yet steadily towards the main fire. But even as the backburn advanced northward, segments of its rear line continued to arch southward, licking at the sky above the track, and I watched with concern as the men battled to extinguish the errant tongues of flame. Every now and then I would notice that one of the men was surrounded by flames and I would shout urgent warnings to him, or scream instructions to the others to go to his aid. Nobody paid any attention to me, however. These men were experts and didn't need my advice.

After about half an hour, large gaps started to appear in the advancing fire line, its momentum broken by the backburn. Within another half-hour the fire was fading and dying. The men relaxed their pace and, using their fire beaters, mopped up the remaining pockets of flame.

By dark the job was done and we headed for home.

A network of firebreak roads, which includes the tourist roads and patrol tracks, divides the park into three hundred units in such a way that each one of these units is contained within safe lanes for backburning. These units are called 'blocks'.

When a fire is driven by a strong wind, backburning can become a difficult and dangerous task, especially when smouldering debris such as dried elephant or buffalo droppings gets blown across the firebreaks, setting adjacent blocks alight.

It is in the late winter and early spring (just before the start of the rainy season) that conditions often become conducive to devastating high-temperature fires. At times like these, the rangers depend heavily on their VHF radios to report major fires and call for assistance.

During September 1985 the park's radio mast developed problems, cutting off all communications for almost two months. The situation was critical. The previous summer had brought good rains and an abundant growth of grass. Throughout the warm, dry winter the sun had turned the grass to straw, and the straw to tinder. Now the air was hot and dry, and there was enough flammable material in the veld and bush to start a conflagration. The refugee problem (people crossing through the park from Mozambique to South Africa) was at its peak, and the risk of man-made fires ran high. The rangers patrolled their sections day and night, watching and waiting.

In the early hours of a Saturday morning, Kobus walked out into the garden and saw the eastern sky flushed orange-red. It was not the rising sun. Within minutes he and the game guards had collected their fire-fighting equipment and were on their way.

They found the fire forty kilometres to the east. It was burning along a vast front from south to north, driven by a strong wind. The crew spread out and set a wide backburn, but the wind retarded the backburn while sweeping the major fire relentlessly on through grass and bush. The men drove twenty kilometres downwind to the next fire-break road and hurriedly set a new backburn. But again the fire beat them into retreat.

As the VHF radios were out of order, Kobus could not call for help.

Throughout the rest of the day the strong wind carried smouldering debris across backburns, creating new blazes everywhere until it seemed to Kobus that the whole world was alight. Aided by his loyal team, he fought back, but was unable to get the fire under control.

In the early afternoon the wind changed course and started sweeping the fire in a westerly direction, towards our house. At dusk I could see the distant glow intensifying into an orange-red corona that stretched across most of the eastern horizon. The birds in our garden fell silent, and not even the chirp of a cricket disturbed the eerie quiet.

My sister's four children were visiting for the school holidays. Luckily all the youngsters were inside playing cards and listening to music. Although they knew about the fire, they didn't yet know that the wind had changed and was bringing it towards us.

I slipped quietly out of the house every half-hour or so to check on the fire. By about nine o'clock, fountains of colour were surging into the sky and ash started to rain down on the garden.

Hettie and her cousin Hennie (my sister's eldest son) were the first to get worried. When they joined me outside and saw the high glow of the approaching fire, they were alarmed. I told them calmly of the plans I had made: if the fire got too close, we would all go down to our boat and row into the middle of the river, where we would be safe. (In 1985 we still had the boat.) I also reminded them that Kobus and his crew were fighting the fire and that they would surely do everything they could to stop it from reaching our house. Reassured, they went back inside to join the others.

I decided we would evacuate as soon as the fire reached the opposite bank of Shibyeni Creek. It now seemed about three, perhaps four kilometres away.

The sound of an approaching range fire is as frightening as the sight of it. First there is the low, steady drone, then a distinct swelling of sound that increases gradually in volume until it becomes a violent, shuddering roar. When the crescendo began to frighten me, I went back inside to tell the children to get ready to leave.

Sandra, always my most pragmatic child, was the most upset, wanting to know what would happen to our dogs, horses and bantams. I told her we would take the dogs with us and release the horses and bantams to make their own escape.

First we all went outside to check on the fire once more. Orange flames were licking at the sky across Shibyeni Creek, but strangely the fire seemed to be standing still, almost as if pausing to reassemble its forces before surging forward once more.

Minutes passed, and still the fire seemed to hesitate.

What was it waiting for?

And then I saw the answer: the wind had changed direction. It was no longer blowing east to west, but south to north. The fire would not cross the Shibyeni. It was being swept northwards.

I felt immensely relieved that we were safe.

But then I thought about Kobus and his men, and my relief gave way to a renewed sense of fear. They had been fighting the fire for more than sixteen hours. I had no way of knowing where they were, or if they were all right.

After the children had gone back inside to prepare for bed, I fetched a long ladder from our storeroom and climbed to the top of our water reservoir. From there I could see the edge of the fire creeping, like a gigantic glow-worm, relentlessly on and on across the landscape to the north. I wished desperately that the wind would drop and give the men a break.

I went to say goodnight to the children, but could not go to sleep myself. I boiled a dozen eggs, sliced up two loaves of bread and made sandwiches. Then I filled two flasks with strong, sweet coffee and packed everything into a basket – just in case Kobus or one of his men came in to fetch it.

At about midnight, I heard the drone of a vehicle and rushed outside. It was Kobus. I hardly recognized him. He was blackened from head to toe by soot. Only the whites of his eyes showed. He told me that they desperately needed more men to help get the fire under control, and asked if I would drive to ranger Dirk Swart's house near Phalaborwa Gate.

'I'll go immediately,' I said.

'Thanks so much,' he said. 'Please drive carefully.' Taking the basket of food I had packed as well as a large container of drinking water, he left in a hurry.

I woke Hettie and asked her to watch over the other children. I told her to row them into the centre of the river should the wind change direction again and bring the fire across the creek. She assured me she would take good care of her sisters and cousins.

Before I left, I checked the wind again. It remained steadily due north. I could only hope it would continue to do so.

I drove fast to Dirk's house, taking just over an hour to get there. His wife answered my knock on the door and roused Dirk. He promised me that he and his team would get to Kobus as soon as humanly possible. I thanked him and left immediately.

While driving back, I watched the tall grasses bending in the wind – it was still blowing south to north. Far ahead on the horizon, I could see the orange-red glow of the fire. From my vantage point it seemed to be standing still, which meant that it was moving in the same direction as I was – from south to north.

Some twenty kilometres from home a sudden gust shook my jeep, and flurries of dust and leaves swirled across the track in front of the car.

The wind was changing direction.

Soon steady gusts of dust and debris were dancing and tumbling across the road in the beam of the headlights.

The gigantic glow-worm on the horizon started to creep slowly but steadily westwards.

I pressed hard on the accelerator. If the fire rose again on the far bank of the Shibyeni, the wind would quickly sweep it into the high trees inside the eastern fence of the garden. Terror gripped me at the thought that Hettie might have fallen asleep and be unaware of the danger.

I sped through the night, intermittently slamming on the brakes to avoid collisions with impala and other game, and swerving dangerously as rabbits zigzagged crazily across the track in front of the jeep.

Some ten kilometres from home, I knew I would not be able to out-pace the flames: the fire had expanded into a blazing front that stretched across most of the northern horizon from east to west. The house seemed right in its path.

Only when I reached the last bend in the road near the river could I see that the fire had passed some distance behind the house. The children were safe. Tears of relief blurred my vision as I turned down the bank and onto the causeway.

Some time during the early hours of the morning the men finally succeeded in getting the fire under control. Dirk and his team returned to their base, and Kobus and his men arrived home shortly before dawn. They were so exhausted they could hardly walk.

After only a few hours of rest they left again to extinguish smoulder-ing tree stumps and mop up other remaining pockets of fire.

After a devastating blaze such as this, a ranger always has the distressing task of tracking down injured animals and, if necessary, putting them down. Kobus requested that a helicopter be sent from Skukuza to assist him, and began his grim search.

One day shortly after the fire, as I was driving to Shingwedzi to visit a friend, I came across an injured honey badger stumbling along at the side of the road in the blackened veld. I stopped next to him and, watching him intently for a while, saw that he had been blinded by the fire. As he struggled painfully to find his way to wherever he hoped to go in the vast, dead landscape, he kept stumbling and bumping into burnt-out stumps and rocks. A huge lump settled in my throat as I cocked my pistol and got out of the car. Aiming carefully, I released him from his agony.

Then I sat down beside the dead creature and stroked his scorched fur.

'I love honey badgers,' I told him softly. 'I once brought one up.'

I sat there for a long time, staring at the ruined landscape, and wept.

TRUMPETS IN THE MORNING

THE RIVERINE BUSH AT MAHLANGENI WAS HOME TO SEVERAL Egyptian goose families. We often saw parent birds with their downy youngsters waddling across the sandy shore to the water. Egyptian goslings are the cutest little creatures.

Karin, who often wished she could get a closer view of the goslings, was delighted when one of the game guards brought her a clutch of five abandoned eggs he had found. She tricked one of our bantam hens into hatching the eggs, and a fortnight or so later the bantam mother was proudly marching her five 'chicks' around the garden.

It made no difference to the hen that her children bore no resemblance to their cousins. Nor did it bother her that the other bantams stared suspiciously at the clumsy-looking brood who waddled when they walked. A mother's love is blind. Eagerly she scratched up juicy insects for them, and dashed about after flying ants and butterflies, clucking excitedly to her chicks to come and get their chow. How baffled she was when they ignored the goodies she got for them and preferred instead to snack on the grass from the lawn. She probably found it strange, too, that her children were growing so fast, despite their pointless diet.

Whenever the loyal rooster – always on the lookout for birds of prey overhead – crowed a warning, the hens would rush their chicks under the nearest plants for cover, and then sit over them with wings spread to protect them. As the goslings were much larger than bantam chicks, it was no easy task for their mother to round up her chubby charges and bully them to safety under a bush, not to mention getting them all under her wings.

The goslings grew and grew, and despite all the trouble they gave to the bantam hen, she remained a devoted mother and spent her days clucking and fussing around her strange brood.

We had a large, meandering fishpond outside our bedroom. Kobus built it in the early days at Mahlangeni, hoping that the watery scene among the shady trees and plants would create a feeling of coolness on those long, hot summer days. It did. And the fishpond was really beautiful. But when stepping out of the sliding doors at night you had to watch your step or you risked falling into it. We tried to keep some fish in the pond, but the kingfishers caught and ate them all. A horde of frogs took up residence in the pond and soon they were driving us crazy with their nightly choir practice.

The goslings were barely two weeks old when they first discovered the fishpond. They took one look at it and their instincts must have told them something, for they promptly plunged right in. Their mother froze, neck stretched forward, eyes blinking rapidly in confusion. As realization dawned, she had a fit. Clucking hysterically, she commanded her children to get out of the water immediately. They wouldn't, of course. They were enjoying their swim far too much. Completely confused, their mother clucked and danced about, and eventually took to flying from one side of the pond to the other, flapping her wings furiously and begging her children to come out of the water. Her frantic calls brought the rooster rushing over to see what was happening. He couldn't believe his eyes either and stood gaping at the scene, shocked speechless and totally clueless about what he should do.

From that day on, the goslings frequented the pool daily, and their poor distraught mother could do nothing but stand at the water's edge, watching anxiously over them.

One day another bantam hen and her brood of chicks turned up at the pond to view the strange scene. As the hen expressed her bewilderment with a series of nervous nods and eye-blinks, one of her chicks became particularly interested in the proceedings and decided that if his cousins could swim, so could he. Walking up to the edge of the pond, he leaned over and was readying himself for the plunge when he lost his nerve and decided to stick to dry land. I had been watching him from my bedroom and was about to rush outside and save the silly chick from drowning when I saw with relief that his bantam instincts had prevailed.

Soon the fast-growing goslings were bigger than their bantam mother. And when they discovered their vocal cords and started honking like hoarse trumpets, she'd had enough. Her children's embarrassing behaviour had become intolerable. She decided that she would, from that day forward, simply get on with her own life and ignore the brats.

Egyptian geese are beautiful birds. They are chestnut and auburn-coloured above and fawn to tawny underneath. Their wings have white shoulder and black flight feathers, and a striking emerald green line along the outer edge.

At the age of about eight months, two of our geese – no longer goslings – decided to move house. With a honking farewell fanfare, they flew over the fence and east along the river until they disappeared from sight. We hoped they'd found a comfortable new home and breeding place somewhere in the riverine woods to the east.

About a month later a third goose took wing and, with a loud parting salutation, left us to seek a new home among the other Egyptian goose families along the river shores.

The remaining two geese stayed with us for another two months before they, too, decided to emigrate. They took off and flew high over the fence – also with a loud farewell fanfare. But they didn't fly far. They landed in the riverine bush along the shore right in front of the house, fell in love with the setting and promptly made it their new

home. Although they spent their days grazing along the shore, they still came to dinner at the Mahlangeni restaurant every evening. Standing on the lawn, waiting for their bowl of porridge to be served, they would honk impatiently if the service wasn't prompt.

A few months after these two had emigrated, they produced their own brood of goslings. While they were hatching and raising their young, the parents took turns to visit us at dinnertime. One of them would stay with the eggs, and later with the young goslings. They also took turns to come for their daily swim on the fishpond. Only when their youngsters had become self-sufficient did they start turning up together again to feed and swim.

Another habit these two had was to arrive at dawn each morning, swooping to a landing on a large rock in the fishpond, and startle us

awake with raucous trumpeting. The purpose of their trumpeting was, of course, to broadcast their proprietorship of the Mahlangeni pond and restaurant to all other Egyptian geese in the neighbourhood, and to warn them that trespassers would be prosecuted.

If you consider the distance their voices had to travel to reach all the goose families along the river, you can probably imagine the volume of noise that hit us in our bedroom early each morning.

GIGGLING THIEVES

I F AFRICA HAS A VOICE, IT IS THE WHOOPING HOWL OF THE HYENA. Rising from nowhere in the deep of night, it drifts through the bush in rising and falling echoes that stir ancient memories of witches and ghosts. And if there is news in the wind of a nocturnal feast, the ghostly howl becomes the prelude to insane arias of cackles, giggles and screams.

Although the hyena is more closely related to the cats than the canines, he looks more like a dog. He is part scavenger and part predator and eats anything that his powerful jaws and teeth can mangle, which is just about everything. He has a massive head and upper chest and a sloping, seemingly half-crippled rear. He moves with a shuffling, shifty gait and he drools a lot and giggles. He also steals.

One night at Mahlangeni a hyena dug his way under our main gates and sneaked into the garden. He ate the girls' riding saddles, plus a brand-new pair of Karin's shoes that she'd forgotten outside and a pair of boots that Kobus had left on the patio behind the kitchen. He also dis-covered my vacuum cleaner in the garage and ate the dust bag.

Kobus had been out on patrol that night and had taken the dogs along. Had they been home, the hyena would never have ventured into the garden. Despite his strength and stealth he's something of a coward.

I wrote a letter to our insurance company to enquire whether we could claim compensation for our losses. They sent me a theft claim

form to fill out, requesting that it be returned to them along with an affidavit. Luckily I had some hyena hairs as evidence. Having found them in the wire of the gate on the morning after the incident, I had gathered them carefully and sealed them in an envelope. Just in case.

Taking the envelope with me, I drove to the police station at Phalaborwa. I showed the hairs to the police officer on duty and told him the story. He misunderstood, thinking I wanted to bring a charge against the hyena. I had to explain to him that I wanted only to swear that it was the truth.

I acquired the sworn statement and mailed it to the insurers.

We were fully compensated.

And we were very grateful.

A few months later, Kobus and I were driving home at night after attending a meeting at Olifants Camp. After two hours on the road Kobus became sleepy, so I took over the driving while he catnapped in the passenger seat. On the winding track near Shabarumbi Creek a hyena dashed out of the darkness, right in front of the car. I slammed on the brakes, swerving, but was unable to avoid hitting the animal. Kobus and I leaped out of the car to see if the hyena was hurt, but it ran off and disappeared into the bush. I was in tears. I had never before collided with an animal. Kobus comforted me, saying that he'd glimpsed the hyena and it did not seem to have suffered any injuries apart from a slightly bruised hip.

Even so, I felt terrible. And one of the car's headlights was completely smashed.

Again I wrote to our insurance company, enquiring whether we might claim compensation for the headlight. They sent me a motor accident claim form to fill out. The questions were tricky, but we really needed the money for a new headlight, so I tried my best to give good, honest answers:

1. Speed before accident: *35 k.p.h.*
2. Road surface: *Bumpy. (Dirt track.)*
3. Width of road: *2 metres.*
4. Weather conditions: *Good.*
5. Visibility: *Bad. (Pitch dark.)*
6. Street lighting: *Poor. (No moon. Only stars.)*
7. Was any warning given by you, e.g. hooting, indicator, etc.? *No. (Animals are not acquainted with these.)*
8. Give details of any road safety signs or warning signs in vicinity of scene of accident: *None.*
9. Damage to other vehicles: *None.*
10. Personal injuries: *(A hyena was injured.)*
11. Name of injured: *(Hyena.)*
12. Address and phone number: *Shabarumbi Creek, Kruger Park. (No telephone.)*
13. Details of injuries: *Unknown. Possibly bruised hip.*
14. Name of hospital where treated: *(He was not treated.)*
15. Connection with accident, e.g. pedestrian, driver or passenger: *Pedestrian.*

There followed a blank space where a sketch of the accident was required. I couldn't think how to draw a picture of a hyena dashing out of the bush in the dark of night. I considered colouring the whole space black and writing underneath it that nights in the bush were so dark one couldn't see a thing.

But it didn't seem a good idea. Though it was true that moonless nights in the bush were very dark, I was nervous of taking any chances in a legal document that required the whole truth and nothing but the truth.

I asked Kobus to help me with the sketch. He made a simple graphic drawing with arrows to indicate our direction of travel, the relative position of the hyena when first sighted and its direction of movement across the road, and a cross to mark the point of impact. I hadn't thought of that. I thought they wanted a realistic drawing of a hyena dashing out of the bush in front of the car.

Again, we were fully compensated. And again, we were very grateful.

On the eastern boundary of the Mahlangeni section there was a ranger outpost called Shipandani. Nestling under tall leadwoods, apple-leaf and umbrella trees on the bank of the Tsendze Stream, it was a beautiful little camp with three thatched huts and a lean-to storage kitchen with an open campfire area. Two reed structures housed a toilet and a shower. To one side of the camp was a boulder-strewn koppie where baboons often played, and where in winter impala lilies bedecked the hillside in a blaze of pink blooms. The camp was not fenced in, and because there were leopard in the area we usually let the dogs sleep inside one of the huts when we camped there.

One night at Shipandani, a hyena sneaked into camp and stole our iron cooking pot and an orange blanket that one of the girls had forgotten outside on a chair near the campfire.

The spoor told us that only one hyena had been responsible for the thefts. It didn't look as though he had made two trips, and we wondered how he'd managed to carry away both the heavy iron pot and the blanket at the same time. The spoor disappeared in the reed thickets along the stream bank, and although we searched the area for our pot and blanket we never found them. We wondered why the hyena had taken them and what he intended to do with them. Hettie reckoned that the hyena was probably wondering the same thing.

A few months later, while doing an aerial census, Kobus flew over Shipandani and spotted an orange object in the veld some distance from the camp to the south of the koppie. He asked the pilot to fly lower so that he could see what it was. It was our blanket. As the area was particularly rocky, there was nowhere suitable for a helicopter landing and so Kobus couldn't retrieve our blanket. I often wonder if it is still lying there all by itself, and why the hyena had carried it over such a long distance before discarding it.

We still haven't found the cooking pot.

A good blanket and an iron pot aren't exactly cheap, but I couldn't bring myself to write another letter to the insurance company. I also didn't want to go to the police station again and report that a hyena had stolen our blanket and pot.

One winter Kobus bought himself a pair of canvas boxing boots. They were thin-soled and light, and Kobus had fancied a pair for a long time. They made his long patrols in the bush feel shorter, at least for his feet, he said.

Shortly after buying the boots, Kobus was part of a team camping at the site of a zebra-catching enclosure, busy with the relocation of some of the animals. The other game rangers teased Kobus a lot about his boxing boots, but he ignored them. They were the most comfortable shoes he had ever possessed. The only problem was that they tended to smell a bit ripe after a day's hard labour. At night he had to leave them outside in order to preserve the fresh air in his tent.

True to form, a prowling hyena discovered the boots. Picking up one of them, he made off with it, only to drop it again some twenty metres into the bush. Considering the smelly carrion that such animals feast on, the boot must have been pretty offensive to put a damper on the hyena's appetite.

When the other rangers saw the hyena spoor in the morning and found the saliva-covered boot close to the camp, they had much to say. One of them suggested putting together a search party to look for the hyena, in case it had fainted and needed to be revived. Another suggested nailing the boots to the zebra enclosure at night to keep marauding lions at bay. This idea was unanimously rejected on the grounds of cruelty to the zebras.

Kobus ignored the comments. Not only were his boots supremely comfortable, they were also hyena-proof.

ELEPHANTS IN THE NIGHT

THE PROBLEM WITH ELEPHANTS IN THE NIGHT IS THAT THEY become invisible. Even if you shine a light on them, you don't really see them. Possibly it's because at night you need to get relatively close to things before you can see them, and the very size of an elephant up close offers no recognizable view of the whole animal. All you see is darkness.

As a rule I tried to avoid driving at night but, one Friday evening after attending a school function with the girls, I had no choice but to drive home in the dark. About halfway home, the massive bulk of an elephant bull loomed up rather too late in the beam of the headlights. He had his head in the bushes alongside the road and his behind on the track directly in front of us. I slammed on the brakes, pulling up right under the elephant's rump. His hind legs buckled at the knees (as usually happens when an elephant is startled) and his enormous posterior began descending onto the bonnet. Waiting for the colossal crunch, I closed my eyes, but luckily the elephant changed his mind about sitting down and charged off, screaming with consternation as he crashed destructively through the bush. The landscape shuddered. My daughters giggled. I was in shock and my teeth chattered the rest of the way home.

Mishak, the driver of the park's transport truck, got held up by engine trouble one day as he was doing his weekly route, delivering provisions to the tourist camps. After failing to get the trouble fixed at Shingwedzi Camp, Mishak borrowed the camp manager's pick-up and left in a hurry for Punda Maria Camp, his last delivery stop. Some distance from his destination, after twilight had merged into darkness, he suddenly found himself on a direct collision course with the derrière of an elephant. As he slammed on the brakes, pulling up underneath the elephant's rump, the elephant's hind legs buckled at the knees and it sat down on the bonnet of the truck, screeching like a tornado. Fortunately for Mishak, it was a young bull still in its teens, and it got up and roared away through the bush. But unfortunately the youngster's screams brought its entire family (a whole breeding herd) out of the bush to investigate the source of the commotion. To avoid infuriating the short-tempered cows, Mishak switched off the engine which, surprisingly, was still running despite the damage to the bonnet. Mishak knew it would be best for him to wait for the herd to take its leave before attempting to move on. The cows, however, weren't thinking of leaving just yet. Trunks in the air, they ambled over to the pick-up. Something

smelled good. It was the sacks of maize meal on the back. Much delighted, they ripped open the sacks and tucked in. Some of the cows unloaded sacks onto the ground, and the calves came over to join in the fun. With his truck surrounded by elephants, Mishak could do nothing but sit and yell at the looters. They paid him no attention, of course. They were enjoying their maize-meal party far too much.

For many days afterwards, tourists reported sightings of white-powdered elephants in the Punda Maria area.

One night, long after Kobus and I had gone to bed, we were woken by the resounding clanging of steel in trouble. Actually I didn't wake up fully but Kobus did. He flew up, saying, 'It's an elephant, breaking the fence of the vegetable garden!'

'Huh? Elephant?' I stammered. About three-quarters of me was still asleep.

'Come on, get up!' he urged me. He had found his torch and was checking the magazine of his rifle.

'Up? Me . . . ? I mean . . . why?'

'To shine the torch on the elephant so I can fire a shot over its head. Come on, hurry! He's plundering the vegetable garden!'

I tried to think of an excuse to stay safely indoors, but it was hard for me to think in full sentences in the middle of the night. So I got up and reluctantly followed Kobus outside into the pitch-black darkness.

We could hear the elephant stripping branches off the sycamore fig in the vegetable garden. I shone the torch in its direction but saw nothing. The closer we got to the feeding noises of the invisible elephant, the more trouble I had keeping the trembling torch steady.

'Good,' said Kobus. 'You're doing fine. Now light his head!'

'Where? I don't see him!'

'But he's right in front of you,' said Kobus.

And so he was. I'd been shining the torch on the elephant's body all along, thinking it was the darkness of the night.

'Light his head!' Kobus repeated.

I moved the beam towards where I thought his head would be, but it was his tail.

'His head's on the other side,' hissed Kobus. 'And where are you going?'

'I'm trying my best,' I protested. 'And what do you mean, where am I going? I'm right here!' But as I spoke I realized that I wasn't right there any more. I'd been walking in reverse gear.

Steadying myself, I bravely lit up one of the elephant's ears, and Kobus fired a shot over its head.

The elephant got the message and wheeled round. As he hurried through the vegetable patches, heading for the break in the fence, his feet obliterated scores of seedlings and pulped vast quantities of mature vegetables. We watched as he stepped gracefully over the broken fence, treading carefully to avoid getting his feet caught in the tangled wire, and disappeared into the night.

When Filemoni saw the damage to the vegetable garden the next morning, he looked up at the heavens and told Someone up there in Tsonga what he thought about elephants. It didn't sound too nice, so I would rather not translate it.

DOMESTIC CIRCUS

IN DECEMBER 1989 KOBUS'S BROTHER, WHO WAS A FARMER, GAVE US two black piglets as a Christmas present. The idea, I think, was for us to fatten them up and eventually eat them. But they were incredibly cute and immediately became part of the family, and so naturally there was no question of us ever eating them.

Since we had no other safe place for them to sleep at night, we put them in the hen house with the bantams. The bantams were not amused and discussed the situation nervously throughout the night for more than a week.

The girls named the boar Fritzie and the sow Fiela. Fiela loved to be cuddled, but not Fritzie – he wanted only to eat.

As the piglets grew older they started snoring and so the poor bantams suffered again from insomnia. Fritzie's snoring was particularly offensive; it sounded almost like the grumbling and snarling of feeding lions. When we saw that the bantams were spending most of their daylight hours catching up on lost sleep, we built a reed shelter with a tin roof for the pigs to sleep in – at a fair distance from the hen house.

Fritzie turned into a pig. A friendly, good-natured fellow, really, but he had few interests in life besides eating and lazing in the mud. Fiela was more winsome and liked to be fussed over. If she spotted one of us in the garden, she'd trot over, press her big wet nose into your hand and, leaning against your legs, wait for you to scratch behind her ears. While you did that, she'd topple onto your feet. Given her astounding weight, it would take some effort to extract your feet from under her sleeping body.

We were very fond of our two fat friends who, in their own special way, contributed much towards the entertainment value of the daytime activities in our garden. Inhabited by two dogs, three horses, twenty bantams, two pigs, a family of squirrels, countless birds and, at intervals, the two Egyptian geese, the garden was never dull for a moment.

We ordered our first horse by mail from the *Farmer's Weekly* in 1982. On the day that he was due to arrive, Kobus drove to the Phalaborwa railway station to fetch him while the girls and I waited at home in excited anticipation. The girls had already decided that they would name him Prins – Afrikaans for 'prince'.

But when Kobus arrived home that evening, a scrawny, scruffy, feeble-looking creature stepped from the pick-up. He looked more like a slovenly mule than a horse and had the bearing of a frightened donkey. The name Prins didn't seem quite so apt any more.

Feeling incredibly sorry for the miserable horse, the girls resolved to make a happy and dignified animal out of him. Much love and tender care, coupled with a course of medication and a healthy feeding regimen that Kobus provided, soon produced results: the horse gained weight, his coat started to shine and his manner became relaxed and affectionate. Sandra christened him Aznar.

Aznar grew so attached to the girls that when they were home he wouldn't let them out of his sight. Often he followed them into the house, and I had to help push him out the kitchen door.

When the girls were away at school he liked to graze along the shore near the house. Always alert, he was quick to sense danger and, at the slightest whiff of a predator in the area, would come charging back inside the fence. The first time he encountered the local elephant herd on the shore, he merely backed off a bit to contemplate the gigantic animals from a respectful distance. The elephants put their trunks into the air to smell him and, concluding that he was a harmless if strange-looking animal, they paid him no further attention. After that, Aznar was often seen grazing peacefully on the shore in the company of elephants.

Some two years after acquiring Aznar, we got our second horse – a handsome Anglo-Arab colt named Apollo. Unfortunately he had a stubborn streak and wouldn't heed our warnings about the dangers of venturing too far into the bush. Aznar fell under the influence of Apollo's obstinacy, and we often had to go looking for the horses and bring them back closer to home and relative safety.

I was alone at home one day when I became aware that the two horses were missing again. Calling the dogs to help me find the horses, I set out to look for them, but as soon as we left through the main gate I heard the thundering of hooves. It was Aznar galloping homewards, wide-eyed and whinnying. As I ran to him, he galloped up to me, trembling and perspiring. Two game guards, who had heard the thundering of the horse's hooves, came rushing over from the village, already armed. Hurrying down the river bank, accompanied by the two dogs, they went to look for Apollo, following the horses' spoor along the shore. I led Aznar to his stable and tried to placate him but he remained extremely upset, whinnying loudly and pawing the ground, obviously trying to tell me that something terrible had happened.

A few minutes later I heard three shots coming from the direction the game guards had taken. My heart started beating in my ears. We'd had Apollo for only two years. He was still so young . . .

I waited with Aznar, wishing desperately that the game guards would come back, leading Apollo.

When they finally returned, Apollo was not with them. They approached me with sombre faces and one of them held out Apollo's tail, offering it to me as a keepsake. They told me that four lions had attacked the horse. They had fired some shots into the air to chase the lions from their kill, and having determined that Apollo was indeed dead, they had cut off his tail to bring to me. I wasn't brave enough to take the tail, but I thanked them for their trouble and thoughtfulness and asked them if they would put the tail in Kobus's office.

Aznar knew his friend was beyond help. He gave a sad, shuddering sigh and pressed his nose into my neck. I hugged him to me and wept.

Soon after losing Apollo, we bought an American saddle horse named Kirby, a handsome, intelligent animal who, if anything, was even more cautious than Aznar. But, unlike Aznar, Kirby refused to believe that elephants posed no danger to a horse. Whenever the local herd turned up to graze along the shore, Kirby galloped home as fast as he could and hid in his stable until the elephants left.

One day when Sandra and Karin (then aged fifteen and ten) were riding along the shore, they saw a lone elephant grazing on the far bank of the river and decided to turn round before Kirby saw the elephant too. But they were too late. Kirby had seen the elephant and, spinning round, broke into a wild gallop. Aznar reckoned that if Kirby had reason to hasten home, he'd better do the same. And so the two horses sped homeward, forgetting to consider their riders. Sandra saw trouble ahead. They were approaching Shibyeni Creek, and the horses were going much too fast to carry their riders safely across the rocky bed. There was a sandbank near the creek, and as they neared the bank, Sandra turned her head towards Karin, yelling, 'Jump off into the sandbank!' Sandra threw herself clear of her horse and landed in the sand. But Karin jumped a second too late and fell hard on the pebble-covered shore. Sandra sat up, rubbing the sand from her eyes and looking about for Karin, then sprang to her feet and ran to her sister. 'Are you OK?'

'I think so,' said Karin, sitting up and looking a little dazed. 'Your voice sounds funny . . .' Then she saw that Sandra's mouth was full of sand and she burst out laughing.

Sandra had been so anxious to find out if her sister was OK that she hadn't had time to spit the sand from her mouth first.

The two girls arrived home, limping and covered in dust and bruises, but went straight to the stables to tell the horses off.

'Kirby!' shouted Karin. 'When will you ever learn that elephants don't eat horses?'

'Aznar!' yelled Sandra. 'Why must you run when Kirby runs? Can't you stop sometimes and think for yourself?'

The two horses looked very remorseful, but still Sandra and Karin decided not to talk to them for the rest of the day.

One day, a lone elephant bull turned up for a swim in the river right in front of the house. Entering the water until only his head and trunk remained above the surface, he cavorted and splashed about, really enjoying himself.

When Kirby saw the elephant he dashed home but, surprisingly, did not head for his stable. He ran through the garden to the front fence and stood there, watching the playful elephant from behind the safety of the wire. He trembled with apprehension but couldn't tear his eyes away from it. Every few minutes he rushed from the fence and, snorting and prancing, went looking for Aznar – no doubt to tell him about the daft elephant. Having done that, he returned to his vantage point once more to study the aquatic elephant.

Our dog Janna, an Australian cattle dog, believed it to be his duty to herd the bantams to the hen house and the horses to their stable every evening. Since the horses knew full well where their stable was and didn't need any help to get there, they would continue onwards at their own dignified pace, completely ignoring Janna's antics.

During the winter months Janna was kept occupied by the resident baboons on their forays to raid our vegetable garden. Lying in ambush between the vegetables, he waited until the raiders climbed over the fence and came within range. As he burst from his cover and did his herding act, the baboons retreated screaming with fright and scaling the fence a lot faster than they did on their way in.

Sadly, our first dog, Simba, died of heat exhaustion in 1987. We buried her, wrapped in her sleeping mat, on the bank of Shibyeni Creek and marked the grave with a stone cairn. She was a wonderful friend and a faithful companion to us all for many years, and we missed her very much.

A few weeks after Simba's death, ranger Johan Steyn brought us a beautiful puppy that looked very much like a wolf cub but was in fact also an Australian cattle dog. We named the pup Wolfie. From an early age Wolfie loved horses and would go wild with joy whenever the girls went riding. While he was still a puppy he was unable to keep up with the horses; by the time they and their riders had crossed the causeway and reached the far bank, Wolfie would be far behind. Sandra would pull her horse up, wait for Wolfie to catch up with them and then lift him into the saddle with her. Before long Wolfie was taking this procedure for granted and, until he was almost a year old, he expected Sandra to take him aboard as soon as they reached the far bank.

As Wolfie grew older he began to look more and more like a wolf. Strangers were instinctively terrified of him. But Wolfie was really a gentle, harmless dog who only put on his fierce act for visitors to let them know that he took his responsibilities as bodyguard to the girls and me very seriously.

When the pigs, Fritzie and Fiela, were six months old, Kobus's nephew Cornelis and his wife Bianca came to visit and brought us a wonderful present: a beautiful four-year-old Anglo-Arab stallion named Tangle.

They arrived in the evening after a long and taxing journey, and the horse looked tense and nervous as he stepped from the horsebox into the unfamiliar surroundings. The girls helped to feed him and make him feel welcome, and he soon calmed down. Then we led him to the camp to introduce him to Aznar and Kirby.

Aznar, being a kindly soul, greeted the newcomer with a gentle gaze and a friendly touching of noses. But Kirby was not at all impressed with the handsome stallion and behaved abominably towards him. He whinnied and neighed, kicked and reared, throwing a disgraceful tantrum. Tangle kept a respectful distance from Kirby and gave voice to his offended feelings with a fair amount of whinnying and neighing of his own.

Kobus suggested that we go inside and leave the two horses to sort out their problems on their own. He predicted that the animosity between them wouldn't last long and that they would soon become friends.

By the time we all went to bed that night, the two horses could still be heard neighing and whinnying, but there were longer intervals of silence in between. Obviously they still didn't like each other, but at least the animosity between them appeared to be fading.

Some time after midnight, Kobus and I were woken by the hurried footsteps of game guards approaching our bedroom across the patio. The chief guard, Corporal Manhique, called to us through the mesh screens: *'Ngala yi khomile hashi!'* 'A lion has taken one of the horses!'

Kobus leaped out of bed. Grabbing his rifle and torch, he rushed outside. I fumbled for my torch and pistol in the darkness, threw on some more clothes and sandals and ran after him, my heart beating wildly as I wondered which horse had been taken. It would be dreadfully unfair if a lion had caught our new horse on his very first night with us. I thought of Aznar and Kirby, and knew it would break my heart if it were either of them.

It was a pitch-black moonless night, and as I approached the camp I saw only the dim spots of light from the torches Kobus and the game guards were carrying. They were already entering the camp. The idea of them stumbling right into the feeding lion in the darkness sent me dashing into Kobus's office to get the spotlight. After clipping the wires to the battery terminals I uncoiled the lengthy cord, then rushed outside and shone the powerful beam into the camp. The light picked out Aznar, standing safely under a mopani tree; then Kirby, behind an umbrella tree, also unharmed. So the lion had taken our new horse! But where was the lion? I played the light from one side of the camp to the other, letting it pause briefly under trees and shrubs to double-check the shadows. Kobus turned and, shading his eyes against the sharp light, signalled me to shine the spotlight into the south-west corner of the camp. I did so. And there stood Tangle! Also unharmed. I moved the beam of the spotlight in zigzag fashion over the whole of the camp area. There was no lion. Kobus and the game guards were talking and laughing now. Relieved, I rushed over to them to listen to their conversation and learn what had happened.

At the time when our guests had arrived the game guards had been in their village and, although they'd heard the car come, they'd had no way of knowing that the guests had brought a horse with them. No-one in the village had heard the horses neighing and whinnying earlier in the night, possibly because the evening breeze had carried the sounds in the opposite direction. At around midnight, Corporal Manhique was woken by the neighing of a horse. He had never before heard one of our horses neigh in such a strange way, so he suspected that the horse was in trouble. His suspicion was confirmed the very next moment by the distinct growling and snarling sounds of a feeding lion. He reached for his rifle and torch and rushed outside, calling to the other game guards.

Apparently there had been another flare-up of tempers between Kirby and Tangle at that time, and Kirby's eerie neighing had indeed sounded like a horse in agony. The 'growling lion' was, of course, Fritzie and Fiela snoring their heads off – especially Fritzie, whose snore could carry over a long distance on a quiet night.

Kobus thanked the game guards for their trouble and we all went back to bed, much relieved at the outcome of affairs.

One day a few months later, while the game guards were out on patrol, they came across three tiny warthog piglets huddled together in the middle of the patrol road. Barely a week old, the piglets were close to death from starvation. Their spoor led from a hollow anthill nearby and, from the signs on the ground, it was evident that their mother had been taken by a hyena a day or two previously. Apparently the starving babies had left the safety of their anthill to search for their mother but had got only as far as the road where they'd collapsed in a little heap.

The game guards gathered up the pathetic creatures and brought them home to us.

I made up a milk mixture and Kobus and the girls helped to coax the frightened little animals to drink from a baby's bottle. But no matter how hard we tried, the piglets would not take the bottles. By ten o'clock that night they still had not fed, and we gave up the struggle. We gently wrapped them up in a blanket and put them in a box, trying to make them as comfortable as possible. We went to bed, feeling sad with the knowledge that they would probably die soon.

I couldn't sleep and, around midnight, got up and warmed up their milk again. Determined to force-feed each one of them, I took the strongest-looking one from the box. Holding him securely in my lap, I pried his clenched mouth open with my fingers and forced the teat into it. Miraculously, he started to suckle right away. Pausing for breath every once in a while, he drank his little tummy full and fell asleep in my lap. By this time his sister had woken and was squealing. I stuck the teat into her open mouth and quickly clamped her mouth shut with my other hand. Surprisingly, she also suckled right away, pausing only for breath and finally drinking almost as much as her brother had before falling asleep. The third piglet was the weakest and smallest of the three and it was obvious that he would not survive much longer without nourishment. I lifted him gently from the box and tried to force the teat into his mouth, but he wouldn't take it. Moaning and wailing with misery he crawled about on my lap. I went off and found a medicine dropper. After quite a struggle I succeeded in forcing a few tiny drops of milk into his little mouth. He liked that and wanted more. When he finally fell asleep with his tummy full of milk, I was confident that he, too, would survive.

Over the next few days, as the piglets grew accustomed to the bottle, they started enjoying the feeding routine so much that they wanted milk every few hours.

Feeding three impatient little warthogs all at the same time was a complicated business. The girls helped during the weekends, and

Kobus helped in the evenings, but when I was home alone, which was most of the time, I had to manage the feeding routine single-handedly. The piglets would not allow me to feed them one at a time. The other two would holler their heads off while waiting their turn and even climb into my lap and rough up the one being fed. In order to cope with three bottles simultaneously, I had to hold one in each hand and grip the third one between them, holding all three bottles tightly together. The trick then was to get all three teats into the yelling warthog mouths without dropping the bottle in the middle. If I dropped the middle bottle, the one who'd lost his bottle would immediately attack the other two to try to get theirs from them.

When each of them finally had a teat in its mouth, there would be peace for a while as the little hogs suckled contentedly. But after a few minutes, one of them would suddenly decide that his teat was no longer to his liking and would want to change it for his brother's or sister's teat. The brother or sister wouldn't want to go along with the deal, and the two of them would start a fight, striking each other with their heads while squealing to high heaven. The third piglet (the weakest one, who suckled more slowly than his brother and sister) would meanwhile suck away contentedly, minding his own business – until it suddenly occurred to the other two that what they really wanted was their little brother's bottle and, attacking the poor fellow from both sides, they would grapple for his teat.

The warthogs soon grew into three very spoilt brats, but they were so adorable and unbelievably ugly that it was impossible not to love them. Their most maddening habit was that they would start screaming for

their bottles whenever and wherever they saw me, regardless of whether it was feeding time or not. Their shrill, grating voices jangled the nerves of anyone within hearing distance. Even the dogs fled from the noise. I would run to the kitchen to prepare their bottles, the three screaming little hogs hot on my heels, and while I mixed their formula and warmed it up, they would dance about on my feet, hollering to high heaven and making me so nervous that I'd spill milk all over myself while trying to fill the three bottles. It occurred to me that a mother warthog needed nerves of steel to put up with such rowdy, demanding babies.

I introduced them to Fritzie and Fiela, hoping that Fiela would display some motherly love towards them. But the pigs would have nothing to do with the little warthogs and ran away from them. I've no idea why. I had thought they would be interested in making their acquaintance since pigs and warthogs appear to speak the same language.

As soon as the warthogs were six weeks old, I started teaching them to drink milk from a bowl. It was a messy business at first as they'd all fall into the bowl and then fight with each other, splashing milk all over the place.

At the age of two months they began to graze on the lawns with Fritzie and Fiela. Still the pigs remained indifferent to the warthogs. Fritzie was, of course, too busy eating to have time for other interests. Fiela allowed the piglets to snuggle up to her when she lay sleeping under her favourite shrub, but I think she slept so soundly that she was unaware of their presence.

One day the Parks Board helicopter flew low over our garden, and as I went outside to wave to the pilot, I heard the two pigs and three warthogs all screaming with fright at the sight and sound of the aircraft. The moment they saw me, they all ran straight to me for protection. As I sat there, hugging the five squealing animals to me, I felt like a pig-mother and wondered what the pilot would be thinking.

*

Feeding time at Mahlangeni was a complicated ritual. At sundown the horses, dogs, pigs, warthogs, Egyptian geese and bantams, as well as numerous uninvited guests (the squirrels and birds), all turned up at the Mahlangeni restaurant for their dinners. Naturally each animal believed that the other animals got more and better food than it did. This made me really mad as Filemoni and I went to considerable trouble to prepare each animal's dinner according to its particular needs and tastes.

The horses had to be fed and locked up in their camp before the dogs were fed otherwise the horses would trot over and, chasing the dogs off, gobble up their porridge, and even their cooked meat if they were in a mean mood. The pigs had to be fed before the bantams or the pigs would steal the bantams' kernels. The pigs, dogs, Egyptian geese and warthogs all had to be fed at the same time, but if there was only Filemoni and me to do the serving, it was impossible to carry all the plates in one trip. And the dogs would eat the pigs' dinners, the pigs the geese's; the geese the warthogs'; the squirrels and birds would eat the food in any untended plate, and the poor little warthogs – the lowest in the pecking order – would be left without any dinner.

Our photo albums are full of pictures of domestic animals. They always seemed to get in the way whenever I took photos of the girls. Aznar is in most of the pictures. Fritzie is definitely the least photogenic of all, looking like an unidentified black blob. Wolfie is very photogenic but often comes out rather wild-looking. Here's a picture of Karin hanging upside down from a tree, her sweater pulled over her head by the crazy wolf who is trying to get her out of the tree. Here's one of Hettie and Sandra, smiling at the camera, sitting in a cloud of dust. The photo was taken when we still had our honey badger, Buksie. The dust cloud is our dog Janna digging up the earth behind the girls. (Janna couldn't stand it that his badger friend wanted to sleep away the daylight hours, and so he was forever excavating all the holes in the garden, looking for Buksie.) Here's a picture of Sandra fleeing from a horse and a dog, both animals hot on her heels. Actually she was training for the school athletics meeting, but the animals thought it was a game.

Sandra became a member of the South African Junior Athletics Team at the age of sixteen. People often teased her that she owed her speed to the fact that she lived in Kruger Park and spent so much time running away from wild animals. What they didn't know was that she actually spent a lot of time running away from domestic animals.

When Sandra first started training at home over weekends, she did so on a stretch of lawn in the front garden. But the domestic animals either chased her or got in her way. So Kobus borrowed a road grader from the park's engineers and constructed a training track for her on the far bank of the river.

Sometimes elephant or buffalo used Sandra's training track for their ablutions, and a clean-up exercise was necessary before she could start training. And sometimes during training sessions, giraffe, kudu or other antelope appeared shyly from the bush, peering through the trees at her as she did her warm-up exercises. But as soon as Sandra launched herself from her starting blocks, they fled. They probably reckoned that if she had reason to take off so suddenly, they had better do the same.

Kobus always accompanied Sandra on her training sessions to keep an eye on the surrounding bush. First they read the signs on the ground to see who was in the neighbourhood. Once, when they found lion tracks, they could hear the lions grunting softly, and they followed the spoor to see how far or near they were. They found the lions not very far away, but they were resting peacefully. Evidently they'd had a recent good meal, and were feeling full and lazy. So Kobus and Sandra continued with the training.

One day when Kobus was away from home, I went with Sandra to do sentry duty, and although I was usually a very good sentry, I must have missed some clues that day, because an awful accident almost happened.

After Sandra had completed her warm-up routine she practised her starts. Even though she was slightly built, the power she put into her starts would knock anyone flying. That day, an enormous warthog sow burst from the scrub at the side of the road at the very moment that Sandra shot out of the starting blocks. The sow dashed headlong onto the track – right in front of my daughter. Sandra's whole body stiffened, and for a terrible moment I envisaged her either crash-landing on top of the sow or diving over her into the hard surface of the track. But Sandra miraculously managed to slam on her brakes in mid-take-off, literally stopping in her tracks just in time to avoid the crash. And then a baby warthog emerged from the scrub and dashed across the track after its mother, its tail straight up in the air. And then another baby followed, and another, and another!

Sandra and I sat down and laughed. The idea of a collision between an athlete and a warthog family just seemed so amusing to us.

THE SEASONS

OCTOBER IN THE BUSHLANDS IS THE PRELUDE TO THE SEASON OF heat, humidity, humility and madness. As the heat builds up and the humidity grows, trillions of insects arrive, snakes sneak into the house, elephants become evil-tempered, and everything else joins forces to make life uncomfortable.

One can learn to cope with snakes, to avoid elephants, to repel insects and to endure other discomforts, but the persistent, oppressive heat will get you if you're not clued up on summer-survival strategies.

Our first summer at Mahlangeni caught us unprepared. As the day-time temperatures soared to 40 degrees Celsius and above, our bodies became sluggish and apathetic and refused to function at a normal level. At night we tossed about on sheets and pillows that were drenched with perspiration, and in the mornings we woke up feeling groggy and irritable from lack of sleep. By the end of January we felt defeated by the heat. But the worst was yet to come.

February and March in the bushlands are the hottest months of the summer. The upper crust of the earth's surface is baked to the extent that even a rain shower will no longer cool it. After a shower the earth steams like a sauna. The night temperatures no longer fall appreciably, and the sultry nights bring little respite from the sweltering days.

Often during that first summer, when I lay awake at night I would hear the girls whimpering in their sleep. Getting up I would go to their bedroom and fan each of them in turn with a towel. Their sighs of relief made it worth the effort.

By the following summer we had become a little wiser and started practising some sensible heat-resisting strategies, such as sleeping under damp towels, drinking litres of cold water throughout the day and taking cold showers at regular intervals – with our clothes on. (For a while your wet clothes keep you marvellously cool.) We also learned to keep hot air and direct sunlight out of the house by closing every door and window, and even the curtains, early each morning. At night we opened everything to let the cooler night air circulate freely through the house. By repeating this routine conscientiously every day of the long hot summer, the interior of the house remained a few degrees cooler than the day temperatures outside – but not cooler than the night temperatures. During the last months of summer the sultry air began to find its way into the house and seemed to get stuck here, preventing the cooler air from entering at night. So Kobus built us a bed out of Lebombo ironwood logs on the patio outside our bedroom. He also placed beds on the screened veranda for the girls.

Every year at the height of the summer, when the nights got too hot to sleep inside, we bathed ourselves in mosquito repellent and, carrying the bare minimum of bedding outside, spent our nights under the stars. In the early evenings Kobus would hose down the paving under and around our ironwood bed several times to reduce the heat retained by the concrete and stone. The evaporation also served to cool the air around the bed.

There was a fuchsia tree growing outside our bedroom, its branches spreading far over the fishpond, the patio and the garden. From our ironwood bed we could see stars hanging among the leaves of the fuchsia tree, caught in the intricate tracery of its branches. A whole family of paradise flycatchers used the tree in summer for nesting, and on moonlit nights we could see their long tail feathers hanging over the sides of the nests above us.

Numerous other birds also roosted in the tree at night. Unfortunately they all woke up before sunrise and greeted the day with a noisy dawn chorus. They also performed their ablutions at that time of the morning. To avoid being on the receiving end, we had to gather up our bedding and flee indoors. The tree was also home to a whole community of caterpillars who, for unknown reasons, plunged from the tree onto our bed at night. And sometimes nectar dripped onto us from the tree's crimson flowers.

One summer, when the nectar and caterpillars were particularly irritating, Kobus spread and tied a tarpaulin across the branches directly above the bed. The caterpillars promptly contrived a new scheme to share our bed. Dropping onto the tarpaulin, they would creep up to the edge and, leaning over to check the bed's position, would dive down at an oblique angle. I can't think of any other explanation. Anyway, the caterpillars won, and the next summer we didn't bother to put the tarpaulin up.

Despite the irksome activities of the tree's inhabitants, sleeping outside was still better than sleeping in the stuffy house.

Another of our summer ordeals was the frogs. They arrived in the spring to take up residence in the fishpond and they stayed there until the end of summer. It was not the frogs themselves that we minded, but their nightly choir practice, which was so loud that normal conversation was impossible. Kobus and I would end up yelling at each other just to communicate.

Whether we slept inside or outside, the effect was the same. The pond stretched right up to the edge of the patio and along one side of it, ending almost inside our bedroom, and so the frogs' voices would resonate throughout the room. The only way to cut down the noise would have been to sleep inside with the sliding doors closed, but then the heat would have been suffocating.

The frog choir consisted of members of various species who croaked in different voices. There were basses, baritones, tenors, altos, contraltos and mezzo-sopranos. They performed a score with a double rhythm section – the one slow, the other lively – which droned and quavered the backing to a monotonous melody. The melody consisted of an un-remitting repetition of crescendos and diminuendos. It was hard to fall asleep with the frogs croaking fortissimo in our ears.

Eventually we would drop off, teeth gritted and fists clenched, but we didn't sleep for long. At a given moment, the frogs would all shut up and the sudden silence would jerk us awake. For a while the respite was heavenly, and we could feel our teeth and fists unclenching. Even the dogs sighed with relief. But then we would suddenly remember that the frogs were only taking a breather and that the lull wouldn't last long. Tensing up, we would wait for the choir to burst into song again. Before long, they did just that. The repeat performance opened with a couple of basso-profundo croaks – which I think was the conductor saying, 'All together now: very loudly!' And, presto! The appalling opera was in full cry again.

We often tried to repatriate the choir. Armed with a torch, a fishing net and a bucket of water, we pounced on the choristers. Catching each and every one of them and scooping them all into the bucket, we trekked down to the river and dumped the lot in the water.

But frogs don't quit easily. They are depressingly stubborn. Within two or three hours our choristers would be back. And despite their exhausting journey up the steep river bank, they'd take up where they left off when we interrupted their performance.

As time passed, we became wiser and changed our tactics. Loading the frogs into Kobus's pick-up we drove them some kilometres downriver before evicting them. For several nights thereafter we'd sleep in blissful peace. Until a new choir moved in. (Or perhaps the old choir?) The choristers would arrive singly or in small groups, and start practising in-dividually for the Great Ensemble Performance. As soon as the ensemble appeared to be plenary, we'd embark on the deportation process again.

In 1986, Kobus built a large swimming pool under the shady trees in the front garden. It was the best thing that ever happened to us at Mahlangeni.

To fall sizzling into a whole pool full of cool water is an experience straight out of heaven. It's like breaking a fever, like quenching a big thirst, like coming alive again after having been baked in a warm oven for too long. The longer you stay in the water, the better – the water eventually cools you down to the core. After a successful cooling-down session in the pool, your body temperature remains under control for quite a while, and you can go on with your work feeling human and friendly again.

In the evenings we'd dive into the pool and wouldn't dry off before lying down. It really worked. If you stayed in the water long enough to cool down to the marrow of your bones and then got onto the bed – wet – your reduced body temperature allowed you to get a really good night's rest. Provided the frogs had been evicted, of course.

Kobus erected a small wall, about forty centimetres high, around the swimming pool to keep the frogs out. Initially the wall also kept the Egyptian goslings out, but when they got bigger they tried to lay claim to the pool. Many a time, on a hot afternoon, as I was floating calmly by myself in the pool, a goose would plummet from the sky and land in the water next to me with a loud splash, startling me almost out of my wits. Then the goose would swim around me, all the while fixing me with an evil look that seemed to say, 'This is *my* pool now. Understand?'

Moreover, the geese didn't always leave the pool as they found it, and we'd have to clean up after them. Kobus said the only way to convince the geese that the pool belonged to us would be to shout at them each time they tried to lay claim to it. We did, and it worked. It's not that we're selfish, but they had the fishpond to swim in as well as the river.

The swimming pool contributed a great deal to our quality of life at Mahlangeni. To float about in the cool water on a hot summer's night, while listening to the sounds of the bush and watching the stars flickering above, is – to quote Kobus – the sort of experience that changes one's whole outlook on life. Before we had the pool, tempers often became so heated in the summer that we wanted to throw each other to the lions.

But once we had the pool, we felt a lot better about life and our summer tempers cooled considerably.

April and May at Mahlangeni were our favourite months. The days and nights became cooler, frogs stopped croaking, snakes went away, bugs and insects disappeared and elephants became friendlier. The mad days of summer were over, and a mood of serene beauty and tranquillity settled over the land.

The savannahs turned blond, the mopani woodlands displayed their autumn finery of golds and bronzes, and the sky became a deeper, softer blue. At twilight, the river sparkled ruby-red in the lazy afterglow of the sun, and the lingering, smoky-blue dusk added a mystical mood to the magic hour.

And so, goodwill was revived and dignity restored as summer mellowed into the halcyon days of autumn. I always wished that this season of graceful living would last for ever.

In June the nights suddenly became so cold that you had to sleep under blankets. The early mornings were chilly and you had to wear a sweater until it got warmer later in the morning. The winter days were mild to warm with an average maximum temperature of 26 degrees Celsius. The crisp air was so invigorating that you found yourself bouncing with energy and chuckling with the joy of life. And you forgot about wishing that autumn had stayed for ever.

As the seasonal pans and creeks dried up in winter, the shores in front of our house became a popular rendezvous for many species of game, including the larger herbivores such as elephant, buffalo and giraffe. A pack of wild dogs put in an occasional appearance, and lions could be heard roaring in the neighbourhood almost every night. Sometimes they roared so close to us that the house trembled.

As the deciduous trees and shrubs shed their leaves and the grasses were grazed short, the bewildering tangle of the summer vegetation disappeared and you could see far and wide into the bush. We loved to go camping, walking and riding at that time of year. The winter

landscapes of pale savannahs and bare woodlands under an azure sky had a stark and classic beauty.

Although winter is usually the most pleasant of the seasons in the park, the end of the season may occasionally be one of scarcity for the animals. When normal rainfalls occur in the late summer, there is sufficient grazing to last the animals throughout the winter. But when the rainfall has been scant, August will herald the appearance of bare patches in the veld.

From 1986 to 1989 our summer rainfalls had been below average. We were experiencing increasingly dry periods and by July 1989 virtually all the grass had disappeared. Then the August winds arrived, dancing through the withering woodlands and across the bleak plains, causing the last of the dry, brittle patches of grass to disintegrate. The earth panted for moisture, and day by day the condition of the herbivores deteriorated.

One evening we saw two bushbuck standing outside our fence, gazing hungrily at our verdant garden. (Our lawns remained green throughout the year as we pumped water from the river to irrigate them.) We opened the front gate for the bushbuck, hoping they would come in. They did, and spent the whole night grazing on the lawns.

From that day on we left the front gate open every evening. At first only the two bushbuck came, then three, and finally six who grazed in our garden every night. We closed the gate once they were all inside to prevent marauding lions from following them in at night. Although Janna and Wolfie, being herding dogs, would dearly have loved to herd the bushbuck, we told them not to, and the good dogs understood and left them in peace. Early in the mornings we opened the gate again, allowing the bushbuck out.

We became increasingly anxious as the drought continued to take its toll on the animals. One afternoon we saw a family of warthogs standing outside the fence, gazing longingly at the garden. A while later they were joined by a small herd of scrawny impala. We hoped that the warthogs and impala would follow the bushbuck in through the gate but, sadly, they didn't. They were too scared of the smell of humans and dogs in our garden. The bushbuck, of course, had spent most of their lives grazing nearby, and so they were quite used to our smell.

On the following evening the warthogs and impala turned up again, and eventually one plucky impala ewe ventured in after the bushbuck, but the others wouldn't follow. I resorted to feeding them from our vegetable garden. Every evening I would harvest two or three baskets of lettuce, spinach, carrots, tomatoes and other vegetables and drop them outside the fence for the warthogs and impalas. In the morning the vegetables were always gone.

Fortunately our vegetable garden was large and we always planted enough vegetables to see us through the winter and to freeze for the hot summer months. I knew I was feeding our precious summer provisions to the hungry animals, but it didn't matter. Their situation was desperate.

As the drought dragged on, our hippos deteriorated rapidly. We could hardly bear to look at their gaunt shapes as they left the river in the evenings in search of food.

One morning I went to the vegetable garden and, harvesting all of our remaining cabbages, piled them into a wheelbarrow. I wheeled them down the bank and across the shore, and dumped them at the waterside. I knew that my attempt to save the hippos from starvation was futile, but I couldn't stand to watch them suffer and do nothing.

I didn't see them eating the cabbages, but by late afternoon I saw that they had disappeared. It gave me little consolation, however, as I knew it was too little too late.

Kobus and I were sitting outside at sundown when we saw a hippo bull shuffle across the shore towards the bank. He seemed so infinitely weary. Then he just stopped and collapsed in his tracks.

We sat very still, neither saying a word. I knew that Kobus was as distressed as I was.

The riverine landscape was bleak and barren, the river only a narrow stretch of muddy water. In the gloom of the fading light, we waited for the darkness to blot out the pitiful landscape. It all seemed so senseless.

Kobus sat silently beside me, gazing towards the horizon. I was about to share my thoughts with him when he lifted his hand and, pointing to the south-east, said, 'Look, lightning.'

I turned and looked. Soon, a distant flash zigzagged above the horizon. A pearl-spotted owl called out, and its sweet melody seemed to linger a while in the quiet evening. A soft breeze stirred through the garden, and soon the south-eastern sky was lit continuously by the distant lightning.

We knew then that the rains would soon come. Perhaps not that night or even the next day, but soon.

The following evening flashes of lightning played continuously across the whole of the southern sky. Later that night, as the distant thunder rolled over the bush, we could smell the rain. It came the following morning. But it fell too hard, stopped too suddenly and disappeared into the parched earth too rapidly.

Yet it was a promise.

Surely the time had come for nature to mend her ways.

And so she did. In the early morning of 22 October, the sun didn't rise and the dark heavens dissolved in rain. It fell gently and steadily throughout the whole day and deep into the night. Before daybreak the next morning, the skies began to clear and the new dawn was bathed in sunshine. The damp landscape sparkled in the sun and the sweet fragrance of the wet earth was everywhere. All day long there was a magic stillness in the air, as if the earth was holding her breath while drinking the life-giving moisture.

At the school hostel, Sandra, Karin and their friends spent the afternoon exploring the surrounding veld and splashing about in muddy pools. They hadn't seen the world so wet for such a very long time, and the sight filled them with wonder and joy.

Hettie went for a walk on her own and, unfortunately, got lost. My bush-wise children never got lost and thought that only dim-witted people did. On that afternoon, Hettie wandered off into the woodlands on the north-east side of the hostel, wading barefoot through muddy pools and following the spoor of small animals in the wet ground. She was eighteen years old, in her last year at high school, a brilliant student and gifted with a passion for music, poetry and fairy tales. Following her dreams into the misty woodlands, she walked on, forgetting where she was. Only when the sun suddenly disappeared behind a dark cloud and it began to drizzle, did she become aware that she had walked much further from the hostel than she had intended to. Turning around quickly, she started to make her way back. After walking a fair distance and not seeing the hostel, she knew she was heading in the wrong direction.

There were no distinct landmarks in the homogeneous mopani woodlands of that area, and once you lost your sense of direction, you were in trouble.

Hettie decided to wait for the sun to reappear from behind the clouds so that she could calculate her directions more accurately. The sky had become so overcast now that she waited almost ten minutes before the sun finally tinged the edge of a cloud. Realizing that she had been heading south-east instead of south-west, she adjusted her course and set out.

Soon the sun disappeared completely behind the thick clouds again, but she continued determinedly in what she hoped was a south-westerly direction.

After a while she saw a flock of vultures perching in a stand of leadwood trees ahead of her. Carefully checking the signs on the ground, she made a downwind detour around the leadwoods. When she tried to correct her course again, she became confused. The sun stubbornly remained hidden behind the clouds, and she could do nothing but stride doggedly on, trying to ignore the spoor of an elephant herd crossing her path.

After more than an hour's walk, she arrived at the main tourist road between Phalaborwa Gate and Letaba Camp. Close to tears with relief, she sat down right there beside the road.

About ten minutes later, she heard a car approaching from the direction of Letaba Camp and stood up so that the driver would see her.

He promptly pulled up alongside her. The driver was a young man, and he looked very surprised at finding her there.

'Hi!' he said. 'Are you in trouble? Where's your car?'

'I don't have one,' said Hettie. 'Could you perhaps give me a lift?'

'Sure! Of course,' said the young man. 'Get in.'

She got in, and as they pulled back onto the road the young man said, 'But . . . if you don't mind my asking, why are you here . . . alone in the bush?'

Feeling embarrassed about admitting it but having no other choice, Hettie told him she'd gone for a walk and got lost.

'You did?' he exclaimed. 'Phew! That's bad. There are wild animals out here, didn't you know?'

'The reason I got lost,' she explained, 'was because it was overcast and I couldn't see the sun.'

'Yeah, that's really bad,' he sympathized. 'But you shouldn't walk out here, you know. The place teems with wild animals – lions, leopards, everything. Honestly, it's extremely dangerous.'

'I don't normally get lost,' said Hettie.

They passed an elephant bull grazing at the side of the road.

'There,' said the young man. 'See what I mean?'

She nodded.

'So, where'd you walk from?' he asked. 'How far?'

'From the hostel,' she answered. 'I don't know how far.'

Looking puzzled, he asked, 'What hostel? Where?'

'It's just inside the boundary of the park,' she explained. 'About two kilometres to the north of the gate.'

He turned in surprise, saying, 'You don't actually *live* here in the park, do you?'

'I do,' she said. 'But this is the first time I have ever got lost.'

The young man asked her many questions about her life in the park, and finally said: 'Well, I've had four terrific days in Kruger. Seen lions, cheetahs, wild dogs, elephants, everything, and – here's the best of all – a lovely, lost girl in the bush next to the road!'

When they reached the turn-off to the hostel, Hettie sheepishly asked the young man to offload her a little distance from the hostel grounds. She didn't want her friends to see her arriving in a car and find out that she'd got lost. He did as she asked, and she thanked him for the lift.

She strolled nonchalantly into the hostel grounds. And so no-one at the hostel, except her sisters, ever knew that she'd lost her way in the bush on that rainy afternoon.

Soon after those first rains had fallen, trillions of seeds germinated under the moist earth and decked the landscape in green carpets of new shoots. Tiny succulent leaves began to bud on the previously barren trees, and then masses of wild flowers sprang up everywhere in a profusion of colours.

The bush was finally alive and well again, and bustling with new life and growth.

WILD HARMONY

O N CHRISTMAS EVE 1990 THE LOCAL HERD OF ELEPHANTS TURNED up, as they often did, to graze in the reeds along the shore. The reverberating, rumbling sounds of their contact calls rolled right into our bedroom. We groaned and pulled the pillows over our ears.

It didn't help.

A baby elephant started shrieking to high heaven, the way baby elephants do when they don't get their way. As the tantrum intensified, some of the other youngsters became fretful and started screaming. The exasperated mothers, aunts and grannies groaned and grumbled. When the mother of the offending infant couldn't take it any longer she screeched a strident warning. Still the impossible imp refused to shut up. So the mother raised her voice to a stunning, full-throated trumpet that resounded to the heavens and could probably be heard in a neighbouring galaxy.

This jangled the baboons' nerves and they began wailing and screaming. Then our dogs started barking. They were tolerant of most animals but our local baboons irritated them beyond endurance, and when the baboons kicked up a shrieking shindy, nothing – not even Kobus's shouting – would stop the dogs from barking their lungs out. There was a hyena somewhere around who would start howling as soon as the dogs began barking. I don't know why. He just did. So he howled. The louder the dogs barked, the louder he howled. The cacophonous concert annoyed the hippos and they complained with booming bellows.

It was difficult for us to fall asleep with the wild concert turned to full volume.

Eventually the elephants left, but our aggrieved neighbours carried on screaming, barking, howling and bellowing into the early morning hours. We finally fell asleep shortly before dawn. Then the two Egyptian geese arrived and startled us awake with their raucous trumpeting.

That's nature for you.

Never a moment of peace.

PART 2

CROCODILE BRIDGE AND PRETORIUS KOP

GOODBYE, SWEET SOLITUDE

IN NOVEMBER 1990 THE PARK OFFICIALS SENT US NEWS THAT WE WERE to be transferred to Crocodile Bridge, a ranger station in the southeast corner of the park.

I could not imagine leaving Mahlangeni. The place belonged to me. Its wild beauty, its moods, its magic were the rhythms of my heart. Who would I be if we moved away?

Another thing that worried me was that I had grown so used to solitude that I had become people-shy.

Although I had never been to Crocodile Bridge, I knew that the southern region of the park was more people-populated than the north. Kobus told me that the ranger's house at Crocodile Bridge was on the bank of the Crocodile River, quite close to the local tourist camp. He also told me that a whole farming community lived on the other side of the river.

What would I say to all those strange people? Strangers expected one to be bright, entertaining and amusing and lots of other things which I had forgotten all about. I lay awake at night, worrying about the prospect of encountering people at Crocodile Bridge.

The girls didn't think that relocating was a good idea either. They had grown up to believe that the natural order of things was for one's home to be a place of freedom and space far removed from the complexities and restrictions of human societies.

*

We moved on a rainy summer morning in January 1991. As we said goodbye to the place that had been our home for eleven years, I remembered a phrase from a story I had read many years before.

The author, I think, was de Maupassant, but unfortunately I don't recall the title, or even what the story was about. I remember only that someone in this story had to take leave of a place that he loved very much, and since he could not bear the idea of never returning to it, he decided that the place would belong to him for ever in his memories. So he said, '*Ici reste mon coeur.*' 'Here remains my heart.'

As the phrase played in my head on that rainy summer morning, I buried my heart at Mahlangeni. And as we drove south to a strange new home almost four hundred kilometres away, I consoled myself that Mahlangeni would belong to me in my memories for ever.

We must have looked like a circus on the road, travelling with three horses, two dogs, two pigs and twelve bantam chickens. I had wanted to take the three warthogs too, but Kobus had said no, they had become self-sufficient and would look after themselves.

Karin, now thirteen, and I drove ahead in my jeep, towing a horsebox. Hettie and Sandra, nineteen and eighteen, followed with their father in his pick-up truck, towing a double horsebox. The dogs travelled with Karin and me, the bantams and pigs with Kobus and the two older girls. The rain wouldn't let up, and the poor animals looked so miserable and insecure. They had never moved home before and they couldn't understand what was happening, or why.

Actually, neither could I.

MELANCHOLIA

THE RAINS FOLLOWED US ALL THE WAY FROM THE MOPANI WOOD-lands in the north to the grassy savannahs of the central region, clearing finally in the area south of Satara where the marula woods stood in soggy silence. The skies became brighter as we travelled along the Lebombo Mountains, and the wet landscapes below us sparkled in the sun. As we descended from the mountains and crossed the Sabie River, the acacia bushlands teemed with wild animals of every description, and it was evident that the south of the park was not only more people-populated than the north, but also more animal-populated.

We arrived at Crocodile Bridge in the late afternoon.

The Crocodile Bridge tourist camp is one of the southernmost camps in the park, and so the main tourist road that runs from south to north through the length of the park starts or ends at Crocodile Bridge Camp, depending on one's direction of travel. The game ranger's house at Crocodile Bridge is about one kilometre to the east of the camp and is reached by a dirt track, turning off from the main road near the entrance to the camp.

We turned into this track and drove slowly, scanning the landscape for a first glimpse of our new home. The track snaked through a grassy savannah dotted with knobthorn, marula and acacia trees, and seemed to lead straight back to the Lebombo Mountains. But after a few hundred metres the track split, and there to our right, on the bank of the river, was a densely wooded patch with a fence around it. We turned towards it, and a few seconds later drove in through the gate of our new home.

We parked under a gigantic fuchsia tree. The parking area faced a subtropical garden where a troop of monkeys were reposing under a mkuhlu tree – much to the annoyance of our two dogs. Leaping from the jeep they promptly evicted the squatters. Screams of monkey consternation filled the air. A flock of red-billed hoopoes responded with an outburst of hysterical cackling.

A paved path led through the profusion of foliage and flowers to the front door of the house. The ranch-style house had sandy-pink walls and a tangerine roof and looked handsome in its lush, wooded garden. For a moment I felt rather charmed by it all. But within the next few minutes a number of alarming facts came to my attention.

The first of these was that the sun was setting in the north. That bothered me a great deal. The second was that a Mozambique spitting cobra was lying at the front door. It reared its head and looked at us disapprovingly before disappearing into a flowerbed at the side of the house. Evidently he was a permanent resident and disliked intruders.

The entrance to the house turned out to be the kitchen. The kitchen led to the lounge where several bats were flying around among wooden beams that supported the ceilingless roof. There were bats in every room. It appeared that they, too, were permanent residents.

It was an interesting house – old, but sturdy and solid. The criss-cross structure of heavy wooden beams under the high roof was particularly attractive, if one could ignore the bats. The layout of the rooms was rather confusing though, and the deeper one went into the house, the darker the rooms got. Most of the windows either opened onto screened verandas or looked straight into the foliage of shrubs and trees, keeping the daylight out. In the dark hall between the lounge and the bedrooms I found a small table on which stood a radio-transceiver and a telephone. A telephone! I hoped I wouldn't be expected to answer it if it rang.

While Kobus and the girls took care of the horses, pigs and bantams, I went out into the front garden which looked onto the Crocodile River. The view was enchanting, but not as breathtaking as the view at Mahlangeni. The Crocodile River was mainly a gathering of streams that burbled their way around islands of reeds. Reeds also covered most of the shores and the banks. I walked the length of the front garden, hoping to see more of the landscape on the far side of the river, but the woods on the opposite bank were so dense that nothing was visible beyond them – or so I thought, until I made a most alarming discovery. Further upstream, through a gap in the foliage on the far bank, I spotted part of what appeared to be a fenced-in garden. And right there, at that very moment, stood a *person*!

It wasn't actually doing anything. It just stood there, contemplating a shrub or something. I couldn't tell whether it was a man or a woman – about three hundred metres separated us. I stared at the disturbing sight with morbid fascination. After a while the stranger turned, spotted me and lifted its hand in greeting. I managed to wave back. But I was shaken. I had neighbours within waving distance! My only consolation was that the river separated us.

Then I saw that the sun was still setting in the north.

Nothing seemed right. But I put a brave face on it and went to see what my family and the animals were doing.

The horses, pigs and bantams were happily ensconced in their new quarters, a large fenced-in area in a far corner of the premises, and were enjoying their meals of lucerne and maize.

'Isn't the sun setting in the wrong place?' I asked Kobus.

'Where do you want it to set?' he asked.

'In the west, of course!'

'So?'

'It's setting in the north.'

He looked at the sun and said, 'Nope. That's west.'

At that moment the furniture truck arrived and so there was no time for an argument. The rest of the evening was filled with the chaotic business of unloading and unpacking. We finally went to bed around midnight, utterly exhausted.

About an hour later we were woken by a cacophony of nightmarish sounds.

I would rather not dwell on what happened that night as the memory of it is too upsetting. In short, a leopard had found its way into our garden (perhaps someone had forgotten to secure the gates properly) and it caught and killed our two beloved pigs, Fritzie and Fiela.

The first thing that went wrong the next morning was that the sun rose in the south. I couldn't understand why, and so I asked the girls to go to the tourist camp to buy me a map of the park. (I had one, but couldn't remember where I'd packed it.) Hettie, Sandra and Karin saddled their horses and, accompanied by our two dogs, rode over to the camp – much to the surprise of the visiting tourists, not to mention the camp manager and his wife. The tourists reached for their cameras, asking the girls to pose for them with their dogs and horses. The camp manager reached for the telephone.

When the phone rang in our house I was unable to identify the unfamiliar sound for several seconds. When it finally dawned on me what it was, I felt too scared to pick up the receiver, so I ran outside to call Kobus. The phone stopped ringing before he could answer it. The camp manager resorted to sending us a note along with the girls.

Kobus and Kobie
Welcome to Crocodile Bridge! Your three beautiful girls created quite a stir in the camp. Not that I mind, in fact I hope they will visit us often! However, I am afraid that their dogs and horses also drew a lot of attention from our visitors, and so I am afraid I have to remind you that domestic animals are not allowed in tourist camps. Do come over for tea this afternoon. My wife, Mariaan, and I look forward to meeting you.
Regards
Johan Schoeman

I felt awful. I had completely forgotten about the park rules. At Mahlangeni the rules hadn't mattered because the nearest tourist camp had been sixty kilometres away. And we were invited to tea! What would I do?

'Don't worry,' said Hettie. 'Think about it later. Look, we've bought you a little present.' She handed me a brown paper bag.

It contained the map I'd asked them to buy me, and . . . a box of chocolates!

'Chocolates!' I gasped. 'Oh wow!'

'We thought you'd need them,' smiled Sandra.

I was in heaven. I'd never imagined that the little shop in the camp would have chocolates, of all things. We hadn't lived near a shop of any kind for ages. Perhaps life at Crocodile Bridge would not be so bad after all. I opened the box and shared its contents with my daughters. And for the next few minutes, while we devoured the whole lot in one sitting, the world and its problems didn't exist. The girls described the camp to me. It was small, they said, compared to other camps, but beautifully laid out with twenty chalets nestling among indigenous trees and shrubs. The shop was tiny and also doubled as a reception office, but was well stocked with a variety of canned food, soft drinks, sweets, biscuits, cheese, milk and eggs.

After we'd finished the chocolates, I studied the Kruger Park map and saw that the Crocodile River was full of twists and turns. In this south-east corner of the park it made a ponderous U-turn in its search for a passage through the Lebombo Mountains. Our house, I discovered, stood on the western leg of the U-turn, facing east onto the river. That, of course, complicated things a great deal. The Crocodile River was the southern boundary of the park, so naturally one would expect our house to be on the north bank of the river, which, in fact, it was. But because of the U-turn, it faced east onto the river instead of south. At Mahlangeni our house had been on the north bank of the Letaba and had looked south onto the river. For eleven years the sun had risen out of the water in the east and sunk into the water in the west.

Here, at Crocodile Bridge, the sun rose directly across the river. It was so confusing.

I went outside to see if I could rearrange my sense of direction but was met by the Mozambique cobra on the paved path outside the kitchen. I froze too late. The cobra spat its venom at me and disappeared into the flowerbed. I looked in surprise at the trickles of venom dribbling down my leg, thinking how fortunate I was that I'd been hit on the leg and not in the eyes. As I rushed back inside to wash the venom away, the telephone started ringing again. I paused for a moment, wondering what to do. Where were Kobus and the girls? I had to wash the venom from my leg without delay. My heart was beating loudly, but the insistent ringing of the telephone was even louder and seemed to command an immediate response. Lifting the receiver hesitantly, I said to whoever was on the line, 'Please wait a moment, I have to wash my . . . uh . . . leg.' I put the receiver down and rushed into the bathroom. I gave my leg a thorough rinse and a scrub, and then sat down and wept because I didn't know what to do about the telephone, nor about the invitation from the camp manager and his wife. My head was hurting and my two beloved pigs were dead. The house was full of bats and the sun rose and set in the wrong places. I felt sick from having eaten too many chocolates. And we had neighbours across the river. I wanted to go back to Mahlangeni.

THE GREAT ADJUSTMENT

IN THE DAYS BEFORE WE HAD MOVED TO CROCODILE BRIDGE, I HAD tried to imagine what my new home would look like, and I had pictured the house facing south onto the river. Evidently that picture had lodged itself in my mind, and now refused to be budged.

No matter how often I stood in the garden at Crocodile Bridge, map in hand, facing the rising sun and trying to reset my sense of direction, I couldn't get it right. 'That's east,' I would tell myself firmly. But it didn't help. In my heart I knew it was south. My sense of direction had been irrevocably scrambled by the twisting river and by the person who had so unwisely built the house on the west leg of the U-turn.

The thing is, if you live in the bushlands, you have to know exactly where the sun rises and where it sets, otherwise you can get horribly lost. I grew up on a bushveld farm, and for as long as I can remember it has been important to me to have a sure sense of north, south, east and west. So when south suddenly became east at Crocodile Bridge, and north became west, it seemed to me that the sun, the stars, the moon, the earth itself and even the shadows on the ground had made a ninety-degree turn. I couldn't rest until I got it right. But I just couldn't get it right.

Often, as I stood in the garden, map in hand, trying to correct my errant sense of direction, I got the feeling that I was being watched. And so I was – by the local troop of baboons. There was something strange and broody about them. Their abode was a sycamore fig on the river bank just outside the south fence of our garden. (Actually it was the east fence, but you know what I mean.) Day after day they sat around in their tree, watching my every move. The moment I left the house, I would feel their eyes on me. What were they up to?

When I mentioned to Kobus one day that the local baboons were acting like a bunch of secret agents that had been commissioned to investigate me, he laughed and told me they were studying the dogs, not me.

We had fruit trees all over the garden: pawpaws, mangoes, bananas, marulas and citrus. My two dogs followed me wherever I went, and the baboons were in fact doing an investigative study of the dogs to find out how seriously they intended to guard the fruit trees. Wolfie, being an Australian cattle dog, was a loyal and conscientious animal who took all his responsibilities very seriously. Flenter, a young Staffordshire bull terrier, was a fighter as well as a fight-picker, and he distrusted all wild animals, especially baboons. (Our beloved dog Janna was no longer with us. A crocodile took him on the shore of the Letaba River during our last year at Mahlangeni.)

The baboons proved to be smart observers, for after a week or so they concluded unanimously that the dogs were to be taken seriously, and the fruit trees to be avoided. I was relieved when they finally stopped watching me. I only wished my other problems would go away as easily.

One night, during our second week at Crocodile Bridge, a couple of prowling civets (long-legged, medium-sized, cat-like animals) devoured my whole brood of bantam chickens. Only the rooster escaped.

I was so upset that I vowed never again to keep bantams.

The rooster decided that henceforth it would be safer for him to be a dog, so he shared the dogs' sleeping place in the garden shed at night, perching on a shelf directly above their heads. He gave up crowing and never ventured far from the dogs during the day. His survival instincts proved sound, for the civets left him in peace.

One morning during that same week I decided that the dogs' sleeping mats needed a spring-clean. As I picked up one of the mats to give it a good shake the resident cobra fell out of it. He landed on my foot, and my foot got such a shock that a ligament in the ankle was injured. The snake hurried away, disappearing into his flowerbed at the side of the kitchen.

His flowerbed was actually more than just a flowerbed – it also contained two trees, numerous shrubs and creepers and it was dense and overgrown to the point of being a perfect hangout for a snake. A whole community of frogs, lizards and geckos also inhabited it, so the snake had abundant food supplies right there in his own home which made foraging outside it unnecessary. He liked to wander a bit though, so we often met him on the paved path in front of the kitchen.

He was a funny snake for a cobra, really. Ordinarily, the Mozambique spitting cobra is a nervous and highly strung snake. Our cobra, it seemed, was neither very highly strung nor particularly aggressive. If you accidentally approached him too suddenly, he'd rear his head, ready to strike, but if you stopped in your tracks and remained frozen, he'd contemplate you for a while and then slither away into his flowerbed. Apparently he had accepted the fact that he would always have human neighbours and that he had no choice but to tolerate them. His philosophy more or less coincided with ours, which was, 'We won't bother you if you don't bother us.' Accordingly my family and I always walked slowly and rather noisily along the paved path to give the snake ample warning that someone was approaching. He would keep his distance, and so neither party would be in danger of an unexpected dramatic encounter.

Wolfie, the cautious dog, kept a discreet distance from the snake. Flenter, the fight-picker, often tried to attack the snake but the snake always spat in his eyes. The first time this happened, Karin rushed the dog to the nearest tap and held his face under the running water until all the venom was washed away. The second time, Flenter ran to the tap himself and waited for one of us to get there and turn it on. On other occasions, when we didn't see the snake spit at him, he would howl at the kitchen door to let us know he needed help. As soon as one of us responded to his call, he'd run straight to the tap and hold his face upright, waiting for the relief of the cool water in his burning eyes.

Our policy of not bothering each other was understood by the snake, but not by the resident bats. They bothered us almost out of our minds.

Bats are mammals that can fly. That makes them pretty unique. But they are not very good fliers. Their navigating systems often pack up and go haywire. When a bat realizes that he has miscalculated a chosen landing spot, he chooses a human as a site for the crash landing, preferably one who is asleep (that is, horizontal and stationary). Sometimes even the crash landing goes awry, and the bat ends up in a basket or some other container from which he cannot escape. Then he shrieks for help until you wake up. When you go to his aid (with murder in your heart), he looks so pathetic as he pleads with you please to help him out that you have no choice but to do so. As you lift him gently out, he bites your hand.

When bats get bored, which is often, they fly round and round in never-ending circles. The only way to stop them from driving everybody (including themselves) insane is to anaesthetize them temporarily. This is done with a tennis racket. You plant yourself in a spot where, by holding the racket upright in the air, a collision is bound to happen. You can also help the collision along a little if you wish. Once the bat is unconscious, you carry him gently outside and leave him on the lawn to recuperate.

Some evenings you'd find almost a dozen bats recuperating on our lawn.

In the beginning we tried very hard to persuade the bats to find themselves another home. But they made it clear to us that the house had belonged to their families for many generations, and that they would never dream of leaving it. I think they mistook it for a cave. You couldn't blame them really. The house was dark and gloomy inside, and the roof leaked a little when it rained, adding moistness to the cave-like atmosphere. We tried spooking them out with an ultrasonic sound device. But it apparently didn't bother them. We tried gassing them out

ABOVE LEFT: The foundling prince.
ABOVE RIGHT: By the age of two months, Leo's eyes were his most arresting feature.
BELOW: Portrait of an upbeat trio – Wolfie, Karin and Leo.

ABOVE: Leo and Hettie entertaining each other.
LEFT: Travelling in regal style.
BELOW: Leo clowning with Sandra and Paul.

ABOVE LEFT: Wolfie teaching Leo herding techniques.
ABOVE RIGHT: A big hug from Karin.
BELOW: Leo and Wolfie watching baboons on the other side of the fence.

Kobus and Leo.
Photograph by Daryl Balfour

ABOVE: Preparing Leo, aged eight months, for his first hunting lesson. Photograph by Daryl Balfour

BELOW: Wolfie, Sandra, Karin, Kobus and Leo on top of Shabeni.

ABOVE LEFT: Karin was Leo's favourite sister.
ABOVE RIGHT: Leo striding over the top of Shabeni.
BELOW: A special bond... Photograph by Daryl Balfour

Onward, Leo. Pamuzinda, 1994.

ABOVE: Resting with Hettie. Pamuzinda, 1994.

BELOW: The Royal Family: Fat Cat, Leo and Happie. Pamuzinda, 1995.

with chlorine, but they didn't seem to notice. We tried worrying them out by keeping the electric lights in the house burning day and night for a couple of days, hoping it might open their eyes to the fact that the house wasn't a cave. It didn't. And remain they did.

Kobus said we should look on the bright side of things. Bats ate insects, including mosquitoes. So we had our own personal mosquito-culling team.

At the end of January, Hettie and Sandra went back to their universities in Johannesburg and Pretoria, more than five hundred kilometres away, while Karin enrolled at school in Nelspruit, our closest town, about a hundred and twenty kilometres away. It was hard for me to say goodbye to my girls, especially to Hettie and Sandra, as they would be away until the start of the autumn holidays near the end of March. Fortunately Karin was able to come home on the school bus every weekend, and this gave me some consolation. Kobus worked very hard and was seldom home. So I was left pretty much on my own during the week to cope with the Great Adjustment.

One night when Kobus was away, camping in the Lebombo Mountains on an anti-poaching patrol, I woke up to a cacophony of sounds. Well, I didn't really wake up fully but my reflexes did, and so I found myself scrambling out of bed, grabbing my torch and pistol and running outside into the darkness – realizing too late that I'd missed the pistol in my haste and picked up an empty coffee mug instead.

Dogs were barking, horses whinnying, and a gate crashed open. Something was also growling, but that didn't register properly because about three-quarters of me was still asleep and the rest of me was thinking only of our three horses. A few nights before, a leopard had growled somewhere in the neighbourhood, causing the frightened horses to crash open the gate of their camp and flee headlong into the dark garden. One of them had collided with an iron structure that had made a nasty gash in his flank, and we had been doctoring the wound ever since.

So, as I rushed towards the source of the uproar, the only thought that surfaced clearly was that I had to prevent the horses from injuring themselves again in the darkness. They were out of their camp and running along the east fence of the garden, straight towards the swimming pool in the south-east corner. As I ran after them, shouting at them to come back, the dogs ran alongside me, barking their heads off. My torch batteries were almost flat, and the faint beam of light didn't do much to relieve the inky blackness of the night. Something else was running along on the outside of the fence, but I had no time to wonder about that. The horses were approaching the pool much too fast. Luckily they veered away in time, dashing through the garden towards the back of the house. Before following the horses, I hurled the coffee mug at the creature that was trying to break through the wire of the fence. The mug struck the wire mesh with a clanging noise, and I hoped that it would frighten away the pestering prowler.

I found the panic-stricken horses at the back of the house and, after a lot of fuss, managed to calm them down and lead them back to the stable in their camp. I thanked the two dogs (who had barked themselves hoarse) for their loyal assistance and then went back inside to make myself a cup of good coffee.

The caffeine startled my mind awake and it was only then, as the fog of sleepy confusion lifted, that I registered the fact that I had actually heard the creature outside the fence snarling at one stage – just like a lion. But I dismissed the thought and went back to bed.

When Kobus came home the following morning, I told him how the horses had been disturbed again in the night, and how I'd had a really hard time calming them down and getting them back into their camp. Kobus said he would do something about the gate to prevent the horses from crashing it open again. But first he went off to see what it was that had worried them in the night. He came back a while later and told me to come and see what he'd found.

First he showed me a trail of lion pugmarks running along the outside of the fence. Then he showed me where a lion had tried to get through the wire by hurling itself against it, leaving a large indentation in the mesh.

I was horrified.

Kobus thought I had been pretty brave, running out into the night to protect the horses. So I didn't explain to him that I had been half asleep.

Adjusting to the wild society at Crocodile Bridge took me a while, but it was nothing compared to my difficulties in adapting to the human society.

Unlike Mahlangeni, Crocodile Bridge is en route to a lot of places. It is only ninety kilometres from Skukuza, and thirty-seven kilometres from Lower Sabie. Across the Crocodile River lives a whole farming community, and the village of Komatipoort is just twelve kilometres away. So I had neighbours everywhere. And people dropped in all the time, mostly to see Kobus on official business but quite often also for a neighbourly visit.

Remembering names became a permanent nightmare for me. Actually, I couldn't even remember faces. A lot of people seemed to look alike.

Strangers often turned up to see Kobus when Kobus wasn't there. That was an ordeal for me because most of the time I wouldn't know whether I had met the visitor (or visitors) previously or not.

After I had proved myself an idiot on several occasions by introducing myself to people who already knew me, I decided it would be best to greet everyone as if I knew them. If they turned out to be strangers, they would point out that we hadn't met, and I would then say: 'Oh sorry, I mistook you for someone I know!' At least that sounded as though I was a person who knew some people. This, at any rate, would be my strategy, and to a large extent it worked.

Except when the visitor, who didn't introduce himself (on the grounds that we'd met before), asked me to give Kobus a message from him. When Kobus came home, I was in trouble. All I could tell him was that someone had left a message that there were elephants on his farm, or whatever. Kobus would ask me for a description of the person, but the only thing I seemed able to remember about people was the expression in their eyes. So Kobus would have to guess whose farm it was and then go out and herd the elephants back into the park.

Naturally, Kobus insisted that I start to get interested in learning people's names. I explained to him that I was very interested, but that my mind seemed to have lost its name-recalling program. He asked how such a thing was possible. So I had to remind him that, during the years we'd lived at Mahlangeni, I had seen very few people other than my own family. Whereas he'd often worked away from home and saw his colleagues and other park personnel, I had been the one who stayed home alone, keeping company with wild animals. This had led my subconscious to the conclusion that it no longer needed to store people's names.

Kobus didn't see my point.

Eventually I learned some names but I would fit them to the wrong faces. At a school function in Nelspruit I kissed the headmaster, mistaking him for one of our kind, elderly neighbours from across the river, much to Karin's embarrassment. At the same function I introduced myself to my dentist, who then explained that not only did he know me, he also knew my teeth.

One day Kobus warned me that someone from Skukuza, who was a good friend of his, would be dropping in the following day, bringing his wife along. Kobus told me their names and reminded me that I had met the couple on a previous occasion.

I was ready for them. I even baked a cake. When the car arrived the next morning, I rushed outside with a warm welcome on my face and hugged them both. 'I'm so happy to see you!' I babbled. 'Come right in, I've baked a cake!'

The lady looked alarmed. 'Well . . . how kind of you,' she stammered, 'but . . . I don't know . . .'

The man only said: 'Uh . . .'

I realized they were the wrong people.

Kobus came out of his office, shook hands with them and introduced himself. The visitors explained that they had been sent by the Department of Water Affairs to research the status of the rivers in the area and that they needed some information from him.

Kobus invited them into his office.

The lady gave me a sympathetic smile. She probably thought I was so lonely for company that I spent all my days baking cakes and waiting for someone to visit.

I tried to comfort myself with the belief that things would get better as time went by. I reckoned that, once I got used to seeing lots of people, my social nervousness would decrease. But it didn't. It grew with each new gaffe that I made.

Remembering names and faces wasn't my only problem. It was the whole spectrum of social graces that eluded me. Each time I opened my mouth, the wrong words came out. But I don't want to give you any examples of these, if you don't mind. Some of them are too embarrassing to bear thinking about.

Nothing went right for me at Crocodile Bridge, not even my favourite pastime – walking the dogs. If tourists spotted me in the bush with my dogs, they'd stop and study me through binoculars – and then go straight to either the camp manager or the game ranger (Kobus) and report me to them.

Kobus had a talk with me, telling me that if I wanted to walk in the bush, I had to do so out of sight of tourist roads. There was a strict rule that tourists had to stay in their cars and drive only on marked roads. If they saw me walking in the bush, Kobus said, they could get the idea that it was safe to do so, and soon everyone would want to do it. And if visitors got trampled or eaten, then the blame would be placed on him because, as game ranger, he was responsible for the safety of the tourists in his section, as well as for enforcing the park rules. I explained to Kobus that I always tried my best to avoid tourist areas, but that it was hard to keep one's sense of direction if the sun set in the wrong place.

Again he didn't see my point. But he gave me a compass for my birthday.

*

On the farm directly across the river from us lived a young couple, Willem and Ilse van Aard. It was their garden that was visible from ours through the gap in the foliage on the far bank, and Ilse who had waved to me on that first day. Although we didn't meet in person for almost two years, we often waved to each other across the river.

I discovered eventually that it was actually quite nice to have a neighbour to wave to, even though she sometimes appeared to be an illusion. (At a distance of about three hundred metres it's hard to tell what's real and what's not.) I might have suspected her of being a phantom neighbour if it weren't for the fact that we occasionally talked on the phone. She'd call to ask me to give my husband a message from her husband. Or I'd call her when I needed information such as where to find a library or a dentist or something.

And sometimes we'd discuss the weather, or the current happenings in the landscape between her house and mine – like the time a marabou stork stood on the shore for half a day watching a crocodile that had a huge dead fish dangling from its mouth. The marabou, being wise to the fact that the croc would have to open its jaws for the swallowing exercise, stood waiting for just that moment to snitch the fish from its mouth. And the croc, sensing what was on the marabou's mind, refused to open its jaws. And so they spent the whole afternoon in each other's company, looking like two frustrated statues. Eventually it got too dark to see them, and neither Ilse nor I knew the outcome of the standoff because by the following morning they were gone.

Another time, an elephant mother chased an innocent buffalo bull right over the horizon after she'd got the idea that he'd threatened her calf. Ilse thought that the calf had probably screamed in fright at the coldness of the water lapping at its feet, and that the mother had misunderstood and assumed the buffalo was the culprit. But I thought it more likely that the mother was simply being outrageous, the way elephant moms usually are.

Anyway, it was nice to have someone to discuss the scenery with.

Scenery was such a good safe topic.

A TROUBLE-SHARING FRIEND

ABOUT SIX MONTHS AFTER WE HAD MOVED TO CROCODILE BRIDGE, another game-ranger family from the north was transferred to the south. Ranger Flip Nel, his wife Annette and their two daughters had been stationed at Shingwedzi for seven years. Annette had loved the solitude and serenity of the vast northern region of the park, and she had been as happy at Shingwedzi as I had been at Mahlangeni. On the day that they arrived at their new home at Lower Sabie in the south, Annette burst into tears. Their house was practically next door to Lower Sabie Camp and within viewing distance of the tourist road.

Lower Sabie was only thirty-seven kilometres from Crocodile Bridge, and I looked forward to having Annette as a neighbour. We'd always been good friends, but up north the distance between her home and mine had been over a hundred kilometres. So we hadn't really seen much of each other.

Shortly after Annette and her family had moved in at Lower Sabie, I drove over one morning to pay her a neighbourly visit.

As I turned into their gate she came out of the house to meet me. I was happy to see that she still looked the same: delicate and gypsy-like with shiny brown eyes and a thick mass of curly, dark-brown hair.

'I've come to welcome you to the south,' I told her.

'How sweet of you,' she said. 'But I don't think I could ever feel at home here.'

'I understand,' I said sympathetically.

'I knew you would,' she said gratefully.

We went inside and made coffee while she told me of a terrible thing that had happened to her earlier that morning. She had gone out into her garden, still wearing her nightie, to look for her three-year-old daughter, Narina. She found her playing in the sand in a far corner of the front garden. Walking over to her, she glanced up and saw a car parked on the tourist road, less than a hundred metres from her house, with tourists leaning out of the windows and studying her through binoculars.

I could hardly imagine such a dreadful experience and I commiserated with her. I told her that at least my house was not in sight of a tourist road but that I had other problems: I had neighbours everywhere; people dropped in all the time, and everybody thought me a blunderhead because I couldn't remember who they were.

Annette agreed that this was most distressing.

She told me that, on a quiet evening, she and Flip could actually hear people talking and laughing in the tourist camp.

I thought that was really awful. I told her that tourists sometimes spotted me when I took the dogs walking. She sympathized and told me that her dog was suffering from a nervous disorder because it wasn't used to having so many people in the neighbourhood.

I felt sorry for her dog.

I told her that I had a telephone in my house. She was shocked.

I also told her that, over at my place, the sun rose in the south and set in the north and that a snake lived in a flowerbed at the entrance to the house.

She said that sounded bad, but not as bad as the telephone.

We were on to our second cups of coffee, and I was about to tell her that I had bats in my house when, suddenly, we both sat bolt upright. Annette's dog, Ngala, was barking outside in a frenzied high-pitched tone. Game rangers' dogs only bark like that when something is terribly wrong. We put our cups down and rushed outside to see what it was.

Three young male lions were running along the outside of the fence, while Ngala, running along the fence on the inside, was barking her head off at them. The frisky young lions wanted only to get at the dog and teach it a lesson, and so they ran along the fence looking for a place to get in. They were running directly towards the gate. The gate was wide open. (Park people seldom close their gates in daytime.) About ten metres inside the open gate, three-year-old Narina was playing in the sand. As she saw the lions approaching, she jumped to her feet and stood frozen to the spot.

Annette shot forth like a launched rocket, sprinting towards Narina and the open gate. I ran after Annette but stopped at my car, which was parked in the drive about twenty metres from the gate. Yanking open the door I got out my pistol. Annette had almost reached the gate by then, and so had the lions. 'I have a pistol!' I yelled to her. 'I'm coming!'

The lions stopped outside the open gate to stare curiously at the petite human female who was boldly charging them. Annette grabbed hold of the gate, swung it shut in their surprised faces and slammed the securing bolt into place.

The crisis was over.

The gardener, Abel, arrived on the scene brandishing a pitchfork and yelling abuse at the lions. Abel's colourful language coupled with Ngala's hysterical barking got too much for the lions and they left.

Annette gathered Narina in her arms and we went back inside.

Narina, a true child of the wild, was only slightly upset and she calmed down as soon as her mother gave her a glass of milk and some cookies.

Annette and I were both shaking. So we spooned more sugar into our coffee.

'You were very brave,' I told her. 'Those lions had a funny look in their eyes. It scared me to death.'

'Me too,' she said. 'When you shouted you had a pistol I thought those were the nicest words I'd ever heard.'

We both laughed and felt much better.

I told her about the lions who had tried to get at our horses one night.

Annette sighed and said: 'Northern lions would never be so cheeky.'

I knew what she meant. Northern lions had more respect for humans, probably because there were fewer humans up north.

We agreed that life in the south wasn't easy.

But as I drove back home later that day I found myself humming a happy tune. Life wasn't too bad really – not if you had an understanding friend to share your troubles with.

THE ALARMING MESSAGE BOOK

CROCODILE BRIDGE WAS A PLACE WHERE THINGS WENT WRONG nearly all the time. There were too many humans and too many animals, and they constantly got into trouble or in each other's hair – the way maddening crowds tend to do.

I wanted only to get on quietly with my own life and to take no notice of the ongoing commotion. But my life didn't belong to me any more. It belonged to the telephone.

People called all the time to report trouble or to complain about the state of things. And they called mostly when Kobus was away from home, which was most of the time. So I kept a large, thick message book next to the phone.

Apart from the animals, the tourists and the farmers – who all had their problems – another source of alarming events was the Nkongoma army base at the foot of the Lebombo Mountains near the Mozambique border. The base was inside the park and fell under Kobus's jurisdiction. At times the army base was a blessing, for if I was unable to find Kobus or any of the local game guards to respond to an urgent call for help, I'd call the base and enlist the aid of the soldiers. Kobus also found the base helpful, for it provided him with an extra source of manpower to assist in apprehending armed poachers or to help fight wildfires, especially those that often came rolling down the Lebombo Mountains from Mozambique.

So naturally, and quite rightly, the soldiers also relied on Kobus and me for help when they encountered certain problems. A fair number of their troubles concerned the driving abilities of the young soldiers. Being young and being soldiers, they drove too fast. Every once in a while, a soldier would drive his truck too fast over the bridge and crash into the Crocodile River. We would hear the loud splash from our house and rush over to help get the soldiers out of the water (before crocodiles got them) and to tend to their injuries. Two soldiers were injured fairly seriously in one of these accidents, but fortunately none was hurt in the others. Trucks, however, got smashed up and the bridge itself was eventually so badly damaged that Kobus insisted the army pay up and fix it themselves.

On other occasions, soldiers crashed their trucks into trees or over-turned them on winding tracks, and they would solemnly report to Kobus that their speed at the time of the accident had been only twenty kilometres per hour. Apart from smashing up their trucks, soldiers also got lost in the mountains, or started accidental bush fires, or got stung by scorpions, or bitten by snakes, or, occasionally, injured by wild animals, and we'd help in whatever way we could. And so everybody in the area had their troubles, and the telephone ensured that my stress levels remained permanently in the red.

I longed constantly and desperately for Mahlangeni – that faraway, magical place where no telephone ever interrupted the solitude.

In the early days at Crocodile Bridge the ringing of the telephone was such an unfamiliar sound to us all that it often evoked no immediate response. Everyone would look up, faintly surprised at the ringing, and for a while nobody would move, until the signal finally registered. But even then we'd all be reluctant to respond to it. We were so used to the formalities of talking on a radio that we had to concentrate on for-getting them when we talked on the phone. On the radio you talked in short sentences and said 'over' at the end of a paragraph. When I talked on the phone I often forgot that I could speak without having to wait for the other party to say 'over' first, and there would be long silences on the line while I waited for a signal that never came. I also got confused if the other person interrupted me. Interruption never happened on the radio. As long as you pressed your mike button in, no transmission was possible from the other party on the air.

Eventually we all got used to the telephone. But then everybody went away and I was the one who was stuck at home, alone with the phone.

As soon as I was fully conditioned to the fact that about nine out of ten phone calls meant trouble, I found myself reacting to the ringing of the phone at full speed and with an appropriate sense of dread. If the problem was serious and required urgent attention, I'd try to contact Kobus on the radio or, if he was unreachable, to find game guards or soldiers from Nkongoma base to respond to the call for help. If the problem was not serious enough to warrant immediate action, I'd write it down in the message book. I often felt sorry for Kobus when he arrived home after a day (or sometimes several days) of hard work to find a list of frantic messages awaiting him.

The following are some of the entries for May 1992. (At that time the water level of the Crocodile River was low, and wild animals frequently crossed over onto the bordering farms.)

16 MAY

- Four elephants eating oranges and bananas on Ten Bosch Farm. Please fetch.
- Herd of 200 buffalo grazing in sugar-cane lands on Whiskey Creek Farm. Please fetch with haste.
- Tourist frightened by bull elephant on Bume Road reversed into ditch. Hitched lift back to camp. Car still in ditch. Please help.
- Four-metre python eating chickens on Hensville Farm.

17 MAY

- Willem van Aard's water-pump attendant dived into river to escape charging buffalo bull. Willem asks please fetch buffalo.
- Family of warthogs raiding mess tent at Nkongoma base.
- Komatipoort police report three elephant bulls walked through village – apparently on their way to Swaziland border post. (Without passports, I think.)

18 MAY

- Customs official at Mozambique border post reports party of Mozambicans brought him present tied up in hessian sack. Official thought it was firewood. Wasn't. Was live crocodile. Presently in his toolshed causing havoc. Please fetch.
- Tourist threatened by bull elephant on Bume Road reversed into tree. Car damaged.
- Four-metre python still eating chickens on Hensville Farm.
- Two hippos taking up residence in irrigation dam at Ten Bosch Farm. Please fetch.
- Large herd of buffalo turned up at municipal offices, Komatipoort.

19 MAY

- Camp security guard Mabasa reports elephant broke into tourist camp. Presently eating sycamore fig tree. Also leopard tracks found in camp this morning.
- Warthogs still raiding mess tent at Nkongoma base.
- Herd of twenty elephant crossed river near confluence. Heading for Border Country Inn. Owner of inn asks what to do.
- Municipal clerk at Komatipoort says thank you for evicting buffalo. Unfortunately they have returned.

20 MAY

- Camp security guard Mabasa reports following: (1) Leopard frightened him in camp last night. (2) Elephant broke east fence of camp again this morning. Ate remaining half of sycamore fig tree. (3) 'Stupid tourists' threw oranges at elephant.
- Soldiers accidentally started fire in Lebombo Mountains. Game guards on their way to check fire.
- Four elephants eating oranges and bananas on Ten Bosch Farm again.

21 MAY

- Hensville farmer caught and brought over four-metre python in sack. It's in your office.
- Tourist startled by bull elephant on Bume Road reversed into car behind him. Both cars damaged.
- Soldiers report warthogs getting 'vicious'.
- Pack of wild dogs chased group of Shangaan women in sugar-cane lands on Whiskey Creek Farm. (Huh?)*

22 MAY

- Aqua-culture researchers intimidated by crocodile while studying larvae. Ask your assistance – if possible, tomorrow or Sunday.
- Tourist ambushed by bull elephant on Bume Road drove into ditch (again). Car still in ditch. (You'd better talk to that elephant!)
- Nkongoma soldiers and warthogs came to blows. Warthogs won.

* *Wild dogs don't normally chase people. They probably followed the women out of curiosity.*

23 MAY

- Komatipoort police report three elephant bulls walking along road towards Mozambique customs office. (Probably the same trio who tried to emigrate to Swaziland last week.)
- Soldier overturned truck in Vurhami Creek. (At 20 k.p.h.)
- Bume Road elephant slapped tourist car with its trunk. Big dent in fender. (Please talk to that elephant!)
- Two hippos in irrigation dam at Ten Bosch Farm again.
- Tourist car collided with impala ram chasing another ram across road in Gomondwane Bush. Car door badly dented. Ram looks dead.
  (PS: Ram is fine. I checked. He's walking around in Gomondwane Bush looking dazed, probably wondering where the other ram went.)

24 MAY

- Bume Road elephant scared visiting Malawian diplomat and his wife(!)
- Bulletin from security guard Mabasa: (1) Warthog sow charged tourist who was taking photograph of her in camp. (2) Camp gardener Elias Sibuyi slapped wife of gate guard Simeon Sibela. Sibuyi says Sibela's wife hit him on head with radio. (3) Snake found in linen room this morning.

25 MAY

- Four elephants eating oranges and bananas on Ten Bosch Farm again.
- Sibela's wife wants to see you.
- More tourists report riotous elephant on Bume Road(!)
- Sibuyi also wants to see you.
- Two hippos having love affair in irrigation dam at Ten Bosch Farm. Farm manager asks please fetch them before they multiply.

26 MAY

- Security guard Mabasa reports following: Baboon broke off aerial of tourist car parked at chalet no. 12 early this morning. Mabasa woke owner of car to tell him. Owner says he's not owner of car, it's a hired car and he asks letter from you to confirm baboon was culprit. Will need the letter to present to the car hire agency.
- Tourists report big tree felled across Bume Road near creek, blocking road. (Guess who did it!)
  (PS: I'm not taking any more messages about that elephant. You'd better deport him.)
- Lone buffalo bull is back at Willem's place scaring pump attendant again.

27 MAY

- WOUNDED LION: Shot on Badenhorst Farm. Fled back into park. Last seen in reeds on north bank 200 metres downstream from Elsje's Point at 8.45 a.m.

LION ATTACK

IN THE EARLY HOURS OF THE MORNING OF 27 MAY, TWO LIONS LEFT the park and crossed the river onto Badenhorst Farm where they caught and killed a cow. Farm manager Hennie Minnaar came upon the feeding lions and fired a number of shots at them, killing one and wounding the other. The wounded lion escaped and fled back into the park. Hennie Minnaar didn't know whether the lion had been fatally wounded or not.

I took the phone call from the farm owner, Phillip Badenhorst, a few minutes after nine o'clock. I immediately called Kobus on the radio. He had left home early that morning to look up the Bume Road elephant and read him the riot act. Luckily he was still on the road when I called and he answered my call on his vehicle radio. He promptly turned back and came home.

After collecting three of his most experienced game guards – Albert Maluleke, Wilson Ngobeni and Albert Malatyi – and our dog Wolfie, Kobus set out in search of the lion. This was the second time during our stay at Crocodile Bridge that a farmer had shot at a lion and wounded it. It upset me enormously. It also distressed me that Kobus had to go out and find these animals. Tracking a wounded lion is a life-threatening business – especially in dense reeds.

Kobus, the game guards and Wolfie met up with Hennie Minnaar at Elsje's Point. Hennie led them to the spot where the lion had re-entered the park. Kobus and his colleagues soon picked up the trail and, after checking their rifles, started tracking the wounded animal.

Wolfie sniffed his way through the long grass and the men followed silently.

For over two hours they followed the spoor through riverine bush, across sandbanks and rocky terrain, through tall grass and, finally, to a dense stand of tall reeds. All signs of the lion's spoor disappeared at the entrance to the thicket. Wolfie sniffed at the long stems while Kobus studied droplets of blood on the reeds.

Still sniffing at the stems, Wolfie moved cautiously into the dense thicket. Kobus ventured into the reeds after the dog. Game guards Wilson Ngobeni and Albert Maluleke followed him. Hennie Minnaar and game guard Malatyi waited at the edge of the thicket.

Kobus and his two colleagues moved ever deeper into the thicket, their senses at full alert. The visibility was less than two metres in any direction. An eerie silence hung in the air. They knew instinctively that the lion was close.

Wolfie, who was about two paces ahead of Kobus, came to an abrupt halt and barked a furious warning. The sudden burst of sound almost exploded the heightened senses of the adrenaline-charged men. Three metallic clicks signalled the release of safety catches. For a few eternal seconds the men stood waiting, rifles at the ready, expecting the lion a thousand times over. But nothing happened.

Kobus slowly parted the reeds ahead of him with his rifle barrel and saw the lion about four metres away. It was in a crouching position, legs gathered beneath its body. It appeared to be resting. Kobus couldn't see the head, only the stomach heaving as it breathed heavily. He signalled his colleagues to retreat. He would approach the lion from a different angle – one that might offer him a better view of the animal and its injuries. If the injuries were not serious, he would choose to give the lion the chance to recover. Before turning back, Kobus studied the formation of the reeds around him, mapping the locality in his mind.

Moving carefully, the men doubled back out of the thicket. As soon as they were in more open terrain, Kobus surveyed the stand of reeds from a vantage point, mentally plotting another route into it. In a bid to reassure himself of the lion's exact locality, he hurled some pebbles into the reeds. But no response came from the lion. Kobus told his colleagues to wait in the clearing and to cover him with their rifles.

Accompanied by Wolfie, he ventured into the thicket once more, moving cautiously in a half circle around the lion's hiding place and searching for a spot where he might have a clearer view through the reeds.

According to rangers' lore, a leopard is silent when it charges but a lion will give a vocal warning before it attacks. Perhaps Kobus had misjudged his distance in the dense reeds, or maybe the lion had moved, but if it had, it had made no sound at all. Nor did it give a vocal warning as it charged. It was only Wolfie who growled a terrifying but belated warning.

As the reeds exploded in front of him Kobus saw only a yellow blur hurtling at him. The lion's jaws closed around his left calf just below the knee. As Kobus hit the earth, his rifle flew from his hands. The lion released his calf and bit into his leg above the knee. Kobus yelled and kicked at the lion with his free leg. The lion shifted its grip again and took hold higher up his thigh. Then it shook Kobus as a dog would shake a rat. Kobus lashed out with his fists. As the lion again adjusted its grip, Kobus managed to strike its open jaw a blow with his left hand. As he did so, a canine ripped the flesh and tendons between his thumb and index finger. The lion suddenly let go and ran off through the shallows.

Kobus saw that Wolfie was still with him, his coat streaked with blood. The dog must have tried to get the lion away from him, but Kobus had no recollection of what either Wolfie or the game guards had been doing at the time of the attack. All his attention had been focused on surviving.

The game guards had stormed into the reeds the moment they had heard Kobus's shouts. But when they saw the lion on top of him, they dared not shoot for fear of hitting Kobus. As soon as the lion let go of him they rushed to his aid, but were so shocked at the severity of his wounds that they did not know what to do. Kobus told them he felt no pain. He took off his shirt and tore it into strips to use as bandages to control the bleeding.

Hennie Minnaar, the farm manager, ran off to fetch his truck. On his return the game guards helped Kobus to the truck, and then Hennie drove Kobus to Komatipoort.

The game guards fetched Kobus's truck and followed.

Kobus told Hennie that he wanted someone to get a message to me. So as Hennie drove past the Badenhorst farmhouse, he shouted a message to a young boy who was standing outside the house.

At about three o'clock that afternoon I had driven to Komatipoort to collect Karin and Laudene (Annette's older daughter) at the bus stop. It was the beginning of a long weekend, and both the girls had come home from school for the four-day break. Shortly after the girls and I got home, Annette arrived from Lower Sabie to collect her daughter.

Annette and I were having coffee in the kitchen and enjoying a nice trouble-sharing session when the telephone rang. An alarm bell echoed in my head as I rushed to answer it.

'Mrs Kruger?' the voice asked hesitantly. It was the voice of a young boy. 'I . . . have to tell you,' he stammered, 'the lion . . . it attacked your husband.'

Suddenly I could hardly breathe.

'How seriously?' I asked.

'I don't know,' the boy said apologetically.

'Where is he . . . my husband?'

'Komatipoort. Someone has taken him to Komatipoort.'

'Yes,' I said. 'Thank you.'

I put the receiver down and rushed into the kitchen.

'What's wrong?' Annette asked.

'I'm going to Komatipoort,' I told her. 'That wounded lion . . .'

I didn't need to finish the sentence. There was instant comprehension in her eyes.

'Let's go,' she said calmly. 'I'll drive you.'

We rushed out of the house to Annette's car. Karin, who was in the garden with Annette's two daughters, saw me and called out, 'Mom! Where are you off to?'

Feeling badly because I'd forgotten all about her, I turned and went over to her. 'I'm going to Komatipoort,' I answered carefully. 'Your father has been bitten by a lion. But it's not serious. I promise to call you on the phone as soon as I get there.'

Her eyes grew wide with shock. 'I want to come with you,' she said.

'No,' I said. 'I want you and Laudene to stay here and look after Narina.'

Karin didn't argue. But her eyes told me that she wanted desperately to come along. I felt sick with guilt. But if Kobus was badly injured, I wouldn't want her to see him. She was only fourteen years old.

Annette drove very fast and talked to me all the way. I don't remember what she talked about but her voice had a calming effect.

For the first time since we'd moved to Crocodile Bridge, I felt grateful that we lived so close to civilization. Komatipoort was a tiny village, but it had a clinic and a doctor and was only twelve kilometres away.

When we arrived at the clinic, the first thing I noticed was that Wolfie was standing at the door, as if guarding the place. There was blood on his coat. The three game guards were also standing silently near the door. They looked shocked. Game guard Malatyi, the youngest of them, was in tears. Hennie Minnaar, the farm manager, was there too. I greeted them all hurriedly and rushed inside, running through the clinic into the emergency room. The floor was covered with blood, mud and blood-soaked bandages.

Kobus lay on the examination table. My eyes flew first to his face and head. No injuries there. Relief swept over me. His shirt was off, his chest bare, scratched and streaked with splashes of mud and blood. I saw with relief that there were no injuries in the chest or abdomen. But the whole of his left leg, from thigh to ankle, was swathed in thick bandages.

His face was the colour of chalk but he greeted me with a smile and said, 'Don't worry. I'm fine.'

The doctor, Jan Maré, was still busy bandaging Kobus's left hand, and he asked if either Annette or I could help fit the drip, as he hadn't yet had the time to do so. Annette, who had been trained as a nurse, expertly inserted the needle into a vein in Kobus's arm and started the drip.

I walked round the bed, taking care not to slip on the blood-splashed floor, and reached for his undamaged hand.

A short while later an ambulance pulled up outside the clinic and two paramedics came inside, carrying a stretcher. After the doctor had secured the leg to a padded splint, they lifted Kobus onto the stretcher and carried him to the ambulance. I also climbed in, intending to accompany Kobus to the hospital at Nelspruit. But then I suddenly remembered Karin. 'Please wait for me,' I told the ambulance driver as I got out. 'I have to make a phone call.'

'I don't think we should wait,' the doctor said. 'Time is fairly important now.'

My heart missed a beat.

I stuck my head back inside the ambulance and told Kobus: 'I have to phone Karin. But I'll follow in my car.' As I said that I remembered that I didn't have my car there. 'I'll go back with Annette to get my car,' I added quickly. 'And I'll bring Karin along. We'll see you at the hospital.'

'No,' Kobus said firmly. 'Don't do that.'

'Why not?' I asked, alarmed.

'It's too far to Nelspruit.'

'I'll drive carefully,' I promised.

'No, you won't,' he said. 'You're too upset. Stay home tonight. You can call me on the phone.'

Before I could argue any further the ambulance driver closed the door. Starting the engine, he engaged the siren and sped off.

Annette was standing beside me. 'I think Kobus really doesn't want you to drive to Nelspruit tonight,' she said.

I hesitated. I badly wanted to follow him to the hospital.

'It's a hundred and twenty kilometres,' Annette reminded me. 'And you know how hazardous that stretch through the mountains can be at night.'

'Yes,' I said after a while. 'OK. I'll go tomorrow.' It didn't seem a good idea for me to have an accident at that particular time.

The doctor was about to leave. 'Are you OK?' he asked me. 'Would you like me to give you a tranquillizer?'

'No,' I said. 'But tell me about Kobus. Is there any chance he might lose the leg?'

He looked me in the eyes for a moment, then said, 'There's a very good surgeon at Nelspruit. He's not going to let that happen if he can help it.'

Wolfie was licking my hand and the game guards were still standing there, watching me anxiously. I gave Wolfie a hug, then turned to the game guards to thank them for their concern and assistance. The corporal, Albert Maluleke, had something on his mind but seemed hesitant to talk.

'What's troubling you, corporal?' I asked.

'We couldn't shoot,' he said miserably. 'The lion was on top of him.'

It came to me that the game guards were feeling guilty because they had been unable to protect Kobus from the attack.

'Corporal,' I said, 'Kobus chose the three of you to accompany him because he trusted you. He knew that you would have the sense not to shoot a lion that was on top of him and risk killing him as well.'

They looked relieved.

'Malatyi,' I asked gently, 'why were you crying just now?'

Tears sprang to his eyes again and he couldn't talk.

Corporal Maluleke answered: 'He's young. He's never seen a lion attack a human before.'

Annette drove me home while the game guards and Wolfie followed in Kobus's pick-up.

As soon as we got home, Annette made us all some strong sweet tea.

About an hour later I got a call through to the hospital and learned that Kobus had arrived in a stable condition. He was in the operating theatre and would probably be there for a few hours.

I persuaded Annette not to worry about me and to go home before it got too dark. She left me reluctantly and only after I had promised to call her on the radio as soon as I had more news of Kobus. She was such a good trouble-sharing friend.

Karin and I spent the rest of the evening discussing the events and making intermittent phone calls to the hospital. Karin was a level-headed, sunny girl whose innate cheerfulness often proved a blessing to me in times of stress. Throughout that long evening I found her company comforting and relaxing.

At about half-past nine, when I made my fourth call to the hospital, Kobus was finally out of theatre and I was allowed to talk to the surgeon. He said the lacerations were extensive but the good news was that there appeared to be no bone fractures. He had scrubbed the wounds and cut away the damaged tissue, and he was treating Kobus with massive doses of gram-positive as well as gram-negative antibiotics to inhibit sepsis. He felt confident that Kobus would not lose the leg.

I was also allowed to talk to Kobus, and although he was struggling to be coherent after the anaesthesia, he managed to assure me that he wasn't in pain and that he was looking forward to a good night's rest. He also spoke briefly to Karin.

Afterwards Karin and I were both smiling with relief. Karin suggested we call her older sisters and tell them about their father.

First we called Hettie at her university hostel in Johannesburg. I told her the news as calmly as I could, but she gasped and dropped the receiver.

When she'd retrieved it, she said: 'OK, Mom, don't worry. I'll see you tomorrow. I'll take the bus to Nelspruit.'

I was moved to tears.

I decided not to call Sandra. She was in medical school and had called us a few days previously to tell us that the head of their department had advised all his students to take a break over the long weekend. Sandra had asked us if she and four of her classmates might use our beach cottage in the Eastern Cape for their break, and we had agreed.

The cottage had no telephone, so the only way I could reach her would be to call an elderly couple who lived nearby and ask them to drive over to the cottage and give Sandra the message. But I hated the idea of spoiling Sandra's short vacation with bad news and, knowing how dreadfully worried she'd be, I decided it could wait until after the weekend.

I phoned my parents. Talking to them had a calming effect on me, so afterwards I felt relaxed enough to get some sleep. Karin and I intended to be up early the next morning to visit Kobus.

THE DAYS AFTER

EARLY THE NEXT MORNING A SPOKESMAN FROM THE BROADCASTING corporation in Nelspruit phoned to warn me that the story of the lion attack would be broadcast on the national news bulletins that day, and he wanted to make sure that the family had been informed. Surprised, I asked him how they had learned of the incident. He said the broadcasting office in Nelspruit regularly checked with the hospital for possible newsworthy events, adding that a lion attack was worth more than just local news and so the story had already been faxed to the Johannesburg office.

I had no choice but to get a message to Sandra. If she were to hear the news on a national bulletin, it would spoil her vacation far more than a personal message from me would. So I phoned Henk and Marie Jonker, the couple in the Eastern Cape who lived near our cottage. They were very sympathetic and promised they would reassure Sandra as best they could.

But as soon as Sandra had been told the news, she rushed to the nearest phone booth and called the Nelspruit hospital. Kobus was surprised to get a call from her all the way from the Eastern Cape, and he did a good job of convincing her that he was fine.

My mother had already informed Kobus's two sisters, so it was only his brother, Cornelis, who still had to be told. (Kobus's parents were no longer alive.)

As I dialled my brother-in-law's number, I found myself shying away from the idea of telling him such awful news. He was sixteen years older than Kobus, and he cared very much for his younger brother. So I tried to think of a way to soften the words 'lion' and 'attack'. I was still thinking as hard as I could when my sister-in-law, Emilia, answered the phone and I found myself telling her that Kobus had been bitten by a cat.

'What kind of cat?' she asked.

'Uh . . . a big kind of cat,' I stammered.

She insisted I tell her its name. So I did, but quickly explained about the nature of the injuries, assuring her that Kobus was fine.

She wanted to know if I was in shock.

'No, of course not!' I said. 'I'm fine.'

'You sound like you're in denial.'

'I do?'

'You said a cat bit him.'

I explained to her that I was only trying to dilute the impact of the news for her.

After I had talked to my sister-in-law, farmers from across the river started calling to ask how Kobus was. Karin and I had planned to drive to Nelspruit at first light that morning, but it was well past eight o'clock before we finally left the house.

On the way to the car, I saw game guard Wilson Ngobeni approaching from the staff village. He was carrying Kobus's rifle and something else that looked like a bundle of dirty rags. Wilson had cleaned the rifle and was bringing it over to the house to be locked in the gun safe. The moment he spotted Karin and me, he dropped the rags behind a clump of grass and, without missing a step, continued on his way, pretending the rags had never existed. I discovered later that the bunch of rags was Kobus's shirt – or what was left of it after he had torn it into strips to use as makeshift bandages. Evidently Wilson had wanted to spare Karin and me the sight of those bloodied strips. I was touched by his thoughtfulness.

As Karin and I got into the car, game ranger Flip Nel from Lower Sabie (Annette's husband) arrived and told me that he wanted to collect the game guards who had been with Kobus the previous day. He hoped they might help him find the wounded lion. I was grateful to Flip for caring about the wounded animal.

Karin and I arrived at the hospital about mid-morning and were relieved to see Kobus looking so well – until a nurse turned up to change the dressings on the wounds. Kobus warned us not to look, but I had seen some bad injuries in my time and I had never been squeamish about such things, so I looked on as the nurse removed the layers of bandages and padding.

The moment the first wound was uncovered I heard someone gasp in a strangled way. It turned out to be me. There was a quick rush of air inside my head and the world started spinning. I had to sit down.

There are no words that can adequately describe wounds inflicted by the jaws of a lion. So I won't even try.

Kobus laughed at me when he saw how shocked I was. He assured me that he felt no pain.

Apparently severe flesh wounds are painful only if they become septic. And then, of course, the pain is excruciating. But as long as lacerations are free from infection, there is no sensation in the damaged tissue.

Ironically, it was the lesser injury to Kobus's hand that eventually became painful.

Probably the surgeon had been so concerned with preventing in-fection in the other wounds that he'd paid scant attention to the laceration between the thumb and index finger. And so it became septic. But prompt treatment soon stopped the infection and relieved the pain.

Kobus had been unable to stop worrying about the wounded lion, so he was pleased at the news that Flip and the game guards had set out in search of it again. He knew that the only reason it had attacked him was because it had felt threatened and wanted to protect itself. He felt sorry for the lion and wished that it could be receiving the same medical care and attention that he was.

Shortly after midday, Kobus was wheeled to the operating theatre again for further debridement of the wounds.

Hettie arrived at the hospital in the late afternoon. She had not come by bus as planned, but with a friend who owned a car. She and her friend, a fellow student named Haddon, spent a couple of hours with us at the hospital, and in the evening we all went home.

We had a lovely, peaceful evening, Hettie, Haddon, Karin and I, talking about life at the university where Hettie and Haddon were studying languages, literature and philosophy.

We drove to the hospital again the following day.

Kobus received numerous other visitors throughout the day: reporters from the media, colleagues and friends from the park, his brother and sister-in-law, and farmers and their families who lived across the river from us. It worried me that Kobus was getting so little rest.

He was scheduled for a third debridement operation in the evening. After he had received his pre-med, we wished him luck, said goodbye and drove home.

As we arrived home, Flip Nel called me on the radio and reported that, after two days of tracking, they had been unable to find the wounded lion. They had finally lost its tracks among other lion tracks in the area, and Flip assumed that the lion had rejoined its pride.

I rang Kobus at the hospital to tell him the news. We both hoped that the lion was doing well and would soon recover from its injuries.

On the Sunday Karin and I stayed home. Hettie and Haddon would leave for Johannesburg around midday and they planned to drop in at the hospital on their way.

Corporal Maluleke and game guards Ngobeni and Malatyi came over to the house in the early morning to enquire after Kobus. They also informed me that lions had caught and killed a buffalo on the river bank some two hundred metres downstream from the house.

Later that same morning, I saw Karin and the dogs heading down the river bank in the direction of the feeding lions. I immediately called Karin back to the house.

She came reluctantly, carrying a four-pound hammer.

'Why can't I go down to the river?' she asked.

'Because there are lions feeding on the bank. And why are you carrying that?' I pointed to the hammer.

'I know about the lions,' she said. 'I saw the vultures early this morning. But I want to finish my tree-house.'

'What tree-house?' I asked in alarm.

Turning, she pointed to a huge sycamore fig overhanging the river some hundred metres downstream. 'I started building it two weeks ago,' she said. 'I would like to finish it this weekend.'

'But, the lions . . . ! How can you even think of going there?'

'Goodness, why would they want to catch me? They have a whole buffalo to eat. And anyway the dogs are with me. And,' she added, lifting the hammer, 'I have this.'

By this time Hettie and her friend Haddon had joined us. Haddon, who was a city person, gaped at Karin in disbelief. 'It seems,' he said to her, 'that you have a morbid wish to follow in your father's footsteps.'

We all laughed. Karin dropped the hammer with a sigh. 'OK,' she said. 'I'll finish my house next weekend.'

I appreciated her consideration of my feelings. The lions would probably not have given her a thought – they were, after all, too busy eating their buffalo. But after Kobus's dramatic episode, I couldn't bear the idea of another member of my family going anywhere near a lion.

The Parks Board owned a flatlet in Nelspruit to be used by park personnel in times of crisis. I phoned the personnel office at Skukuza and got permission to stay at the flatlet while Kobus was in hospital.

On the Monday morning I drove to Nelspruit again, dropped Karin off at her boarding school and moved into the flatlet.

It was nice to be so near the hospital. But living in a bustling, people-packed town was hard for me, and by the end of the week I was suffering from acute claustrophobia. My ears were also hurting, being unaccustomed to discordant and continuous sound. So when the surgeon agreed to let Kobus go home for a few days I was very grateful. The condition, however, was that I would have to take over his nursing and clean and dress the wounds every few hours. The idea filled me with dread, but living in a town was even more dreadful, so I agreed.

Luckily Sandra and a classmate of hers from medical school, Paul Meyer, arrived at the hospital that afternoon to visit Kobus and to spend the weekend with us. I immediately commanded the two medical students to watch the nurse demonstrate the wound-cleaning and dressing procedure so that they could take over the nursing for the weekend.

After picking Karin up at her boarding school, we all drove home.

It was awfully good to be home again. Kobus had not been able to sleep properly in the hospital and he was looking forward to a really good rest in his own bed and his own house.

Sandra and Paul proved to be experts at cleaning wounds. They scrubbed their hands with disinfectant and put on sterile surgical gloves before touching the wounds or any of the instruments needed for the flushing and cleaning exercise. I watched each time, hoping that by the end of the weekend I would be able to take over from them without wanting to faint all the time. The worst part of the procedure was inserting a tube filled with disinfectant right into the wounds and then squirting the solution into the surrounding tissue.

At about midday on Sunday, Sandra and Paul had to leave us and I was really sorry to see them go. They had been so very helpful.

For a number of days after this, I was full-time nurse to a lion attack victim and I am proud to say that I eventually became quite adept at flushing and dressing the wounds. The flushing was done with EUSOL, and I even manufactured my own when our supply ran out. I remembered reading once that EUSOL was made up of nine parts boiled water to one part ordinary household bleach. EUSOL was invented by medical students at Edinburgh University. The name EUSOL is in fact an acronym for Edinburgh University Solution.

One day, as I was dressing his wounds, Kobus told me how difficult it was to tear a khaki shirt. He was referring to the day of the attack, when he'd had to tear his shirt into strips to bandage his wounds. No matter how hard he'd tugged at the fabric, he told me, it had simply refused to tear. Hennie Minnaar tried to help, but all that happened was that the sleeves came off. So Kobus had taken over again. If it hadn't been for the high level of adrenaline pumping through his system, Kobus reckoned, he would probably never have succeeded in tearing the shirt.

I think the manufacturers of khaki uniforms should take note that a game ranger could bleed to death while trying to tear his shirt into strips.

At the end of that week I took Kobus back to the hospital. It was time for his skin graft operations.

On 22 June, after several operations and almost one month after the lion attack, Kobus was finally discharged from the hospital. When we came home he went straight to bed and slept almost non-stop for more than forty-eight hours. When he finally woke up he said he was feeling better than he had felt during all the weeks since the attack. He wanted to know what was for supper and looked very happy when I told him I had made minestrone soup. He even got up and walked to the kitchen to inspect the soup.

As we sat in the lounge, sipping our soup, Kobus gave a contented sigh and said, 'You can't imagine how well I'm feeling.'

I looked at his pale, unshaven face, the dark rings under his eyes, his dishevelled hair and the equally dishevelled bandages that hung about his leg from thigh to ankle. 'I'm glad you're feeling good,' I smiled. 'You don't really look so.'

He looked down at his untidy bandages with a frown. After a while he unwound and removed the bandages and studied his leg. The scars were big and ugly, despite the very successful skin-grafting operations.

Still contemplating his leg, Kobus remarked, 'It probably won't win me first prize in a Mr Pretty Legs Competition. But no matter. It can walk.'

'Did you know,' I asked him, 'that there had actually been a possibility that you might lose the leg?'

He nodded. 'The surgeon told me, yes.'

We studied his scarred leg some more and agreed that it wouldn't get him far in a Mr Pretty Legs Competition, but that it most definitely was a prize-winning leg in every other respect.

CARING FOR A SERVAL

A T THE END OF JUNE, A WEEK AFTER KOBUS HAD BEEN DISCHARGED from the hospital, a farmer came to our house, bringing us, in a wire cage, a very distressed, wild serval kitten. After a fire had swept through the sugar-cane lands on his farm and into the adjacent riverine forest, he had found the kitten, abandoned and with an injured paw, on the river shore.

The kitten, a female about three months old, snarled and hissed at us, and lashed out with sharp little claws if anyone tried to touch her.

It broke my heart to see her so frightened. Opening the cage door and ignoring a vicious swipe that left my arm bleeding, I gathered up the terrified kitten. Lifting her out and pressing her firmly to me, I carried her to a quiet room where I sat down with her and held her tightly to me for a long time until I could feel the tension leaving her body. As soon as she was reasonably calm, I put her gently down and left her in the room, closing the door behind me.

I returned a while later, bringing her a saucer of warmed milk and some raw minced meat mixed with egg. She was hiding under the bed, still too frightened to eat, so I left her alone, giving her the time to get orientated in her new surroundings.

The serval is a large cat, smaller than a cheetah but much larger than the domestic cat, rather slenderly built with a proportionally small head, large oval upstanding ears, and elongated legs. The yellowish coat is heavily marked with black spots, bands and stripes.

A serval kitten at the age of three months is too old to become tame, but too young to survive on its own. Knowing this, we hoped only to be able to provide solace and a temporary refuge for the kitten until she was old and strong enough to return to the wilds.

The injured front paw was badly swollen and appeared to be causing her pain, so I phoned the veterinary clinic at Skukuza.

Dr Cobus Raath came out to our house and, after anaesthetizing the frightened kitten, he diagnosed a broken paw and set it in a plaster cast.

When the kitten woke up she was distraught, unnerved by the strange, heavy plaster cast, and even wilder than before.

It was evident that it would take her a long time to accept her captivity.

It seemed she knew this too, and an expression of sheer misery settled in her eyes.

The girls came home for their winter holidays and spent long hours lying flat on the floor next to the bed under which the kitten hid day and night, talking soothingly to her, willing her to trust us and accept us as her surrogate family.

Eventually the kitten became a tiny bit tamer, allowing us to reach out and stroke her fur.

As soon as her broken paw had healed and the plaster cast had been removed, she became more interested in her surroundings, and wandered through the house inspecting the various rooms. Still she remained wary of us all, and allowed us only remote contact with her. We respected her wishes and kept our distance, never picking her up, hardly ever touching her, stroking her fur with an outstretched arm, and only if she allowed us to.

One evening in August, when she'd been with us for almost two months, she jumped into my lap as I sat reading in the lounge. The gesture came as such a wonderful surprise to me that I was moved to tears. I stroked her head, and she settled down in my lap and began to purr.

Hettie came home in September for a two-week break, and the kitten decided to move into Hettie's bedroom, where she spent most of her days curled up on Hettie's bed or playing with Hettie's teddy bears. Hettie sat quietly next to her, studying for her exams.

Though the kitten was eating well and looking healthy, and seemed contented during the day, she was restless at night, often sitting on the sill of an open window, staring longingly through the gauze screen into the dark garden. As she was a nocturnal animal, the sounds and smells of the night called out to her, and she was yearning for her natural life-style.

It was time to set her free.

She was about six months old when I opened the gauze screen for her. She left immediately, silently, a little hesitantly, and disappeared into the night.

'Goodbye, sweet little serval,' I said softly, and I prayed to the god of wild things to be good to her.

To my surprise and utter joy, she returned early the next morning, jumping in through the window that I'd left open for her, and went straight to Hettie's room. Curling up on the bed among Hettie's teddy bears, she fell asleep.

Every night she left through the open window, returning in the mornings, until she was almost eight months old.

Then the call of her serval nature began to take her ever further afield, and she would return to us only once or twice in a week for a brief visit, a good meal, a quiet day of resting and reassembling her courage and determination to seek her kin and the world to which she had been born.

Eventually she left us, never to return.

I hoped she had found her kin, and peace and happiness.

THE FOUNDLING PRINCE

AT A ROCKY OUTCROP NEAR A HIPPO POOL IN THE CROCODILE RIVER, some eight kilometres upstream from the camp, there is a place where tourists may leave their cars and walk down to the water to view the hippos. A game guard is posted there every day to escort and protect the visitors.

On the evening of 1 December 1992, security guard Daniel Mabasa, who had been on duty at the hippo pool that day, reported to Kobus that a small animal had been crying all day long somewhere on the rocky east bank of the pool. He'd heard the same cries on the previous day, he said.

Kobus asked Daniel to mimic the cries. When he did so, Kobus believed them to be the meowing calls of either a lion or a leopard cub. Worried that the cub was in distress, Kobus went to the hippo pool to investigate.

He left his truck on the nearby track, and as he started climbing up the rocky slope of the east bank, he heard the forlorn sounds of an abandoned cub calling its mother. Guided by the meowing, he reached a wide ledge that led to a crevice underneath a boulder. He paused a while, listening carefully for any sounds that might indicate the presence of the cub's mother. Then, when he felt reasonably certain that the cub was alone, he moved across the ledge and reached into the crevice.

He found a tiny lion cub.

The umbilical cord was still in place and not yet dry – the cub was no more than two or three days old. Its voice was hoarse from crying. Kobus knew that if he left the cub there it would die.

Gathering the little animal in his arms, he wrapped it in his shirt and carried it down the slope to his truck. Then he called me on the radio.

'I've found a lion cub abandoned by its mother,' he told me. 'What shall I do?'

I knew what that question meant. He was asking if I was willing to be its foster mother.

For one brief moment I thought, me, mother to a lion? I'm just a harmless, vulnerable primate.

But I said: 'Bring it home.'

As soon as I saw the wretched little bundle that was crying its heart out for its mother, I forgot that I was a vulnerable primate and became a lion-mother.

The cub was dehydrated and hypothermic, as abandoned carnivores usually are. We bathed him in warm water and dried him with a thick towel. Then I filled a sterilized baby's bottle with a solution of homogenized milk and glucose. I was worried that the cub might not be able to drink, but as soon as I'd managed to get the teat into his mouth he started sucking and couldn't seem to get enough.

The cub didn't know whether to feel comforted or threatened by our presence. After he'd finished drinking, he hissed and made brave little growling noises at us. When he growled, his whole face puckered into a fierce-looking crinkle.

We wrapped him in a blanket and put him in a pillow-lined cardboard box in our bedroom. Hoping that he was comfortable and would sleep for a while, we left him there and went to have our evening meal in the kitchen. But the moment the cub sensed that he was alone, he started meowing pathetically. So we fetched him and kept him in his box next to us. He was immediately comforted.

Although his eyes were still closed, he appeared to be very much aware of our presence. If we touched him or picked him up he would growl, but if we left him alone in a room he whimpered and called to us.

He seemed very tired and weak, but spent a peaceful night in his box next to our bed.

Early the next morning Kobus and four of his game guards set out in search of the cub's mother. Combing a wide area around the cub's birthplace, they searched all day long but found no signs of the lioness. Kobus wondered why she had abandoned her cub. Perhaps she had gone hunting on an adjacent farm and had been shot.

Meanwhile the cub was beginning to settle down, sleeping most of the time between feeds. After his first night with us, he no longer growled or puckered his face at us.

As it was against the park's policy to keep wild animals in captivity we would need permission to raise the cub. So Kobus went to Skukuza a few days later to see the director of conservation and research, Dr Willem Gertenbach. Although we had been foster parents to an array of orphans and strays over the years, we had not needed permission to adopt them as they had belonged to species that adapted easily to their natural lifestyles after fostering. Despite having been hand-reared, all of our previous foster children had eventually returned successfully to the wild.

The problem with large carnivores is that once they have been hand-reared, they are unable to fend for themselves in the wild unless an appropriate rehabilitation programme can be provided. A male carnivore also needs a hunting territory not yet occupied by other carnivores of the same species. A lion, being a social animal, also needs hunting companions to help defend the territory. Reintroducing a hand-reared lion into the wild, or at least finding a suitable alternative home for it, can be a complicated business.

But we would worry about that later. First of all we needed official permission to keep the cub.

Kobus told Dr Gertenbach that we were fully aware of the problems of our proposed venture and assured him that we would not take our responsibilities lightly. After considering the matter and discussing it with the park warden, the director gave us permission to raise the cub. And so our foundling prince was granted the right to live.

Unfortunately, the first few weeks of his life proved to be a struggle. Although he was drinking well he wasn't gaining weight properly, and after a week he started losing his fur. We thought that external parasites were to blame for this and so we took him to the veterinary clinic at Skukuza. Dr Dewald Keet gave the cub an anti-parasite injection together with a shot of vitamin A. The cub didn't mind the injections, but when the vet inspected his ears he howled his little head off at the indignity of it all.

In spite of our efforts, the cub didn't get better. He grew weaker, lost more fur and his tummy became abnormally distended. I couldn't understand why. He seemed hungry all the time, even though I fed him every two or three hours. He drank fast, clawing and slapping his bottle with his front paws in an impatient way. Only later, with hindsight, would I realize that the reason he seemed so impatient with his bottle was because, no matter how much he drank, he was unable to satisfy his hunger.

One morning, when he was about two and a half weeks old, he woke up so weak and ill that he was unable even to crawl about. His little belly was enormous, but despite the acute discomfort that he must have felt, he never cried or complained. Kobus and I watched helplessly as the cub tried to get up but failed, and it almost broke our hearts to see how stoically he accepted his fate.

Once again we drove him the ninety kilometres to Skukuza to visit the vet.

This time, Dewald diagnosed malnutrition and gave the ailing cub a steroid injection. He also gave me a copy of a scientific article on an analysis of lion's milk.

After reading the article I felt sick with guilt and quite appalled at my own stupidity. Since lion cubs feed only two to three times in a twenty-four-hour period, allowing the mother time to hunt, lion's milk has a much higher protein and fat content than cow's milk. I had been feeding our cub ordinary, sterilized cow's milk. And although I had added glucose, vitamin syrup and cod-liver oil to it, the formula had been hopelessly inadequate. The cub's swollen belly indicated enlarged, bloodshot kidneys, a serious and often fatal condition in cubs suffering from malnutrition.

The recipe for lion's milk, as formulated by an animal nutritionist, Dr De Waal, consisted of Puppylac powder (a commercial substitute for dog's milk) dissolved in full-cream cow's milk, egg yolk and cream. It seemed an incredibly rich solution to me, but as soon as I started feeding it to the cub he drank more slowly and seemed less impatient with the bottle.

Unfortunately the awful symptoms of malnutrition didn't disappear right away, and for several days the cub remained very weak and ill. The girls, having arrived home for their summer vacation, took turns with me to hold and comfort him. He was such a good, uncomplaining baby. We hoped that if he realized he was loved and cherished, he would fight harder to survive.

And so he did.

After about a week he started to show signs of recovery and even became playful. Lying on his back and offering his tummy to be tickled, he would swipe mischievously at us with his front paws. Gradually he gained weight, grew new fur in the bald patches, and turned into a chubby, happy, healthy little lion-baby.

His eyes had opened on his fourth or fifth day of life (and how handsome he looked with those large, open eyes!) but until he was about four weeks old they remained covered with a blue film. Unable to see properly, he would clumsily bump into things as he started exploring the house. When the blue film finally disappeared, his beautiful rust-coloured eyes became his most arresting feature.

The girls named him Leo.

NOBLY BORN

DESPITE MY MANY YEARS OF EXPERIENCE AS A FOSTER MOTHER (TO a banded mongoose, a honey badger, a bantam chick, a squirrel, three warthogs, two scrub hares, a marsh owl and a serval kitten), nothing could have prepared me for the intensity of emotions and the level of involvement that come with fostering a lion.

A lion cub is the most placid and self-contained of all infant creatures. It never whines, is never dissatisfied, doesn't scream for its bottle, doesn't demand attention, asks nothing of you except to know that you are around somewhere. Occasionally it may come looking for you, and when it finds you, it will gaze at you with an expression of perfect contentment that says, 'Ah, there you are! How nice.'

Often, when I found the cub staring at me with those enormous, expressive eyes, I'd ask, 'What is it you want, Leo? What can I do for you?' And his gaze would become soft and sweet with an expression that seemed to say, 'I only wanted to know where you were.'

How can one not love a creature who talks with his eyes and who asks nothing of life except to know that he has a mother?

Although Leo was a totally contented baby, he was by no means a sedate one. He possessed a great talent for living joyously and abundantly, and he spent all of his waking hours playing himself into a state of exhaustion.

He had an assortment of toys: a tattered teddy bear, a ball of wool, an

old rag doll, a tennis ball, an empty coffee tin and a stuffed toy duck. He loved them passionately and would run straight to them the moment he woke up. I kept them in a basket for him. He would dive into it often with such speed and clumsiness that the basket would topple over and roll some distance with him inside it.

Most small animals instinctively respect or fear any animals bigger than themselves. Not Leo. Coded with the knowledge that he was the king of them all, he perceived other animals either as lesser creatures or as admiring fans and treated them accordingly.

We introduced him to our dogs when he was six days old and he took it for granted that dogs would naturally love lions. The dogs instinctively took fright at the smell of the cub and backed off. But as soon as they saw how tiny and harmless he was, they approached him cautiously and, as a gesture of welcome, licked him all over, proving what the cub had known all along: dogs love lions.

The horses were quite shocked at the sight and smell of the creature that we brought over to show them. But after a while they approached carefully, studied him in the aloof way horses have and decided that if a lion was to become part of the household, then that was that, as long as it wasn't expected that they should love him.

When Leo was five weeks old we were invited by Kobus's brother and his wife to spend New Year's Day with them on their farm near Lydenburg. Not wanting to leave the cub alone at home, we packed him, his bottles, his formula, his sleeping box, pillow and blanket and his beloved toy duck into the car and set off.

Leo spent most of the three-hour journey on a lap, either mine or one of the girls', contentedly sucking a finger. (He was an incurable finger-sucker.)

When we arrived at the farm, I carried Leo to the barbecue area where the family was assembled. After everyone had had a chance to admire and cuddle the cub, I sat him down on the grass close to my chair.

An arrogant-looking little dachshund came trotting out of the house. Spotting the cub sitting on the grass, he charged right over, barking his head off. I was about to rescue Leo, but saw to my surprise that he was totally unruffled by the approach of the hysterical dachshund. He sat calmly, happily, waiting for it. As soon as the dog was within slapping distance, up came Leo's front paw – one swift, well-aimed swipe – and the dog was making a hasty U-turn in mid-air and clearing the distance back to the house a lot faster than is normal for a dachshund.

The silly dachshund had no doubt mistaken the cub for an alien dog and got the shock of his life when he realized it was a lion.

Leo was still sitting where I had placed him on the grass, looking dignified and, as usual, totally contented. He knew, of course, that lions – like all good royalty – never get hysterical.

Two turkeys and a bunch of farmyard chickens came over to inspect the cub. Though they seemed unable to grasp that he was a lion, some-thing in their primeval memories was evidently sending them urgent messages, for they circled the cub at a safe distance for a long time, necks stretched forward, eyes blinking rapidly, all the while discussing the strange visitor excitedly among themselves. Leo sat like a prince, con-templating his admiring audience with a benevolent air.

When he grew sleepy, I gave him his bottle and put him to bed in his box with his pillow, duck and blanket. This seemed to persuade the birds that Leo was a human baby, so they lost interest in him and resumed their everyday business.

When we got back the following day, Leo recognized his home and was so happy to be back that he spent a whole hour gambolling and cavorting all over the place and checking every room to see if all was still the same. He was a clever boy. He knew that a lion belonged in its own territory.

At the age of about six weeks Leo became interested in hunting, and so his toys became 'practice prey'. Taking advantage of any cover available, he would carefully stalk a toy that was lying unprotected by itself and, waiting patiently for just the right moment, would pounce on the unsuspecting object. The coffee tin gave him a big scare, for instead of perishing after receiving a vicious slap, it rolled aggressively towards him. Startled by the tin's behaviour, he decided to ignore it and concentrate on his other toys instead. When they had all been successfully demolished, he tried once more to attack the coffee tin but it wouldn't co-operate, so he looked about for more obliging prey. He soon discovered a host of them: pillows, books, baskets, shoes, towels and so on.

Until he was two months old Leo was a house lion. He would venture outside only if accompanied by one of the family. Luckily he was easily house-trained. With the fastidiousness of all cats, he preferred to make his little puddles and messes outdoors. As he got older and no longer needed encouragement from us to do his bathroom routine, he would, at the call of nature, march out through the veranda door and use the daisy border at the side of the patio. Considering that he never left the house on his own except when he needed the bathroom, I think he was a very good little lion. The daisies died eventually, but at least the house remained free of lion puddles.

At the age of about three months he started venturing outside on his own more often to explore the garden, but still only within close range of the house. Belonging as he did to a species of competitive, territorial predators, he was coded with the knowledge that a lion should stay within the boundaries of his family's established range. Stumbling into the territory of an alien pride could mean trouble, especially if the dominant males weren't kind to interlopers. And so Leo deemed it wise to stay close to the house until he learned where the boundaries of his home range were.

As he became more outdoor-orientated, it dawned on him that dogs and humans would be great as practice prey. He chose the snake's flowerbed at the side of the kitchen as his favourite spot to lie in ambush. It was a good choice, of course, being right alongside the paved path – the main approach route to the kitchen door. And so any un-suspecting human or dog who happened to be approaching or leaving the house got pounced on by a lion, or spat on by a cobra, as it were.

Even at a tender age, Leo proved to have a good memory. He never for-got his favourite people. When Hettie and Sandra went back to university at the start of the new term, they wondered if the cub would forget them. He never did – regardless of the length of their absence – and was always overjoyed to see them again. Every Friday afternoon, when Karin arrived home, he rushed straight into her arms to greet her with a prolonged display of affection.

Annette fell desperately in love with Leo and tried her best to per-suade me to trade him for any or all of her personal possessions, including her husband. I wasn't willing to trade, of course, not even for her husband (he was a great guy, but I already had one), so I said thanks a lot, but no. She accepted her fate stoically but often came over with Narina to play with Leo. Leo grew very fond of Annette and Narina, and even when he started treating other people as outsiders he always treated them as family.

Often, while Annette and I were enjoying a nice trouble-sharing session over coffee, Leo and Narina would stalk and chase each other all over the place until both of them collapsed with exhaustion. Then

Narina would climb onto her mother's lap to rest, while Leo climbed onto mine to suck my finger.

Whenever Leo got tired or sleepy he needed a finger to suck on. He would not ask for one, he would simply climb onto an available lap and seize the owner's hand. Gripping it between his front paws, he would select a finger for himself. Once your finger was in his mouth, you were stuck. Caught between his tongue and palate, the finger would remain firmly in place, glued by suction, so to speak. And any indication from you that you wished to extract your finger would prompt the razor-sharp dewclaws to tighten their grip on your hand. The only way to get your finger back was to wait patiently until he nodded off, and then take care not to wake him while extracting it. It was cute, of course, but exasperating, especially if he took a long time to fall asleep and you had other things to do.

Annette suggested I buy him a dummy, and I often considered doing so. But what if he became an incurable dummy-sucker? It didn't seem quite fitting for a prince. I wanted to bring Leo up in ways as close as possible to what his real mother would have done. Not being a lion myself, I wasn't sure exactly how she would have gone about it. I could only guess.

But I knew she wouldn't have bought him a dummy.

A ROYAL CUBHOOD

A T THE AGE OF FOUR MONTHS LEO WAS A BOISTEROUS, AFFECTIONATE little lion with an immense personality. He possessed the spontaneous gaiety of one who never doubts his own adorability. He loved being hugged and cuddled and would often leap from the ground into our arms to embrace us fondly and to lick our faces.

But in addition to being totally adorable he was also inexhaustibly playful and, being a lion, he could never resist stalking us and pouncing on us. We developed the habit of glancing nervously over our shoulders. If we noticed him frozen in a crouched position with intent, mischievous eyes, we would hastily brace ourselves for the impact of the pounce. Running away did not help – he was faster than us.

Initially he was a bit rough and careless with his claws, and our arms and legs often got rather severely scratched.

In repose, a lion's claws are sheathed; they are exposed only in deliberate attack. The razor-sharp dewclaw, the equivalent of our thumb, is a most vicious weapon. Fortunately, Leo soon developed more control over his claws and learned to keep them sheathed when playing with us. By the time he was six months old and capable of inflicting serious injury, there was far less likelihood of lacerations than when he was younger.

Leo had a beautiful nature and he never showed any signs of aggression towards us. If he did something that we didn't think was a good idea for a lion, we disciplined him with a firm tone of voice. He understood this and would try to make amends by rubbing his body against our legs and uttering soft, sorrowful moans. Once, when I scolded him rather severely for stealing my washing off the line, I felt so guilty when I saw the hurt look in his eyes that I resolved never again to get angry with him.

At the age of five months Leo was satisfied that the boundaries of his pride's established territory were the fences around the garden, and he was delighted with his wooded playground of almost two acres. The many trees, shrubs and flowerbeds offered a nice variety of cover for a lion whose favourite game was stalking unsuspecting prey – us, the dogs, visitors and any washing left unguarded on the line.

Although we had started taking him for walks in the bush when he was three months old, he never ventured outside the garden on his own, even though the gates always stood open during the day. Visitors were often surprised that we left the gates open and would ask us if we weren't worried that the lion would escape.

I am sure the question would have mystified Leo. Why would he want to leave his family and his safe haven? Where would he want to go?

Whenever Kobus spent a day or two at home to catch up on office work, Leo would frequently bound into his office for a fond greeting and a cuddle. Often, while Kobus was talking to a colleague on his office radio, he would unexpectedly find his head clasped firmly between large paws and his face smothered with lion kisses. His colleagues soon learned to accept that his sudden silences on the radio meant only that he was being strangled by an affectionate lion.

Initially Leo shared our bedroom at night but at the age of three months his sleeping box got too cramped for him, so he went in search of a better arrangement. He chose the guest bed on the screened veranda and enjoyed his new-found comfort so much that he abandoned his habit of getting up at dawn to greet the family. Instead he would stretch out on his back, paws dangling in the air while the rays of the early sun played on his chest and tummy. Often when we found him there, stretched out on his bed like a lazy prince, he would look at us with an expression that seemed to say, 'Why are you up so early? It's so nice to be in bed still!'

We didn't mind him sleeping on the bed. In fact we thought it a nice idea that he had a bed all to himself rather than have him trying to climb into bed with us. But two months later, when he was about five months old, he discovered that his mattress was great fun to chew, and so he demolished it. When he started hauling mattresses off other beds to play with, we realized it was time to teach him to sleep outdoors. (By this time he had already chewed up several pillows, shoes, books and other valuables and had left tooth marks on some of the furniture. Our house was beginning to look very lion-inhabited.)

We fetched a large wooden crate from our storeroom and set it on its side on the patio outside the veranda. We also spread a tarpaulin over the crate to make it rain-proof.

The first time Leo was banished from sleeping in the house, I spent half the night in the crate with him. For two more nights I spent an hour or so in his crate with him, and after that he was left on his own. Before long he realized that he was a semi-nocturnal animal who didn't need a crate to protect him and so he began to spend his nights out in the open, even when it rained.

One night, when we were having a rather frightening thunderstorm, I went outside with my torch to see if Leo was all right. I couldn't find him in the garden so I went to check his crate. Not wanting to shine the torch right inside in case he was in there and I frightened him, I got down on all fours and, while calling his name, stuck my head into the crate. Receiving no answer, I decided he wasn't there after all. But a huge paw suddenly seized my shoulder and pulled me right into the crate. The next moment a very rough lion tongue was licking my face in greeting.

A lion's tongue is like sandpaper. Our necks, faces and arms often bore the scars of Leo's friendly attentions.

Leo still enjoyed having toys, so I stuffed a few hessian bags with rags, tied each to a length of rope and hung them from trees. These proved to be excellent as practice prey and also as swings.

When Leo was six months old, we introduced him to an old tyre. He would rush after it as it was rolled along the ground and try to trip it up with a circular swipe of the front paw. As soon as the tyre was downed, he would pounce on it triumphantly. Once, when I rolled the tyre along the downhill slope of our front lawn, the tyre gained speed too rapidly and Leo was unable to catch up with it. It crashed into the garden fence and, bouncing off the mesh, came rolling back straight towards him. Believing that the tyre had suddenly turned aggressive and was chasing him, Leo uttered a startled grunt and fled. After that he didn't trust the tyre for quite a while and refused to run after it when it was rolled for him.

The older Leo got, the more demonstrative he became. By the time he was six months old, he insisted on greeting each member of the family several times a day with a ceremonial touching of heads and cheek-rubbing.

We had to kneel for the greeting ritual, of course.

But we didn't mind.

He was, after all, a prince.

LEO AND WOLFIE

ONE DAY, AS LEO AND FLENTER WERE BOTH CHASING A TENNIS ball, Leo got to the ball first, but Flenter tried to take it away from him. So Leo slapped him playfully on the head with his front paw. This sent Flenter into a rage and he attacked the cub. Surprised and hurt by his friend's aggressiveness, Leo slunk off. When he returned a while later to make amends, Flenter would have nothing to do with him.

Flenter was actually becoming a bit of a problem dog. He had never really cared much for wild animals, and the bigger the cub got, the less Flenter liked him. Being a Staffordshire bull terrier, he wanted to be the leader of the pack. But since his pack consisted of one Australian cattle dog and one fast-growing lion, he had a bit of a problem.

Wolfie he could handle, for although Wolfie was bigger and heavier than he was, Wolfie was not a fighter and chose to be submissive rather than to invite attack. But Leo wasn't getting any smaller, and so Flenter was worried. How was he to control his pack if its youngest member was already twice as big and strong as he was? (And there was obviously no end in sight to his expansion.) Moreover, he had a nagging suspicion that the outsized youngster was related to the king.

The poor dog didn't know how to cope with his troubles, and so he vented his frustrations on Wolfie, attacking him at every opportunity and demanding total submission from him. But no matter how often Wolfie pledged submission, Flenter was never satisfied.

Eventually Wolfie wasn't even allowed to play with Leo any more. Flenter would attack him.

Wolfie, being a gentle soul who always tried to avoid any unpleasantness, started slinking about the place, trying his best to keep out of sight of Flenter. The whole situation was becoming intolerable, and we knew that something would have to be done about it.

There was a farmer across the river, Johan Boshoff, who had a special fondness for Staffordshire bull terriers. He admired them for their courage, tenacity and strength, and found them incomparable as guard dogs and companions. He owned a Staffordshire bitch and was looking for a mate for her. Whenever Johan came over to see Kobus, he would spend some time playing with Flenter. One day he asked us if we would consider selling Flenter to him, and Kobus and I both said no, sorry.

But as time went by and Flenter's repeated attacks on Wolfie became unbearable, we reconsidered.

Although Flenter did not tolerate other animals, he loved humans and took easily to strangers. Wolfie, on the other hand, was tolerant of all wild animals, but he did not take to strange humans. He loved only his own family. If strangers tried to befriend him, he would look the other way with a distrustful, suspicious glint in his eyes. He especially hated having a stranger pat him on the head. He would lift his upper lip at one corner, exposing a canine. It was only a fair warning, to be translated as: 'If you try to become any more familiar with me, I'll bite you.'

Wolfie was the kind of dog one could never dream of giving away. It would be too cruel.

But would Flenter mind all that much? He seemed genuinely fond of Johan Boshoff.

So, one morning, after Flenter had again attacked Wolfie and bitten him rather severely, we asked Johan if he still wanted the dog. He did, and offered to pay any price we asked. We wouldn't have dreamed of selling our dog; we only wanted a good home for him.

And so, for the first time in our lives, we gave a dog away. It was a very hard thing for us to do. I remember the day that Johan came to fetch Flenter: as he was driving out the gate with Flenter on the back of his pick-up, I called out to my dog and waved goodbye, tears streaming down my cheeks.

But Flenter, busy sniffing the deck of the pick-up, where Johan's Staffordshire bitch must have left her scent, was so intrigued by it that he forgot to look up when I called his name in farewell.

Johan kept in touch with us and we learned that Flenter had adapted well to his new home and was, in fact, charmed with his girlfriend.

When Wolfie finally realized that Flenter was not coming back, he stopped slinking about the place and became a very happy and relaxed dog, smiling most of the time. And he enjoyed being able to play with Leo without being attacked by Flenter.

In due course, Wolfie became Leo's most trusted friend and companion.

People often asked us how a lion's intelligence compared with that of a dog.

I think a dog is more intelligent in terms of its relationships with humans. It can learn to understand a fair amount of human vocabulary and to respond to vocal commands. Leo appeared to have a very limited capacity for understanding the vocal index of human language, but his ability to interpret body language was remarkable. It was a sensitivity that enabled him to recognize a variety of human moods and emotions and to appreciate differences in human personalities.

Leo had a unique relationship with each member of the family.

Kobus was his father, and the dominant male of the pride. Leo loved, respected and admired him. I was his mother, much loved but not respected as much as his father. He trusted me and depended on me for motherly love and care but, in a mischievous mood, he would tease and bully me. He never bullied his father.

Karin was his favourite sister as she came home more often than the others, and her sunny, boisterous nature always provided for a lot of fun.

Sandra was the sister for whom he had the most respect. He sensed her quiet determination of spirit, and although he played with her and challenged her as he did everyone else, one harsh look or stern warning from her would instantly turn him into a well-behaved lion.

He sensed Hettie's passionate nature and showed remarkable perception in his responses to her moods. If her mood was joyous he would be an exuberant clown, and the two of them would play with such happy abandon that I sometimes feared Leo would unintentionally hurt her. (There were in fact a few accidents, but fortunately nothing serious.) If her mood was wistful, he would sit quietly beside her, groaning softly or licking her arms and face to comfort her. He would never tease her or try to play with her when she was in a melancholy mood.

Sandra's classmate at medical school, Paul Meyer, had since become a regular visitor, accompanying Sandra whenever she came home. Although Paul had grown up in a town, he took to our way of life right away and fell madly in love with the bush.

To Leo, Paul was the best brother any lion could wish for: Paul not only knew how to play wonderfully wild and rough lion-games, he also had a talent for inventing them.

Whenever I was awoken in the early hours by the sound of human feet racing around the house followed by the thud-thud of lion paws, I would know that Paul and Leo were playing Cops and Lions again, or Lions and Crooks, or whatever. (Paul usually carried a water-pistol for self-defence.)

Leo also had a unique relationship with Wolfie. Wolfie was his trusted companion and friend, his tutor and his mentor. He respected Wolfie and never broke the rules that Wolfie set down for him. Even when Leo eventually weighed a solid one hundred kilograms more than the dog, he still regarded Wolfie as his superior.

Wolfie could be strict with Leo at times, but for the most part he was extremely tolerant of him, often allowing Leo to chew his ears, or his tail, and to bully and pester him to a point that no other dog would dream of enduring. Leo loved to run directly behind Wolfie and to trip him up with circular swipes of his front paw.

Wolfie, ignoring the discomfort of a hind leg getting swiped from underneath him every now and again, would earnestly continue his own business of sniffing the ground and running along whichever spoor he was following. Only occasionally, when the tripping game truly hampered his exploratory endeavours, would he pause momentarily to turn his head slightly towards Leo, lifting his upper lip at one corner to expose a canine, evidently telling Leo: 'Do that one more time and I'm going to bite you!' Leo would back off immediately and behave himself.

Leo loved excursions into the bush. Whenever we told him that we were going for a walk or a drive, his eyes would light up with excitement. But being unable to distinguish between the words 'drive' and 'walk', he would pay close attention to Wolfie's reaction to see which it was to be. If it was 'walk' Wolfie would head for the gate, if it was 'drive' Wolfie would leap onto the truck. And Leo would do whatever Wolfie did.

Leo seemed to realize that Wolfie understood a lot of human language, and so he relied on the dog as his interpreter. It was very useful to have Wolfie in this role. Whenever we wanted to give Leo a specific command, we would give it to Wolfie instead, knowing that Wolfie would respond and that Leo would follow his example.

Wolfie caught on that we were using him as an interpreter, but he didn't mind. Being a conscientious dog who took his responsibilities seriously, he co-operated as best he could, even though the job sometimes required a lot of patience. If Leo wasn't paying attention, for instance, Wolfie would have to repeat the required action several times until Leo got the message.

One of our favourite Sunday afternoon outings was to drive to Mpanamana, a beautiful pan at the foot of the Lebombo Mountains. The pan was home to a family of hippos who always performed dramatically at the sight of us. They plunged and splashed about, raising gaping jaws in our direction and bellowing threats at us. Leo loved to sit and watch the hippos perform.

The trouble was that when we wanted to go home, Leo wanted to stay longer. Wolfie, loyal, obedient dog that he was, would respond promptly to the command to get onto the pick-up, but Leo would pretend not to hear.

Until he was about six months old, we were still able to carry him to the truck if he refused to listen. But as he grew heavier and stronger, he got wise to the fact that if he struggled while we carried him, we had to release him immediately. And so we had no choice but to rely on Wolfie to get Leo onto the truck. We would ask Wolfie to please disembark, fetch Leo and jump back onto the truck again. Wolfie would jump off, go over to Leo, look him straight in the eyes to get his attention, then turn and run back to the truck and jump on it again. Leo seemed to reckon that if Wolfie wanted him to get onto the truck so badly, then there probably was a good reason for it. And so he would follow. But when Leo was in a difficult mood, Wolfie sometimes had to repeat the performance several times before Leo would obey.

Eventually Wolfie became so conditioned to this procedure that whenever he jumped onto the truck and saw that Leo wasn't following, he would jump right off again, without waiting for a command from us, and repeat the performance until Leo followed him.

It was during these outings into the bush that we realized that Leo considered Wolfie to be his mentor.

Lions are born with the hunting instinct, but they are not born with the skill of hunting. This they learn from their mothers. It is a fine and complicated art, and a mother lion spends up to two years teaching her offspring to hunt successfully.

Something in Leo's instinctive memory must have told him that there were important things in the bush for him to learn. For some reason he didn't look to Kobus or to me for an education, but to Wolfie. He strongly suspected Wolfie to be the guy who knew all the things that it was crucial for a lion to learn.

But he was mistaken. There was nothing, really, that a herding dog like Wolfie could teach a lion about hunting and survival. And Wolfie had no idea that Leo was looking to him for an education. So he would run about the bush in crazy zigs and zags as dogs do, sniffing the ground and reading all the messages left behind by hordes of wildlife. Leo would follow Wolfie like a shadow, but instead of sniffing the ground like a dog, he would watch Wolfie's face and body language intently, hoping to pick up some useful clues to whatever secret knowledge Wolfie possessed. If Wolfie started digging furiously into abandoned termite hills or aardvark burrows, Leo would stand right in front of him and study the dog's busy face with a look of intense puzzlement that seemed to say: 'Huh? What are we doing now?'

In the bush Leo often had that huh? expression on his face. Poor chap. We felt sorry for him. He was badly in need of a proper tutor.

*

Wolfie never chased or harassed wild animals, but on the few occasions that he was surprised by a sudden close encounter with mongooses, warthogs or other small game, he would herd them for some distance and then leave them in peace.

One day Wolfie poked his head into a burrow to check who was inside and out charged a warthog mother, followed by three warthog babies. Wolfie, making a hasty retreat, reversed into Leo who was standing right behind him. The dog nevertheless managed to get out of the way in time. Not Leo. He was still saying 'Huh?' when the sow collided heavily with him. She made a U-turn and headed in the opposite direction, followed by her screaming children. As soon as Leo recovered from the surprise of the sudden blow inflicted by the sow, he saw that Wolfie was in hot pursuit of the warthogs. He bounded after them and, being a lion, soon caught up with them. By this time Wolfie was running alongside the warthog family, doing his herding act. Good student that he was, Leo followed suit and ran alongside the startled warthogs, watching them with an expression of happy achievement on his face. He obviously thought he was learning fast.

The dog and the lion herded the family of bewildered warthogs for some distance, and then Wolfie decided generously that enough was enough and gave up the chase (or the herding act). He came trotting back to us, followed by Leo. We always praised Wolfie for being kind to animals and for not hurting them. On this occasion we had no choice but to pat Leo on the head as well. We knew, however, that this was not helping his education along.

Leo was growing up to be a herding dog.

This worried us. He was already way behind in his educational curriculum. It was time we started teaching him the things his mother would have taught him. He would never be a successful lion if he continued to believe that his food came from the refrigerator and that the bush was a place where a herding act was required.

The problem was how and when to teach him. As game ranger, Kobus was on call twenty-four hours a day, every day of the week, and he was lucky if he had more than an hour a day free to spend with Leo.

The only solution, it seemed to me, was that I would have to take over our lion's education. Kobus could give a helping hand whenever he had some time to spare.

A CONFUSED SCHOLAR

THERE WERE NUMEROUS GAME TRAILS TO THE NORTH AND WEST OF our house, and I liked to follow them when walking with Leo and Wolfie, knowing that we would come across the local waterbuck, wildebeest, kudu and impala populations who would be on their way either to or from the river.

I loved the way the animals stopped and stared at us with a big question mark on their faces: 'What is this primate doing in the company of a fat wolf and a lion?'

In the beginning the sight of Leo gave them a fright and they would flee. But Leo never gave chase, for the simple reason that Wolfie didn't. He would stand and look at the animals with that huh? expression on his face. The animals soon cottoned on that this was a dim-witted lion and so they lost their fear of him.

Even though the local game populations grew quite used to the sight of the three of us together, they never stopped wondering about us. And while they were standing and staring, we would walk carefully up to them until we were almost close enough for a friendly chat. Then we would all stand and stare at one another.

There was one waterbuck bull who often gave in to curiosity and approached us nonchalantly, stopping very close to us and studying us with a perplexed expression, sometimes stamping a hoof impatiently on the ground as if demanding an explanation. I loved to deepen his bafflement by crouching between Wolfie and Leo and putting my arms around them.

The impalas sometimes forgot that they had seen us together on previous occasions and bounded away upon sighting or smelling us. But as soon as they realized we weren't giving chase, they would stop and stare, and that same question mark would be on their faces.

When I decided it was time to start Leo's hunting lessons, I was troubled by a moral question. How could I, having won the trust of the local antelope populations, now do an about-face and start teaching my lion to hunt them? It didn't seem fair. Yet, how else could I teach Leo to hunt? Not being a lion myself, I wasn't really sure how to stalk animals. Stalking these semi-tame antelopes would at least be a lot easier than stalking wild ones who didn't trust me.

I felt like a traitor. But I had my responsibilities as a lion-mother. So I tried to harden my heart and decided to go for the impala. At least they were less intelligent and more forgetful than the others.

This is how I tackled the first hunting lesson.

It was late afternoon and the three of us — Wolfie, Leo and I — were following a game trail, looking for the herd of impala who would be on their way back from the river at about that time. As soon as we spotted them, I crouched in the long grass and commanded Wolfie to do the same. He sat down obediently and Leo, Wolfie's faithful shadow, did likewise. The herd was moving towards us at a leisurely pace, grazing as they did so.

I threw a handful of dust into the air to test the wind. 'Stay here,' I whispered to Wolfie. Leaving behind one obedient dog and one puzzled lion, I crept off towards the river, keeping well out of sight of the impalas. I moved carefully in a semicircle around the herd until I reached a spot where I was directly opposite Wolfie and Leo with the herd between us. Then I waited for the wind to carry my scent to the antelopes. Wolfie and Leo were still hidden from sight in the long grass.

Grey herons stalked fish in stilt-legged slow motion on the opposite shore, and cormorants and egrets perched spread-winged on rocks that showed above the water. A sudden rustling sound in the tall reeds some distance upriver caught my attention. I quickly got to my feet, commanding Wolfie to stay close to me. Leo raised his nose to the wind, then bounded off and disappeared into the reed thickets.

Wolfie uttered a soft yelping noise.

'No,' I told him. 'Stay with me.' I stood quietly, straining my senses for some clue as to what might be going on inside those ominous thickets. And where was Leo? What was he up to?

Again the reeds rustled, but nothing happened. The landscape appeared to be frozen in time. Some sixth sense told me to get out of the way. As I turned and ran towards the river bank behind me, the reed thickets to my left began to wave wildly. A herd of buffalo burst from them and came stampeding across the shore. I sprinted up the bank. As soon as I reached the top, I turned and saw the herd running downriver, followed by a playful lion doing a perfect herding act.

After a while I sent Wolfie to fetch Leo.

Wolfie scampered down the bank and across the shore, barking at Leo to come back. Leo turned and came bounding towards the dog, looking immensely pleased with himself. As he met up with Wolfie, he touched heads with him in greeting and told him all about it. Then he came running up the bank towards me, and the expression on his face seemed to say, 'Did you see me herding the buffalo? Wasn't I great?'

'Come along,' I heard Karin saying to Leo late one afternoon. 'You're not a cattle dog. You're a lion. And I'm going to teach you to hunt.'

I saw the three of them leaving through the gate. Karin, Wolfie and Leo.

I wondered how she was going to accomplish her mission.

Later, when dusk started to settle, I began to worry about the trio and set out to look for them. As soon as I walked out the gate, I saw them. They were on their way home. Wolfie was trotting towards me, followed closely by Leo who was trying to trip him up. Karin approached with stiff-legged strides, swinging her arms in the way she does when she's irritated. Her face, clothes and arms were covered with dust.

I went to meet her.

'So, how did it go?' I asked.

'He's so stupid,' she replied. 'I organized a perfect hunting situation for him. I crept up to a couple of resting wildebeest and chased them right towards him. They never even saw him. They almost collided with him. But you know what he did? He charged right past them and caught me!'

'I know just how you feel,' I said sympathetically.

Some days later Kobus had a few hours to spare and he decided it was a good time to help with the hunting lessons.

We set out in the pick-up with Wolfie and Leo on the back. Though we encountered lots of animals along the way, Kobus didn't stop. He was looking for guinea fowl. They were such muddle-headed birds, he reckoned they would be a sensible choice as practice prey for a slow-witted lion.

Some ten kilometres from home we finally came across a big flock of guinea fowl. They were marching down the track right in front of us. Kobus drove off the track, kept alongside the parade for a few metres and then turned back onto the track again, stopping more or less in the middle of the procession. Leo and Wolfie bounded off the truck and started chasing the front half of the flock. The startled birds fled down the road, sprinting comically on short legs, necks stretched forward, and intermittently taking off in brief bursts of flight.

Leo enjoyed the chase, thinking it was a new game. The idea of catching a guinea fowl never entered his head. After a while Wolfie decided to turn back. As he did so, so did his faithful shadow, Leo.

Kobus and I turned to see where the other half of the flock had gone, and saw that they were standing right behind us! Apparently they had been watching the proceedings down the road with as much interest as we had. But as soon as they saw the dog and the lion approaching, they turned and fled up the road. Wolfie and Leo again gave chase. Meanwhile the front line of the flock returned to the site of the commotion, and as we turned we found them right behind us, gawking at the proceedings up the road. As soon as Leo and Wolfie returned, they herded the current audience down the road again. Meanwhile the up-road half of the flock returned to watch the proceedings down the road . . . and so on. It had the makings of a never-ending story.

The next day Kobus took us for another drive and shot a guinea fowl for Leo. The fowl had been sitting in a tree, and as it fell to the ground Wolfie rushed towards it, followed by Leo. Kobus told Wolfie not to take the bird, and the good dog obeyed, leaving it for the lion. It took Leo a while to understand that the bird was dead and that it was his. Snatching up the dead guinea fowl in his mouth he ran off with it – where to, no-one knew. Not even Leo himself. After a while he returned, the dead bird still dangling from his mouth, his eyes asking: 'What should I do with it?'

I suggested to Kobus that he cut the bird open so that Leo understood that it was edible. But Leo was very possessive and wouldn't let Kobus touch it.

When we decided to go back home, Wolfie had to do his get-onto-the-truck routine several times before Leo obeyed. But as Leo jumped up the bird slammed into the side of the pick-up and fell out of his mouth to the ground. With a yelp of anguish Leo leaped off the truck to retrieve his bird, and poor Wolfie had to do several more reruns of his getting-off/getting-on act before Leo finally followed, the bird gripped firmly between his teeth.

When we got home, Leo spent the rest of the day running all over the garden with the dead bird in his mouth, tossing it into the air, catching it, rolling on it, wrestling with it, even sitting on it. Eventually the bird started to disintegrate, and it was distressing to see its entrails, feathers and limbs scattered everywhere. Leo himself was a disgusting sight, with feathers and bits of bird sticking to his coat and whiskers. Ugh.

He never ate the guinea fowl.

A RIOTOUS ADOLESCENT

O N THE FIRST DAY OF KARIN'S SPRING VACATION FROM SCHOOL, SHE looked forward to spending the afternoon relaxing in the garden. She carried a book, a cassette player and a blanket outside and made herself comfortable under a shady tree.

Leo spotted his favourite sister on the lawn and bounded over to her. Pouncing on her blanket, he yanked it out from underneath her and made off with it. Karin gave chase, screaming at the lion to bring back her blanket.

I was inside the house doing some sewing, and I watched the comedy show through a window.

Karin returned a while later, carrying her blanket and looking angry, followed by Leo. After threatening the lion with murder if he didn't behave, she made herself comfortable on her blanket again and proceeded to read her book. Leo lay quietly on the grass next to her, pretending to be a very good lion.

After a while one of his paws sidled ever so slowly onto the blanket, and then another paw followed. Soon the rest of his body started to move in gradual instalments. Karin reached out to pat his head, and as she did so, he snatched her book and ran off with it.

'Hey!' Karin yelled as she jumped up and ran after him. 'That's a library book! I'll get into trouble!'

A few minutes later she returned, carrying her library book, looking very angry and, of course, with Leo in tow. He had an apologetic, almost sorrowful look on his face, as if he couldn't believe his own naughtiness.

'OK,' Karin muttered crossly as she sat down on the blanket. 'I'll give you one last chance. But if you dare to even think of bothering me, I'm going to punch you on the nose.'

Leo looked even more regretful.

'And look at this!' she added, shoving the library book at him. There were lion tooth marks through the cover. 'How will I explain that to the librarian?'

Leo looked at the book and his face was a study in self-recrimination.

Karin settled down to her book and her music. Leo lay quietly at her side, trying his best to be a good lion. And for a while he actually succeeded.

But after about five minutes the effort proved too much for him, and he started irritating Karin in small ways. One paw edged forward, just an inch or so at a time, until it ended up either on her book or on her cassette player. Karin slapped the offending paw away, muttering threats. And for a while Leo would try to behave again. But it was hard for him. He couldn't stand the fact that she would rather read than play with him.

Suddenly the urge to play was overwhelming. He leaped up, pounced on her and, as she rolled over to get away from him, he sat down on top of her. Karin punched him on the nose and a short, fierce wrestling match followed, human and lion limbs flailing in all directions. Karin ended up the winner, sitting on the lion's chest and pinning his paws to the ground above his head. She bent over, bringing her face very close to his, and then hissed at him, like an angry cat. That was more than Leo could bear. He moaned in a tone that seemed to mean: 'Please don't hiss at me like that! It frightens me.' Karin let go of him, rolled over onto the blanket and continued reading her book. Leo decided that it would be better for him, after all, to behave. So he lay peacefully next to her on the blanket, and she stroked his fur.

*

At the age of ten months Leo was a handsome youngster with a strong and determined character. Though he was more boisterous than ever before, he was very obedient and seemed to realize that he had to co-operate with us.

We, in turn, tried to limit any restrictions on his behaviour and raise him as a lion, not as a domestic pet. For his own sake, as well as ours, we wanted him to remain the unfrustrated, even-tempered animal that he was. He was as affectionate as ever and he enjoyed being close, often either leaning against us or sitting on us. Whenever the girls came home, Leo insisted on greeting them with a lengthy ritual of head-touching, cheek-rubbing, embracing and cuddling, accompanied by a series of soulful grunts and groans.

He still loved bounding into Kobus's office for a hug and a cuddle, but he was now so huge that he would just about knock the desk over when he jumped onto Kobus's lap. If Kobus was talking on either his radio or the phone, it would land on the floor along with anything else that was in the way. At the end of the fond greeting the whole office would be in chaos.

Leo also still loved chasing and jumping on us, but he was so heavy now that he often brought us crashing to the ground. So we had to teach him to respect the fact that we were a lot more fragile than he was. Eventually he learned that we didn't want him to chase and catch us any more, but the idea baffled and perplexed him. It was such fun. Why give it up?

He couldn't altogether bring himself to abandon his favourite game, but he was willing to modify it: he would stalk us and launch himself at us, but slam his brakes on in time to break the impact of the pounce. And so he would catch us more 'gently', clasping us around our waists with his enormous paws. We didn't mind that too much, as long as he didn't try to drag us down for a playful wrestling match, which he often did.

He also possessed a rather exasperating sense of humour: whenever he saw someone bending over, he would sneak up from behind and give the unsuspecting bottom either a playful chomp or a toppling shove.

The flowerbed at the side of the kitchen was still his favourite ambush spot, and since he loved to test the reactions of strangers, I was forced to go out and meet all visitors at the parking area and escort them safely indoors. Fortunately, Wolfie always barked to announce the arrival of visitors, acting as our official doorbell.

I loved gardening, but when Leo also became interested in this activity, things got complicated. He only wanted to help, of course, but our ideas tended to clash, and so a newly planted flowerbed would end up looking like an excavation site.

Moreover, the telephone often interrupted my gardening, and whenever I dashed off to answer it, Leo would think I was inviting him to a game of catch. I would spend so much time and energy wrestling the lion off me that, by the time I answered the phone, I'd be too breathless to talk.

One beautiful morning in October, as I was trying to do some gardening, the telephone started ringing. And, as usual, Leo caught me long before I reached the house. After a short but vigorous battle I managed to disentangle myself from the lion and, with a stern warning to him to leave me alone, I tried once more to reach the house.

Breathless, I arrived at the paved path – and a lightning movement at the edge of my vision froze me.

It was the cobra.

Rearing himself up high, he fixed me with a cold reptilian stare. I stopped breathing. He was much too close. While the steely eyes studied me carefully, judging my case, I remained as still as I could, praying that the noisy pounding of my heart wouldn't annoy him to the point of pronouncing me guilty. Meanwhile Leo evidently thought that the reason I had stopped running so suddenly was because I wanted to play some more. The snake had just reached his generous verdict of 'not guilty' and was about to retreat when the lion caught me from behind and brought me tumbling to the grass.

The snake didn't like that at all, and spat at us. The venom spray caught me on the leg. I kicked the lion off me and hastily got to my feet to inspect the damage. The poison was dribbling down my leg straight towards a bleeding scratch on my ankle. Keeping the ankle raised, I hopped over to the nearest tap and managed to rinse the poison off before it reached the scratch.

My head was spinning and my heart was doing flip-flops from the crazy variety of shocks that I had just experienced and – I could hardly believe it – the stupid telephone was still ringing its head off! I rushed inside, snatched up the receiver and tried to make my voice sound normal.

I was rather surprised to hear the voice of a dear friend, Riaan Cruywagen, at the other end.

Riaan and I had been at school together and had stayed in touch ever since, writing to each other about once a year.

On this day, while I struggled to regain my breath, Riaan told me the reason he was calling was that he had just made a most alarming discovery. He'd been to the dentist that morning, he said, and as he paged through an old magazine in the waiting room he came upon an article telling the story of a game ranger who had survived a lion attack. When he read that the game ranger was Kobus, he almost fell out of his chair. He checked the date on the magazine and saw that it was June 1992. He then remembered that he had been on vacation at that particular time, which was why he had not heard about the attack. Even so, he said, he felt awful about it and hoped that I hadn't thought him terribly insensitive for not having called to offer condolences and to enquire about Kobus.

I was about to tell him not to worry, that it had all happened a long time ago, but if he still wished to offer condolences he might offer them to me – I had just been attacked by a lion *and* a cobra. But naturally I couldn't expect him to believe that, so instead I told him not to feel badly, that it was really my fault that he hadn't known about the attack as I should have written and had been meaning to, but time had simply been getting away from me.

We had a lovely chat, and eventually I told him about the cub we were raising. At some stage while Riaan and I were talking, I heard Wolfie barking outside, but I took no notice. It was only after I had put the receiver down that I suddenly got the feeling that I had ignored an important signal. And then it struck me – the doorbell! I rushed out of the house to warn the visitors about our lion.

Too late. Leo had already caught himself a soldier and they were wrestling on the lawn.

The soldiers from Nkongoma base all knew about our lion, but this was a new recruit, and judging from the look of alarm on his face he had not been forewarned. I rushed to his aid and got Leo off him.

'I am so terribly sorry . . .' I stammered. 'Are you OK?'

Scrambling to his feet, he assured me that he was.

He was a young boy, barely out of his teens. I admired his gracious attitude, and told him so.

He confessed that the sight of the lion rushing at him had been quite a shock. But fortunately, he said, the lion had caught the dog first. And since it hadn't eaten the dog, things looked a little brighter than they would otherwise have done.

I invited him in for a cup of sweet, strong tea, which I was sure he needed. But he declined, saying that he was in a hurry to get back to the base. He had come to deliver a letter to Kobus from his commanding officer. As he said that, he realized that he'd misplaced the letter. He turned to look for it and spotted the envelope caught between the leaves of a bush-fern in the flowerbed. As he bent over to retrieve it, I tried to warn him not to – but, again, it was too late. Leo chomped him in the rump and the cobra peeked out from behind the bush-fern. Fortunately the snake decided to retreat, disappearing under the leaves of a neighbouring delicious monster plant. I snatched up the envelope and, after further apologies, sent the soldier on his way before things got any worse.

It was obvious that we would have to take better care of our visitors in future. So I decided I would put up a sign next to the paved path:

BEWARE OF THE LION AND THE SNAKE.

But this struck me as sounding a little dramatic, so I thought perhaps BEWARE OF THE FLOWERBED would sound better.

But I wasn't sure.

IN A WORLD OF HIS OWN

WE OFTEN TRIED TO INTRODUCE LEO TO OTHER LIONS – AT A respectful distance, of course. But until he was almost eleven months old, Leo had never seen another lion in his life.

That, however, was not our fault. We had come across lions in the bush several times, and as soon as we'd spotted them we had tried to show them to Leo. But instead of looking in the direction that we were pointing, he would stupidly stare at the finger that was doing the pointing. On a few occasions we actually grabbed hold of his head and swung it in the direction we wanted him to look, but he would roll his eyes upwards and look at us instead.

Often, when lions roared close to the house at night, I would rush into the garden with my torch to see how Leo was reacting. I usually found him sitting up and listening, not too intently but at least with some interest. I'd put my arms around him and say: 'Do you hear that, Leo? Those are your kin! Do you understand what they're saying?'

But Leo would yawn, or lick my face, or stretch out on his back, inviting me to a cuddle. He found the calls quite interesting, but not *that* interesting.

This worried me. Did Leo know he was a lion? If not, what did he think he was? A dog? Or a human? I desperately wanted him to know that he was a lion. It seemed very important to me. But how could I teach him that?

I thought back to the days when he was still a young cub, and I couldn't help believing that he had been closer to realizing he was a lion then than he was now. Could it be that the long period of his association with us was responsible for the fading of his instinctive memories? Did his total acceptance of us as his family blot out all earlier knowledge? If so, it was most important that we started making serious efforts to introduce him to other lions.

Kobus came home late one afternoon and told me that he'd seen a pride of lions resting in the Vurhami Creek, only two kilometres from the house. We called Wolfie and Leo and set out immediately in the truck, hoping that we might at last be able to introduce Leo to his own kind.

When we got there, the lions were still resting on an open stretch of sand in the creek, some hundred metres upstream from the causeway. Kobus parked the truck on the causeway and we got out quietly. As Wolfie and Leo jumped off the back, we commanded them to stay close to us. Kobus took out his rifle, checked its magazine and slung it over his shoulder. There was also an R4 rifle in the cab and I decided to take it along, just in case Leo might need some protection.

We climbed down the side of the causeway onto the sandy creek bed. Two of the lions spotted us but remained lying down, just lifting their heads to study us. They had probably had a recent good meal, and were feeling full and lazy.

We approached them slowly. Taking care to look casual and relaxed, we hoped our body language would communicate that we meant them no harm.

Leo and Wolfie kept close to us. Leo appeared apprehensive, his gaze fixed warily on the lions. Wolfie was his usual composed self.

The landscape was very quiet, the only sound being the sand crunching underneath our feet. The Vurhami was a beautiful creek with its scattering of perennial pools, its wide sandy bed and its high, densely vegetated banks.

All the lions were wide awake now and studying us with alert expressions. The pride consisted of five lions (or so we thought at the time): one adult male, two adult females and two sub-adults who appeared to be only a few months older than Leo.

The closer we got to them the more restless they became. For a while, however, their bafflement at the sight of a young lion in the company of two humans and a fat wolf overrode their fear of us, and so we were able to get quite near before they decided to turn tail.

I was about to ask Leo what he had thought of the lions when a shocking, reverberating growl immediately to our left shattered the afternoon silence. As we spun around to face its source, a lioness burst from the dense undergrowth of the bank and charged us.

Our reflexes taking over, Kobus and I raised and aimed our rifles, releasing the safety catches. I was standing directly behind Kobus. Wolfie launched himself at the lioness. Three cubs appeared from nowhere and fled up the bank. The lioness turned to see where her cubs were going. Wolfie ran up the bank after them. With an angry growl, the lioness turned and charged again, coming at us in a yellow blur of speed, abruptly pulling up very close to us. Then she suddenly turned away and ran after Wolfie and her cubs.

Kobus shouted to Wolfie to come back. The dog needed no persuasion and came tearing down the bank. (Had he gone after the cubs in an attempt to lure the lioness away from us?)

The lioness and her cubs disappeared over the top of the bank. Kobus and I relaxed our aims, feeling extremely grateful that it had not been necessary to fire a shot.

We looked about for Leo. He was missing. As we turned to look towards the causeway, we saw him jumping onto the back of the truck. He had cleared the distance between the truck and us in record time – even for a lion.

Poor fellow. His first meeting with wild lions had not gone well.

When we reached the truck, we patted and hugged Leo and tried to tell him that lions weren't usually so aggressive, and that the only reason the lioness had charged us was to prevent us from getting any nearer to her cubs. Leo rubbed cheeks with us and, in his own language of grunts and groans, shared with us his personal views of the adventure. I knew he was telling us that he had never been so scared in his life.

A few days after our encounter with the lioness, I overheard Kobus discussing the incident with two of his colleagues, Tom and Brian. They obviously didn't know I was near, or else they might have used nicer language.

KOBUS: Then all hell broke loose – a lioness burst from the thickets and charged us, and *directly* behind my back came the sound of Kobie releasing her rifle's safety catch . . .

BRIAN: NO!

TOM: AAUGH!

KOBUS: I felt too threatened to breathe . . .

BRIAN: @*%#!

TOM: Crisis! What a nightmare.

KOBUS: . . . trapped between two nervous females, each with so much destructive power . . .

At this point I decided that I didn't need to listen to such nonsense, so I walked out of earshot.

Leo was almost twelve months old (and weighing close on a hundred kilograms) when it finally dawned on him that he was stronger than his parents. It had taken him a surprisingly long time to become aware of this, but when he did, the idea gave him so much self-confidence that he started challenging rhino and elephant.

Late one afternoon, as we were driving home after a visit to Mpanamana, we came across a rhino bull grazing next to the road. As was our habit, we stopped to let Leo and Wolfie admire the animal, but to our surprise Leo jumped off the truck and playfully charged the rhino. With a startled snort, the bull spun round, lowered his head and charged – aiming a most formidable horn at Leo. We held our breath.

Luckily Leo caught on immediately that the rhino's sharp end was to be avoided. Hopping out of the way, he dashed around the rhino in figures of eight, scrambling the beast's sense of direction. Soon the spinning, horn-swinging bull began to feel a little dizzy, so he had to stop and stand still for a while to reorientate himself to his surroundings. Leo darted away and, with swinging tail and comical body language, invited the rhino to chase him – which the rhino promptly did. Leo disappeared into a thicket. The rhino charged right past him. As he slammed on his brakes, wondering where the lion had gone, Leo reappeared. And so the game, with its prelude of dizzy-dancing, started all over again. Eventually the rhino got tired of it and, totally ignoring the pestering lion, began grazing again. Leo tried his best to persuade the rhino to play some more, but the beast had had enough and started moving off into the bush.

Leo went after him. We called to him to come back. But he ignored us, moving ever deeper into the bush with his new 'friend'. Dusk was setting in and we wanted to go home. Kobus even started the truck's engine to let Leo know we were about to leave without him. It didn't help. We called again, but we knew that when Leo was in an arrogant mood he wouldn't even understand his own name.

We were not keen to send Wolfie after Leo – the rhino might decide to take his frustrations out on the dog. After a while we began to get worried, so the three of us ventured some distance into the knobthorn thickets. There was no sign of either Leo or the rhino. It was getting too dark to see properly, and so in the end we had no choice but to rely on our faithful dog to find our lion for us.

'Wolfie, please fetch Leo,' we told him, and off he went.

About fifteen minutes later the splendid dog returned with the naughty lion in tow.

We decided, as we had on many previous occasions, that Wolfie deserved a gold medal.

From that day on, Leo could never resist challenging rhino and elephant, and so we no longer stopped the truck when we came across these animals but instead tried to get past them as fast as possible.

On a number of occasions when we were held up by elephants in the road, Leo jumped off the truck and challenged them. I almost died of fright each time a screaming, trumpeting giant charged my cub. But Leo would nimbly hop out of its way and caper about in zigs and zags, teasing and confusing the elephants until they got thoroughly fed up and decided to move on.

Leo evidently enjoyed himself enormously, and it always took a lot of persuasion from Wolfie to get him back onto the truck again. I am sure Wolfie often prayed as hard as we did that we wouldn't encounter elephant or rhino along the way.

On a hot morning in November, Sandra and Paul, who were home for their summer vacation, decided to go fishing.

'Come along, Leo and Wolfie!' they said. 'Let's go fishing.'

Leo loved fishing, but being a little dim in the verbal department he thought they'd said, 'Let's go jogging.' So he said no thank you. It was much too hot a day for a lazy lion to go jogging. And he knew Paul and Sandra: they would jog all the way to Vurhami Creek and back without stopping for a rest. Now why would a lion want to give up his snooze for that?

'Come on,' Sandra persisted. 'You'll be sorry you stayed behind!'

Leo lifted his lazy head from the ground, gave her a fond gaze as a gesture of thanks for her concern, but again declined the invitation. He definitely wasn't in the mood for jogging.

Eventually they left without him.

There was no gate leading from our front garden down to the river, so one had to leave through the back gate and walk all the way round the western and southern fences to reach the trail that led to the river bank.

Enjoying his snooze, Leo registered distant sounds coming from the direction of the river. He opened one eye and spotted three figures disappearing over the river bank. Good heavens! They were going fishing!

With a surprised grunt he leaped up and ran to the east fence, calling out to them to wait for him. But by this time they were over the bank and unable to hear him above the sound of the river.

'Auh-wu! Auh-wu! Auh-wu!' Leo called.

But they didn't come back. He ran all the way to the back gate, and called again. No good. The gate didn't even face the river. So he summoned all his courage, walked out through the gate (something he never did on his own), ran along the fence, turned the southern corner to face the river – and then stopped. Surely it would be too dangerous for a lion to venture any further on his own? So he stood there, calling his heart out. He so much wanted to go fishing with them!

When he realized that no-one was coming back for him, he decided to go and tell his parents.

'Auh-auh! Auh-auh!' he called while running back to the house.

Kobus came out of his office and I came out of the house to see why our poor lion was crying so pathetically.

'Leo,' we asked, 'what's the matter?'

He came running straight to us, grunting and groaning a stream of complaints.

Game guard Albert Maluleke, who had been cleaning his rifle in the garden, told us the whole story, explaining that the children and Wolfie had gone fishing and that Leo had misunderstood the invitation to go along with them.

'Don't be such a baby, Leo!' I told him. 'You can go down to the river by yourself!'

'Au-wuh, au-wuh,' he moaned.

'But you play with rhinos and elephants,' I reminded him. 'So what are you afraid of?'

He looked at me with huge, innocent eyes that said, 'I don't know exactly. But I think I'm still too young to go so far from home on my own.'

In the end, Kobus and I walked him down to the river. As we went down the bank Leo spotted the children and Wolfie on the shore and ran to them, complaining loudly at their lack of consideration for his feelings. Paul offered him a fish, and so Leo forgave them.

Leo was an avid fisherman – not that he fished himself, but he would sit quietly next to Paul and Sandra, his gaze fixed on the line. As soon as a fish was pulled out, he would leap up, ready to lend a helping hand if necessary. If it was not necessary, he would study the fish with an expert eye and nose. He knew he was allowed only to look and smell, and not to taste. He was, however, allowed to guard the catch, and if a fish tried to get away he would slap it right back where it belonged. It was worth the trouble, of course, for in the end he would be rewarded with a fair share of the catch. Occasionally, when he thought no-one was looking, he would quickly open his mouth in case a fish wanted to jump inside. But he would never blatantly steal a fish.

Leo adhered to an inborn code of ethics concerning his and his family's food. He would never try to pilfer our food, nor would he expect us to share with him while we ate. At the same time, he was very possessive of his own food and would allow no-one except me near him while he fed. Perhaps the reason he trusted only me was that I was the one who always fed him.

Kobus occasionally shot an impala for Leo, but most of Leo's food was donated by the park's research department. Whenever the veterinarians required a carcass, they would ask Kobus to shoot the animal for them, and since they needed only the stomach and occasionally the lungs for their research purposes – usually they were checking for signs of tuberculosis or other diseases – they would donate the rest of the carcass to Leo.

There was a small kitchen attached to our guest cottage in the garden, and we converted it into a butchery for Leo's meat. A carcass could hang there overnight to be cut up the next day and stored in Leo's freezer (donated to Leo by my parents). We couldn't afford the luxury of letting Leo have a whole carcass to feast on. He wouldn't be able to finish it by himself in one sitting, and so a lot of meat would go to waste.

Our policy of not wasting any meat helped ensure that Leo never had to go hungry. There were times, however, when the meat supply ran low, and if Kobus wasn't home to shoot an impala I had to buy Leo chickens from the market in Komatipoort. To Leo, a whole raw chicken was always a special treat.

One day an army truck from Nkongoma base turned up at our gate, and two soldiers came up to the house to tell me that their truck had collided with an impala ram. The antelope had been killed on impact. They offered their apologies and wondered if it would be OK if they donated the carcass to our lion.

Leo's meat supply was running low at the time and I had been thinking of driving to Komatipoort to buy him some chickens, so naturally I was rather grateful for the unexpected meat delivery. I asked the soldiers if they would be so kind as to offload the carcass at the door of Leo's kitchen and help me hang it inside.

They explained that they had already offloaded the carcass and that Leo had started feeding on it. I thought to myself that at least Leo was discovering what it felt like to have a whole carcass to himself. On the other hand, a lot of meat would go to waste if I didn't try to salvage some of it. It was a very hot day and, if left outside, the meat would soon become smelly and attract hordes of blowflies.

I went off to assess the situation. The moment Leo saw us approaching, he clutched the carcass to him. Flattening his ears, he growled a distinct warning at the soldiers. I suggested to them that they retreat and wait out of sight for a while. As I walked carefully up to Leo he showed no signs of aggression towards me.

Karin, who was home for the weekend, came out of the house. I called to her to bring me a large kitchen knife.

As she approached with the knife, Leo became nervous of her presence so I told her not to come closer.

There was a dense shrub border at the edge of the lawn, about an arm's length from the spot where Leo was feeding. I asked Karin to creep quietly up to it from the other side. I would cut off a chunk of meat for Leo and, when he wasn't looking, I wanted her to reach out, get a grip on the rest of the carcass and carefully pull it away into the shrub border.

I had to sit on the carcass in order to cut it up. Leo probably thought I wanted to share in the feast, but he didn't mind. I was, after all, his devoted mother who would never allow her cub to go hungry. I saw that he had been chewing on various parts of the carcass, apparently unable to make up his mind where to start. So I cut open the stomach for him, and he took an immediate interest in the entrails. That kept him busy for a while, so I started cutting off a whole hind leg for him.

Soon he became interested in the hind leg I was cutting off and decided to sample it. By the time I finally had the leg free from the rest of the carcass, Leo was happily chewing on it. Karin reached out from her shrub cover behind us and started pulling the rest of the carcass slowly towards her. It was too heavy, however, and I had to lend a helping hand. Very slowly we pulled the carcass towards the shrubs. Leo turned his head to contemplate its altered position, then looked at me with an expression that seemed to say, 'It's OK. Have some if you want it.'

So we pulled the carcass away. Together we lifted it onto a wheelbarrow and wheeled it to Leo's kitchen. The soldiers came over and helped us hang it inside.

Leo didn't seem to mind that a big part of the carcass had gone missing. His tummy was already so full that breathing was becoming difficult.

Until he was a year old, Leo's fare had consisted mostly of impala, chicken and the odd antelope that had to be destroyed. On 28 November, which we presumed to be Leo's birthday, the park veterinarians asked Kobus to shoot a buffalo for them – they needed to do a spot check for tuberculosis on a certain herd in the area. And so Leo got his first taste of buffalo meat as a birthday present.

A buffalo is an incredibly big animal. We saw that only about a third of the meat would fit into the freezer, so we donated the rest of it to the local game guards and camp staff.

Being so large, the carcass couldn't be accommodated in Leo's kitchen, so it was hung on an iron hook from a high branch of the mkuhlu tree in the barbecue area. Leo looked on wonderingly as Kobus and the game guards hoisted the enormous carcass into the tree.

We didn't usually skin carcasses but cut them into lion-size chunks, leaving the skin on so that Leo would have a fully balanced lion diet. On this day, however, the part of the carcass that would go to the staff village had to be skinned.

Leo watched the skinning and cutting-up procedure with keen interest. He wasn't sure whether the buffalo belonged to Kobus or to the game guards but, whichever, he accepted that it wasn't his, and so he was a very well-behaved spectator. Eventually Kobus offered him the entrails. Leo gratefully accepted the generous gift, dashing off to a far corner of the garden where he could enjoy his feast in solitude.

They were the best entrails he had ever tasted, so after devouring them he went back to watch the proceedings – just in case another handout might be considered.

Kobus offered him a chunk of liver, and Leo accepted with much gratitude. A while later he returned again – just in case.

By the end of the day his stomach was practically dragging on the ground. And so he was a very full and happy lion on his first birthday.

Early the next morning, Leo saw that a large piece of the buffalo skin was hanging from a low branch of the mkuhlu tree. It was within easy reach for a lion – but to whom did it belong? Dashing over to Kobus's office, Leo called to him: 'Auh-wuh! Auh-wuh!'

Kobus came out of the office to see what Leo wanted.

Leo led him to the tree and showed him the skin.

'You want the skin?' Kobus asked.

Leo rubbed his body against Kobus's legs, uttering soft, pleading grunts.

'OK,' said Kobus. 'You're such a good boy. You may have it.' He reached up, pulled the skin down and handed it to Leo.

Leo's heart almost burst with happiness. He spent the rest of that day and most of the following week dragging the buffalo skin all over the garden, wrestling with it, rolling on it, sitting on it and parading it to anyone who happened to come along.

We wondered why the buffalo skin made him so happy. Was he playing a game of make-believe, pretending to himself and everyone else that he had killed the buffalo single-handedly? He certainly acted like someone parading a trophy. We all played along, pretending to believe him. Only Wolfie refused to be taken in by Leo's preposterous story.

At the age of one year, Leo's large, rust-coloured eyes were still his most captivating feature. Expressive and intelligent, they revealed his moods, his thoughts and even his questions so effectively that I never doubted what he was telling or asking me when he looked at me.

It was only when Leo looked at the sky – which he often did – that I didn't know what he was thinking.

Curious to know what he was seeing, I would look up myself. And I would spot a bird, usually far, far above, circling lazily in the great blue yonder. It was obvious that Leo had exceptional vision. But why did he study the heavens like that? Did wild lions do that too?

Sometimes I would ask him: 'Leo, what do you think of when you look at the sky like that?'

He would turn to me and, concentrating his gaze on me with love and trust, would seem to say: 'I am only dreaming – the same as you do sometimes.'

And I would find myself reacting with mixed-up feelings of wonder, joy and sadness at the knowledge that such an exquisite bond was possible between a human and a lion.

SANDRA'S WEDDING

A FEW MONTHS AFTER PAUL AND SANDRA FIRST STARTED DATING, they made the astonishing discovery that Paul's mother and I had been room-mates at university. She and I had lost contact shortly after we had both married and moved away to far places. I didn't even know that she had a son named Paul, nor did she know that I had a daughter named Sandra.

And – this sounds almost like a fairy tale – Paul's mother's name is Sandra. I had named my second daughter after my erstwhile best friend.

Naturally she and I were both bowled over by our children's discovery. Shortly after, she drove all the way from Lichtenburg in the Northwest Province to look me up.

The renewal of our friendship was such a success that we decided to have a proper family get-together as soon as possible.

Paul and Sandra had both started their university careers as medical students, but after completing two years of medical studies they had each decided to change their courses – Paul to veterinary science and Sandra to nutritional science. Although their two years of medical training gave them some discount on their altered courses, several years of study still lay ahead for both of them. Neither wanted to wait that long before getting married and so they consulted us, asking if we would give them permission to marry at the end of their third university year. Naturally we gave our permission – and our blessing.

So when Paul's family arrived for the promised visit in July 1993 we celebrated the engagement.

The wedding date was set for 11 December.

The children decided they would like a simple, small, rural-style wedding. Paul suggested that it be held in our garden. Kobus agreed that a garden wedding was a wonderful idea. But Sandra (junior) said that she didn't fancy being pounced on by a lion in the middle of the ceremony. Paul promised that he would protect her with his water-pistol. But Sandra said no, that would look too silly for words and, anyway, she wouldn't like Leo to pounce on any of the guests during the ceremony either. Hettie reminded us that Paul's father was a medical doctor and casualties could be treated on the spot but even so, she said, a garden wedding probably wouldn't be practical. There was the cobra to think of as well.

I also sided with Sandra. I wouldn't want our guests to be looking over their shoulders, worrying about the whereabouts of the lion instead of paying attention to the sermon.

And so it was settled that the two of them would get married in the quaint little stone church in Komatipoort.

The sugar-cane farmers across the river owned a community hall on the south bank of the Crocodile River, and we asked them if we might hire it for the reception. The farmers generously offered to let us use it free of charge. The hall was set in a beautiful garden surrounded by bushlands and had a magnificent view of the river and the park beyond it.

Sandra and Paul made their own invitation cards, sending them to relatives and close friends. All in all, we expected between fifty and sixty guests. My good friend Annette offered to bake the wedding cake, supply the flowers and turn the reception hall into fairyland with the assistance of her sister, Lien, who had a magic touch with flowers.

The church ceremony was scheduled for five in the afternoon and the reception for about an hour later.

We held a family meeting to discuss the menu and decided on barbecued meat, mixed salads, home-baked bread (which Paul's mother graciously offered to supply) and chocolate trifle for dessert. Paul's father kindly offered to provide the drinks.

Sandra would make the pudding. Hettie and Karin would prepare the salads on the morning of the wedding. My task was to make the wedding dress.

I didn't really like sewing and I wasn't good at it. I did it only because I had three daughters and because a game ranger's salary wasn't big enough to allow for a clothes budget. Fortunately Sandra's taste was pure and simple to the point of austerity. So the pattern she designed for her wedding dress was actually quite straightforward. Even so, it took me ages and a good deal of agony to get the dress made. I so much wanted it to be perfect.

The preparations for the wedding started in earnest at the beginning of December.

Everything went smoothly until two days before the wedding.

Then everything went less smoothly.

The mercury rose to 44 degrees Celsius in the shade. I couldn't get on with my sewing as my hands were slippery with perspiration and I was terrified it would leave stains on the satin. The wedding dress was almost finished, but not quite. I decided to wait until dark and continue in the cool of the night.

I still had nothing to wear to the wedding myself. But fortunately my mother had once given me a whole trunk full of pretty dresses that she had owned when she was young. So I unpacked the trunk and found a beautiful dark-blue dress in a sheer, silky fabric. It had long sleeves and a high collar – which wouldn't do in the suffocating heat. But that was no problem. I would cut off the sleeves and the collar, make a few small alterations and *voilà*!

Hettie found a lilac-coloured dress of soft sateen in the trunk and decided it would be her outfit for the wedding. She looked stunning in it, the pale lilac setting off her silky blond hair and blue eyes. Karin tried on some of the stuff in the trunk, but eventually decided that at her age (sixteen) she looked a little incongruous in such old-fashioned outfits. So she drew all her birthday money from her savings account and bought herself a short, white chiffon skirt with a dark blue silky linen top. It was the first outfit she had ever bought herself (all her clothes were either inherited or home-made). She looked striking in it and I was very proud of her taste.

All my daughters were going to look so beautiful at the wedding – the very thought of it brought tears to my eyes. We had never before, as a family, all dressed up like this for an occasion.

I waited for nightfall to get back to my sewing. Apart from the final touches to Sandra's dress, there were still the alterations to be made to my own outfit.

Then a sudden thunderstorm just before dark brought a terrific gale that upended a large coral tree in the garden. It crashed into the power lines, cutting off our electricity! I couldn't go on with my sewing.

Kobus and the game guards spent most of the next day sawing the fallen tree into transportable chunks and carting them off.

Just before noon the power supply was finally turned on again and by that time the mercury had once again risen above 40 degrees Celsius. Paul's parents, two brothers, sister and sister-in-law arrived at midday and Leo tried to pounce on all of them, so we had our hands full.

At two in the afternoon a BBC film crew arrived. They were filming for a programme called *The Really Wild Show*. The director, Joanna Sarsby, had phoned us all the way from London a few days earlier, asking permission to film our cub for their documentary. Kobus had told her that we were anxious not to expose our lion to publicity for various reasons, one of them being that hand-rearing a lion in the park was a sensitive issue. Joanna explained that the theme of the programme was in fact a debate on the issue of hand-rearing wild lions and whether they should be reintroduced to the wild or whether suitable alternative homes should be found for them. She added that the programme would be screened only in England.

Kobus nevertheless asked her to contact the park warden first and seek his permission. She did this, and permission was granted. So she called again and asked if she and her crew could come on 10 December, the day before Sandra's wedding. Unfortunately no other date suited them, but they promised not to keep us more than two hours at the most.

Naturally we were curious to know how these people had learned about our lion. It turned out that Joanna had heard from a friend, who had heard from a colleague, who had heard from Gareth Patterson. (Gareth Patterson is the young Englishman who worked with George Adamson in Kenya shortly before Adamson's death at the hand of poachers, and who adopted Adamson's orphaned lion cubs and moved them to a safe place in Botswana. Renowned for his understanding and love of lions and for his dedication to the protection of wildlife, he is known in Africa as 'the Lion Man'.)

I wondered how Gareth Patterson knew about our lion.

The answer came that same afternoon.

I received a telephone call, and was immediately entranced by the caller's British accent and the melodious inflection of his speech. When he said he was Gareth Patterson, I was astonished. I said that we had been wondering how to contact him but that, quite frankly, we hadn't thought it possible to make contact with a mythical person who lived somewhere in the wilds of Botswana.

Gareth told me he was calling from Pretoria and that he had just been interviewed by the same BBC crew who were on their way to us. He explained that he had heard about our lion from an acquaintance, who had heard from a friend, who, on a recent visit to Kruger Park, had met a game ranger who had mentioned our lion.

This is how news travels in Africa.

The reason for his call, Gareth said, was to enquire about our future plans for Leo. I told him that that was the very reason why we had been hoping to contact him – to discuss Leo's future. We needed help. Gareth said he was on his way back to Botswana right then, but promised to contact us again early in the new year.

Now to get back to the day before the wedding.

As soon as the film crew arrived, Leo turned into a mischievous monster.

He stalked and caught each one of the four crew members while Kobus and I were trying to introduce ourselves to them. They had just come from Letaba Ranch, a ranger's outpost in the north of Gazankulu where they had filmed three other hand-reared lions – lazy, well-behaved adult lions who were kept in a large fenced-in camp near the ranger's house. The crew were surprised (or perhaps horrified) to find that our lion not only roamed free, but also behaved abominably. While we were trying to explain the 'rules' to them – don't bend over, don't crouch, never run away, stay together in a group and avoid eye contact – they were breaking more or less all the rules. So Leo had a field day. Joanna saw him coming at her and tried to run, but he caught her around the waist and wrestled her to the ground. While Kobus was rescuing Joanna, the sound man was bending over his equipment, so Leo charged straight at him and chomped his behind. The cameraman, setting up his camera, was also bending over, and he got a chomp in the rear plus a toppling shove.

Paul's family wisely stayed indoors, watching the goings-on through the windows. When Paul saw that Kobus and I were having a really hard time trying to control Leo, he came out to help. The moment Leo spotted his favourite brother, he charged straight at him. Paul, being an accomplished athlete, dashed round the house, Leo hot on his heels. When they turned the last corner and came into sight again, Leo caught up with Paul and pulled his shorts off, exposing his green underwear. The cameraman was happily impressed. But Paul had had enough. He was camera-shy anyway and not at all anxious to appear on British TV in green undergarments, so he fled back into the house.

Meanwhile Leo disappeared into the flowerbed, emerging a few seconds later as a yellow blur and landing on top of me. I fell flat on my back, and as Leo sat down on me to prevent me from getting up, the cameraman swung his lens at me. I felt so angry I could have murdered Leo, but I didn't want the British visitors to know this, nor did I want them to realize that I had no control over the lion. They probably wouldn't believe me if I told them that Leo had never been as naughty as this in his whole life. Kobus pulled Leo off me and gave him a smack on the bottom plus a piece of his mind in Afrikaans.

Joanna wanted the narrator, Chris, to interview Kobus and me. But each time Chris approached Kobus, microphone in hand, Leo pounced on one or the other of them. Eventually Kobus wrestled Leo down and, while pinning him to the ground, managed to say a few words into the microphone.

Chris started the interview by saying: 'Kobus, now this is not a domestic pet. Surely a little blood gets drawn now and again?'

As if on cue, Leo struggled free from Kobus's grip. Kobus had started replying: 'Uh, yes, Chris, but—' Before Kobus was able to finish the sentence, Chris was flat on his back, Leo on top of him, and Kobus was rushing to rescue Chris from the lion who seemed intent on proving to the narrator that he most certainly was *not* a domestic pet.

At least the cameraman, when he wasn't being attacked himself, got some highly interesting footage of our 'riotous' pet – as Joanna called him.

Joanna said she would like to film some footage of Leo playing with our daughters. So Hettie and Karin came outside but told Sandra to stay safely indoors. They knew that Leo was in an impossible mood, and they didn't think it would be a good idea for their sister to walk down the aisle on her wedding day covered in lion scratches.

Hettie and Karin tried to placate Leo, but Leo pounced on Karin and brought her crashing to the ground. She tried to get up but Leo was being far too rough with her. I told the cameraman to cut and was about to rush to Karin's aid, but Paul came charging out of the house with his water-pistol and, after pulling Leo off Karin, he squirted the lion full in the face. The cameraman again swung his camera into action, but Paul didn't want to be seen on British television shooting a lion with a water-pistol, so he dashed round the house, out of sight of the lens, with Leo hot on his heels. He kept Leo busy until both of them were exhausted and Leo flopped down on the grass for a rest. I was so grateful to Paul for his help.

While Leo was resting, Chris finally managed to interview Kobus and me. It didn't go well for me though, as I was feeling thoroughly beaten up and probably looking too awful for words with my hair and clothes soaked with perspiration. Hardly able to think coherently, I described Leo as 'a very gentle and affectionate animal'. Surely no-one would believe that when they saw the visuals.

The crew left at about five o'clock that afternoon, and Leo immediately turned into a well-behaved lion.

Perhaps his outrageous behaviour had been his way of telling strangers with cameras that he wanted to be taken seriously.

Fortunately Leo didn't seem to feel patronized by Paul's family, and since they all adhered to the 'rules' he left them alone.

Late that evening, after everyone had gone to bed, I tackled my sewing again. I finished Sandra's dress at about midnight, and mine an hour or so later.

When I finally went to bed, utterly exhausted, I realized that the guests would start arriving in the morning, and although we had booked chalets for them in the tourist camp, they would probably want to come over to the house to say hello.

I wasn't looking forward to another day of trying to protect visitors from Leo. Kobus would be away most of the morning, transporting the food, drinks, ice, cutlery and so on to the reception hall and getting the fires started for the barbecue. Paul would be helping him and setting up the music system in the hall. And I myself had about a million things to do before the church ceremony at five in the afternoon. So I devised a plan to immobilize Leo.

I got up at dawn that morning, went out to Leo's kitchen and removed about fifteen kilograms of buffalo meat from the freezer, adding it to the five-kilogram portion that I had removed the previous day. Leo usually got his daily meal in the evening, but I had other plans for him on this day.

So I called him and offered him the thawed portion for breakfast. Then I carried the frozen pieces to the veranda and placed them in front of an east-facing window where the heat of the sun would soon thaw them.

At nine o'clock I called Leo for a second breakfast, offering him a chunk of meat that was almost thawed but not quite. Leo, although surprised at receiving yet another unscheduled meal, didn't mind at all and happily carried the piece off in his mouth.

A while later I noticed him puzzling over the coldness of his food. He pawed it and frowned at it. Eventually he turned it over. No good. It was still cold. He tossed it in the air, and when it landed he inspected it hopefully. Still no good. It was as cold as it had been at take-off. Then he sat on it. That may seem like a brilliant move to you. But Leo often sat on things – including us – when he wasn't sure what to do next, and I believe the reason he sat on the meat was to prevent it from running away while he tried to think things through. Anyway, it helped speed up the thawing and he was soon able to enjoy his extra meal.

At ten o'clock I offered him the rest of the meat. And by eleven o'clock, when the first of our visitors arrived, his tummy was so full that it was difficult for him to move. So he flopped down next to his outsized tummy and spent the rest of the day in a horizontal position. Naturally, our visitors were terrified of the lion and gave him a wide berth. But as soon as they realized that he was comatose, they fetched their cameras and took dozens of pictures of the serene, fat lion.

*

Organizing a wedding is an enormous task that has a way of multiplying and breeding new, small tasks all the time. My family and I worked very hard until about an hour before the ceremony.

By the time I finally found myself sitting in the church, I was so tired that I could hardly think straight. But as soon as the entrancing strains of Wagner's *Lohengrin* filled the church and Sandra came walking in on her father's arm, a surge of exhilaration swept my fatigue into oblivion. With her shiny red hair and radiant smile, Sandra was the most beautiful bride I had ever seen. And Kobus, in a dark suit, looked so handsome that I almost cried. I hadn't seen him in a suit for ages and ages. Karin, who had never seen her father in a suit in her whole life, thought for a moment there had been some mistake. Wasn't he supposed to be in khaki uniform?

The sermon was both stirring and amusing, its theme being that faith and love inspire courage and determination. To prove his point, the minister indicated the groom and reminded us that this young man had succeeded in winning the hand of a game ranger's daughter. 'A game ranger,' said the minister, 'who is reputed to be fiercely protective of his daughters and who also owns a lion.'

(Personally, I didn't believe it was prayers or passion that gave the young man his courage: it was his water-pistol.)

When we came to the part where the rings were to be exchanged, my sister's teenage son, Kobus Frick, stepped up to the couple with his violin and played Andrew Lloyd Webber's beautiful song 'Love Changes Everything' for them. (I learned later that it was Hettie who had secretly arranged for her cousin to provide this glamorous touch.) The young virtuoso performed the melody with an exalting grace that turned it to pure magic. Paul's mother touched my hand to let me know how moved she was, and as I turned my head to smile at her, I caught a glimpse of Paul's father beside her – with a tear spilling down his cheek.

After the ceremony, everybody got into their cars and followed us north out of Komatipoort to the reception hall in the heart of the bush.

Annette and her sister Lien had indeed transformed the hall into a fairyland. Blue and green tablecloths, dozens of blue and green candles, blue and green balloons, and masses of foliage and flowers everywhere. The abundance of blues and greens created a cool, forest ambience – which was just what we needed in the heat.

As soon as all the guests had been seated, Paul's oldest brother proposed a toast to the couple, and then Paul made a nice, short speech to thank and welcome everyone. Afterwards, the guests carried their drinks outside into the garden to admire the magical bushveld sunset and to enjoy the aroma of the meat roasting on the fires. A soft breeze rolled down from the Lebombo Mountains and stirred the trees, bringing sweet respite from the day's heat. On the far bank of the river, a family of warthogs was enjoying a mud bath, and a lone fish eagle swooped low over the bush, its piercing calls echoing through the landscape. From the wooded hills to the west of the river, the stirring cry of a jackal rose, and birds everywhere performed their end-of-day songs. The sun disappeared behind the hills in a blaze of carmine and magenta. Dusk settled, and the sweet, quavering call of a nightjar started the evening serenade.

Lowveld (bushveld) air is richer in oxygen than other air. And the more oxygen humans breathe, the hungrier they get. I don't know why. They just do.

As soon as the meat was done, the highly oxygenated guests dashed for the serving tables and stacked their plates with heaps of home-made bread, spicy barbecued meat and a variety of delicious salads. After second and third helpings, some were groaning with indulgence fatigue, but they nevertheless helped themselves generously to Sandra's exquisite chocolate trifle.

When everyone was full and happy, Paul and his brothers moved the tables and chairs from the hall to the patio outside. A cassette player was switched on and dance music spilled through loudspeakers into the hall.

Paul and Sandra opened the dancing with extraordinary style, gliding across the floor in perfect rhythm to the music, in perfect harmony with each other, and somehow combining grace with abandon. I was fascinated. Where did they learn to dance like that, this astonishingly handsome couple?

The rest of the young people joined in, and a striking young girl caught my eye – slender and graceful with silky golden hair and . . . ah! I knew that face! Hettie!

Then a gay, tinkling laugh drew my attention to another incredibly lovely girl – it was Karin!

Now where, I wondered, did I get such beautiful children?

More people joined in the dancing, and the smiling faces of friends and relatives floated by – my brother, my sister, their lovely families, Paul's delightful parents, my good friend Annette, my gracious in-laws . . . all these charming, wonderful people, come from afar to celebrate my daughter's wedding, dancing in this forest fairyland of music and magic.

Amazing.

How did all this happen?

A tall, handsome guy came over and asked me to dance.

'Do I know you?' I asked him.

'I hope so,' he replied. 'I'm your husband.'

'Ah, yes!' I said. 'The fierce game ranger with the lion? You are not so easy to recognize tonight, you know. The suit disguises you.'

We danced and talked and laughed, and our hearts were young and gay.

We helped ourselves to wedding cake and coffee on the patio, gazed at a million stars and enjoyed the feel of the velvet night.

Then we danced some more in celebration of all that was good: the wedding, the beautiful night, life, the universe and everything.

MOVING WEST

DURING OUR THREE-YEAR STAY AT CROCODILE BRIDGE, KOBUS managed to engage the co-operation of Mozambican government officials in the campaign against poachers, and by the end of 1993 the poaching problem on our eastern boundary had been dramatically reduced. So the director of nature conservation decided to transfer us to Pretorius Kop, a ranger station in the south-west region of the park.

I wasn't sure how I felt about the transfer.

Despite all the madness of life at Crocodile Bridge, there were things that I liked about the place and that I would miss – the enchanting landscapes at the foot of the Lebombo Mountains, for instance, and the abundant variety of wildlife in the area. And, of course, our beautiful subtropical garden. Naturally I would not miss the hysterical telephone. Or the bats. And it occurred to me that, actually, I wouldn't miss the beautiful garden too much either. There were times, especially in the rainy season, when everything grew too fast and too furiously, choking up the garden and making me claustrophobic. I like open landscapes where you can see far and wide. Our garden often got so dense and overgrown that you could see only as far as the nearest view-blocking profusion of foliage. We kept pruning and chopping things back to keep them out of our way, but the pruning only inspired more aggressive growth. It worried me sometimes that the wild tangles of vegetation appeared to be groping at me. One day the trailing stems of a delicious monster actually caught me round the throat and tried to strangle me.

The two things that I would miss most about Crocodile Bridge were, strangely enough, two people: my phantom neighbour Ilse and my trouble-sharing friend Annette. Apparently I had become a slightly altered version of my former self who had lived so happily in isolation at Mahlangeni.

Annette and I would still be able to visit each other, of course, but Pretorius Kop was almost a hundred kilometres from Lower Sabie. We wouldn't be able to meet very often.

We moved in January 1994, about four weeks after Sandra's wedding.

All in all, saying goodbye to Crocodile Bridge wasn't too hard. There had been plenty of good times and exuberant moments but, in the greater scheme of things, my heart still belonged to Mahlangeni.

On the day that the furniture truck arrived, I again fed Leo into a horizontal state to prevent him from bothering the furniture movers.

The game guards all came over to say goodbye to Leo, and it was obvious that they would miss their feline friend. Kobus took photographs of each one of them posing with Leo, and promised to send them as soon as the film was developed.

All our children were on holiday in the Eastern Cape, so Kobus and I moved alone with Wolfie and Leo. We left in the evening to avoid encountering tourists on the road. (They wouldn't understand why we had a lion and a dog together on the back of the truck.)

It was a difficult journey. Leo insisted on travelling in regal style on the roof of the cab, his front paws dangling over the top of the windscreen and his tail hanging past the back window.

There were numerous creeks along the way, and each time the road dipped down a steep bank, Leo started sliding off the roof and across the windscreen. I would thrust my arm out through the back window, grab hold of his tail and hang on with all my weight to prevent him from falling off. When driving up a bank, Leo would clutch the mounting of the roof aerial for support. We worried that the aerial would snap so we ordered Leo to get off the roof, but he wouldn't listen.

Eventually the journey in the dark began triggering his predatory instincts. Every time we spotted eyes alongside the road, he jumped off the truck – from the roof onto the bonnet and then onto the track right in front of us – and Kobus would have to slam on the brakes to avoid colliding with him. Leo then disappeared into the darkness and we had no choice but to wait patiently for him to return from his explorations. Calling didn't help – he was in an arrogant mood. And we didn't want to risk sending Wolfie after him. Dogs were easy prey for nocturnal predators.

At Mitomeni Creek we encountered two cheetahs alongside the road, and Leo promptly jumped off the truck again. He'd never met a cheetah in person before and was eager to make their acquaintance. But the shy cats took one look at the king and fled.

So Leo ran after them.

We waited . . . and waited . . . and waited . . .

When he finally came back about twenty minutes later, Kobus ordered him to get on the truck and to stay there, or else.

But believe me, there is nothing much that one can do about a difficult passenger who happens to be a lion.

Pretorius Kop was about two and a half hours' drive from Crocodile Bridge, but Leo's antics kept us on the road for more than four hours, so we arrived very late that night. The chief game guard at Pretorius Kop, Sergeant Sambo, had been waiting for us, and as we pulled up at the gate of our new home, he opened it for us, saluting smartly. We got out of the truck to shake hands with the sergeant and thank him for waiting up. Leo and Wolfie jumped off the truck, but Leo took one look (or one smell) at the new house and decided it wasn't a safe place for a lion, so he jumped straight back onto the truck.

Sergeant Sambo had heard about our lion, and although he kept a respectful distance, he realized right away that Leo wasn't a very brave fellow.

He informed us that the camp manager, Pieter du Plessis, had heard that our furniture truck would not be arriving until the next day, so Pieter had sent over two beds together with bedding and towels for us. We thanked the sergeant, and after Kobus had discussed arrangements for the following day with him, we bade him goodnight.

Clever Wolfie caught on immediately that this place was to be our new home. So he got right down to the business of marking things that needed to be marked.

But Leo remained timidly on the truck, all his earlier arrogance forgotten.

'Come on, Leo,' I said to him. 'Don't be a baby. Come and explore your new home!'

He looked at me with a perplexed expression that seemed to say, 'This place smells of strange humans and dogs. I'm scared of them.'

'They've left,' I told him. 'It's only their smell that's still around. It will go away eventually.'

Leo didn't know whether to believe me or not.

'Trust me, Leo,' I said. 'It's our place now.'

He jumped off the truck and ran straight to Wolfie, almost colliding with him. And for the rest of the night and all of the following day he would not leave Wolfie's side. He obviously trusted his friend to protect him from dangerous aliens, even though his friend weighed about a hundred kilograms less than he did.

The night air was crisp and fragrant and full of cricket concerts and frog serenades. We followed a paved path that led through the dark garden to the house.

Opening the front door we stepped into a spacious lounge. Every room in the house was huge. But what delighted us most was the distinct absence of bats. Never again would we have to duck their idiotic crash landings. All the rooms had large windows that opened directly onto the outside world. We looked forward to having the daylight streaming into the house, and to not falling over things in dark rooms any more.

Wolfie knocked at the front door. He wanted to see what the house looked like inside. So we invited him and Leo in for a quick tour of the empty house. Wolfie gave every room a thorough sniffing-over, but Leo didn't trust the strange human smells in the house and concentrated only on staying close to the dog.

Afterwards I fetched their sleeping mats from the truck and spread them on the front patio. Leo was so relieved at the sight and smell of his familiar mat that he immediately sat down on it to prevent it from going away. But Wolfie was in no mood for sitting around – the whole of the garden still needed to be inspected. So off he went. Leo called Wolfie to come back, but Wolfie paid him no attention. It occurred to Leo that Wolfie would probably be a better bodyguard than his mat, so he leaped up and ran after him.

Kobus and I had the sandwiches and coffee I had packed for us, took a shower and went straight to bed. It had been a long day.

But despite my exhaustion I was unable to fall asleep. I lay watching the stars and the dark silhouettes of trees through the bedroom windows, wondering what the place would look like in daylight.

A barn owl called out from a tall palm tree in front of the bedroom. Soon another answered. I loved the call of barn owls. They reminded

me of forsaken places inhabited by nothing but the wind, the moon, the stars and barn owls.

Finally the hypnotic strains of distant frog concerts made me sleepy, but as I was about to drift off, I heard the most fascinating meowing call. I couldn't imagine what it was, so I woke Kobus to ask him.

We lay quietly for a while, listening. The strange meowing call rose again, and was answered by another.

'Genets,' Kobus told me.

Genets! I was thrilled. They were dainty, shy creatures that looked like a cross between a domestic cat and a mongoose. I didn't know they had such exquisite voices.

I got up and stuck my head out through the window. And as I listened to the sweet, plaintive calls, it gave me great pleasure to be welcomed to my new home by a genet serenade.

At dawn the next morning I dashed outside to see if the sun was going to rise in the right place. It seemed strange not to have a river in front of the house, and for a moment I felt lost. But I remembered the route that we had travelled the previous day – first west, then north-west, then north. And some inner feeling told me that east should be behind me and somewhat to my right. So I turned, and in the dusky gloom I could make out a wide, wooded valley. And right above its horizon a splash of tangerine streaked the sky.

A wave of relief swept over me.

After three years of confusion, the sun was finally back in its proper place.

ENCHANTED DAYS

THE CAMP AT PRETORIUS KOP IS ONE OF THE OLDEST AND LOVELIEST in the park. It has over a hundred chalets scattered attractively among magnificent trees and dapple-shaded lawns. Wild flowers and songbirds are in abundance, and busy little vervet monkeys are often seen scrambling along the fences.

The surrounding countryside is verdant and beautiful. In summer the tamboekie grass is tall, and the sickle-bush, marula and kiaat trees in splendid leaf. In springtime the coral trees are laden with blood-red flowers, the wild pears with snow-white blossoms and the tree wistarias with pendant sprays of sky-blue blooms.

One of the dominant tree species in the region is the silver cluster-leaf. Its branches form lovely patterns, often growing out horizontally from the trunk and drooping at the ends. The long, silver-grey leaves are borne in bunches on slender twigs. These graceful trees grow in abundance in sandy areas and on the slopes of valleys. In midsummer, when the trees are laden with clusters of pink fruit, the trees are no longer merely silver, but both pink and silver.

Also unique to the Pretorius Kop region are the granite koppies that thrust up from the wooded plains. Their rocky slopes are draped with flame creepers, bauhinia and honeysuckle, while rock figs send out long roots that hug the boulders and penetrate the fissures. The koppies have lovely Tsonga names: Shabeni, Manungu, Shitungwane, Matupa, Mlaleni.

*

Our sandy-pink house was the shape of a barn, square and plain from the outside but attractive and sunny inside with its abundance of large windows that opened into the wooded garden of almost two acres. The garden didn't have the subtropical character of the Crocodile Bridge garden – it was more spacious and open, and the vegetation didn't look so aggressive. The front garden faced north into a marula wood. To the east was a valley of silver cluster-leaf trees, and to the west a stretch of mixed bushwillow, marula and acacia bushlands. A dirt track ran along the outside of the south fence. Directly across the track were the houses of the two local trail rangers, and beyond them those of the camp manager and other personnel. Adjacent to the staff village was the tourist camp.

Leo spent his first day at our new home pretending to be Wolfie's shadow.

When the local game guard corps came over to meet Kobus, they found an outsize lion trying to hide behind a medium-size dog, so naturally they took him for a retarded lion. But the only reason Leo appeared so timid that day was because he didn't yet know where the boundaries of his safety zone were.

Wolfie, of course, knew exactly where the boundaries were, and so he spent the better part of the day completing his business of marking every fence-post, outbuilding, tree and shrub. Leo trusted Wolfie's superior knowledge in these matters, and so he stayed close to the dog and paid attention.

In the early afternoon, a troop of vervet monkeys scaled the south fence of the garden, advanced across the lawn and climbed up a mango tree. When I saw the interlopers gorging themselves on our mangoes, I went up to the tree and warned them that if they didn't leave right away, I would call my dog. They peered down at me through the foliage and shrieked abuse.

'Listen,' I told them, 'I also have a lion. If you don't leave right this moment, I'll call my dog *and* my lion!'

They didn't believe a word I said and went right on cheeking me.

I turned towards the house and called Wolfie in the tone I use when I need him urgently. The dog and his shadow came tearing round a corner of the house. Wolfie immediately sensed the whereabouts of the intruders and launched himself at the mango tree – followed by his shadow.

For a brief moment all the monkeys were shocked speechless at the sight of the lion. Then they fell out of the tree in unison, screaming their heads off and heading for the fence at breakneck speed. Some of them were too shocked to remember where the fence was and dashed crazily all over the place. Wolfie and Leo had a lot of fun herding the hysterical delinquents out of the garden.

By the end of the day Leo felt confident that the whole garden, as marked by Wolfie, constituted his and his family's new safe haven. So he became more relaxed and stopped crowding the dog. Wolfie was noticeably relieved when the lion finally allowed him more breathing space.

When the game guards turned up early the next morning, they found a more arrogant lion following them through the garden to Kobus's office. They increased their pace, glancing nervously over their shoulders. As Kobus came out of the office to meet them, Leo launched himself at Kobus for a fond hug. Some of the game guards thought for a moment that Leo was attacking Kobus, and they promptly stepped forward in case he needed help.

Kobus was touched by their loyalty, but quickly explained to them that this was Leo's way of greeting him. He then gave them all a thorough lecture on how to control Leo. He warned them never to run away from Leo if he wanted to play but, instead, to stand their ground and to talk Leo out of it with an authoritative tone of voice. He also suggested they carry a stick whenever they entered the garden. (Carrying a stick normally lends an air of authority to one's body language.) Even if you brandished only a puny twig at Leo, and said, 'No, Leo!' he would back off right away.

Though the game guards remained wary of Leo for a while, they soon learned the correct way of controlling him and eventually became quite fond of him.

We had a gardener at Pretorius Kop called Aaron. Leo liked the man, evidently thinking he and Aaron had a lot in common since they were both interested in digging up the soil. He enjoyed following Aaron around to see how he could help. But Aaron didn't appreciate sharing his job with a lion. So one day, when things got a bit out of hand, Aaron grabbed a wheelbarrow and charged Leo with it. Leo got a dreadful shock and ran for his life.

After that he was terrified of the wheelbarrow and wouldn't go near it. And whenever Aaron caught Leo demolishing the flora again, he would get the wheelbarrow and chase the lion with it. Leo would come running to the house, calling for help and uttering streams of complaints about the wheelbarrow. I had to explain to him that wheelbarrows weren't normally aggressive – only when lions got destructive in the garden.

At the edge of the marula woodland, just outside the north fence of the garden, was a small pond where various antelope often came to drink. Initially they were terrified of Leo, but as soon as they realized that he didn't know they were edible they lost their fear of him.

One day a troop of baboons turned up to feast on the ripe marulas in the woodland. As they were gathering the fallen fruit under the trees, Wolfie spotted them and gave a warning bark, probably telling them that he was now the new boss in the area and that his job included keeping baboons out of the garden. The baboons looked up and, seeing the dog, muttered to themselves: 'Goodness, what a serious-looking dog. We'd better stay out of his garden.'

Meanwhile, Leo, who had been enjoying a snooze, woke up wondering what Wolfie was barking about. Getting up, he went to investigate and found the dog standing at the northern fence, keeping a watchful eye on the baboons. So he decided to go over and join him.

One of the baboons, glancing up, saw Leo and screamed: *'Whazat? A lion?'*

In no time the entire troop had dashed up the marula trees, yelling in consternation.

Wolfie gave a few more imperative barks.

Leo only said: 'Huh?'

I was watching them from the veranda, and decided to fetch my camera and take a few pictures of Leo and Wolfie contemplating the baboons.

All the baboons were in the marula trees now, and they were so busy screaming their heads off that they didn't even see me leaving the house and walking to the bottom of the garden. I had a zoom lens on the camera, so I chose a spot some distance away from Leo and Wolfie, hoping to get some nice shots of the way their faces were reflecting their respective thoughts. Wolfie clearly took a dim view of the hysterical clowns, but Leo was having a hard time trying to puzzle out the reason for their behaviour.

After a while some of the baboons began to realize that the lion wasn't really doing anything. He just stood there, gaping at them. Maybe he didn't know how to scale the fence. The idea calmed them somewhat, and soon they got a bit braver, barking defiant battle cries while hopping up and down on the branches. Some of the larger males displayed their power by breaking off small branches and hurling them to the ground.

The war-dancing and power-displaying deepened Leo's puzzlement by several degrees.

Wolfie eventually decided that the sabre-rattling was just too silly for words and that he didn't need to watch it any longer, so he retired to his favourite siesta spot at the side of Kobus's office. Leo gave up trying to fathom what it was all about and flopped down on the grass for a snooze.

The baboon concert went into diminuendo as the war cries changed to nervous chattering. I shut my camera and decided to go back indoors. But then I looked at Leo lying stretched out on his back, and I couldn't resist the urge to go over and give him a big hug.

I forgot that the baboons wouldn't understand what I was doing.

The moment they became aware that I was approaching the lion, there came a murmur of panic and disbelief from the onlookers. What was this stupid primate doing, walking up to a lion? Soon their screams resounded to the heavens. I couldn't tell whether they were trying to warn me or whether they were reacting out of sheer dread, like a crowd of teenagers watching a horror movie.

Leo was still lying stretched out on his back when I reached him, and as I sat down beside him for a hug, a huge front paw reached up and around my neck, pulling my head affectionately to his chest. The baboons got so hysterical that some of them lost their voices and could only whimper. I am sure that a number of them actually shut their eyes to avoid witnessing the sight of me being devoured by the lion.

After a while I started feeling sorry for my distressed audience, so I got to my feet to show them I was still alive. I also waved to them. A number of them just went right on shrieking and whimpering; perhaps their eyes were still closed. Others stopped their screaming and began uttering all kinds of strange sounds, probably telling themselves that surely this was just a bizarre dream – it couldn't possibly happen in real life.

The two trail rangers across the road, Bryan Haveman and Bruce Leslie, soon made friends with Leo and learned how to control him, which was good because they often had to come over to Kobus's office to discuss things with him. But apart from the two trail rangers and the game guards, the rest of our neighbours chose to keep a respectful distance. They often came up to the fence, however, hoping to catch a glimpse of Leo. And Leo, who enjoyed having admirers, would amble over to the fence and graciously grant his fans the pleasure of his royal company.

We didn't want any tourists to know that we had a lion, so we asked all our neighbours not to mention it to anyone in the tourist camp. If people started flocking over to our house to meet the lion, I would constantly have to protect visitors from Leo. Although most people are thoughtful and intelligent beings, there is always the odd one who does strange things and who might not realize that even a tame lion can be a very dangerous animal. And it goes without saying that, unless you are intimately acquainted with lions and know how to control them, you shouldn't try to play with them. You might end up dead.

Hiding Leo from tourists wasn't always easy, though.

Whenever Kobus wasn't home by dusk, Leo would sit at the gate, calling for him. Although his voice wasn't capable of a full-volume roar yet, his calls could be heard over quite a distance, and certainly in the tourist camp. Fearful that tourists might get curious about the calls, I would rush outside and try to persuade Leo to do something else. Fortunately, tourists who heard Leo calling never seemed to realize exactly where the calls came from. They probably thought they were listening to a wild lion calling somewhere in the bush.

The roads in the area presented us with another problem: the patrol tracks and tourist roads sometimes crossed each other, making it difficult for us to avoid being seen by tourists when taking Leo and Wolfie for a drive. Usually tourists would drive right past us before actually registering that there was a lion on the back of the truck. As soon as they did, they would slam their brakes on and reverse at top speed, hoping to get another glimpse of us.

Occasionally people would report the unusual sighting to the tourism official on duty at the camp. And the good officer, wishing to protect us from public curiosity, would tell them that he knew nothing of such a lion and that he had no idea why it would be travelling on the back of a truck.

A baffled tourist once reported to the officer that he'd spotted a lion and a dog together on the back of a game ranger's vehicle, and he wanted to know how it could have happened. Had the lion jumped onto the truck as it passed? And, if so, why didn't it eat the dog?

The silver cluster-leaf valley to the east of our house became my favourite area for walking Leo and Wolfie. Though there were no tourist roads in the valley, there was one at the top of the far rim, so I always took care to turn back before we reached it.

But one day, just as we'd almost reached the far crest and were about to turn back, Leo spotted something, and off he went to investigate – straight towards the tourist road and the sound of an approaching car. Fearful that he might get run over, I ran after him, calling him to come back. I estimated the road to be about another forty or fifty metres away, but I miscalculated.

Leo had just crossed the road, chasing after a herd of zebra, and the delighted tourists slammed on their brakes to admire the lion – when stupid me came charging out of the thickets and across the road right in front of them, yelling at the lion to come back. When I realized my predicament, it was too late to do anything about it, so I just carried on running and disappeared into the bush at the other side of the road, praying that the people would not believe what they'd seen.

Fortunately they never reported me. Perhaps they thought it had been an illusion. Or maybe they were too shy to report that they'd spotted a lady and a fat dog chasing a lion. Who would believe them?

All in all, our first summer at Pretorius Kop remains in my memory as a time of enchanted days. I loved my new home and its surroundings. And perhaps I also realized the importance of cherishing each magic moment, for my foundling prince was nearing adulthood and I would not be a lion-mother for much longer.

THE LION MAN

GARETH PATTERSON PHONED AGAIN TOWARDS THE END OF February, asking how long Kobus and I wished to keep Leo. I told him that we would like to keep him for ever, but that it was against our park's policy and that we had in fact already received a formal letter from the park warden, enquiring about our future plans for Leo.

Gareth apologized for not contacting us earlier – his work in the Tuli bushlands of Botswana had kept him busy. But Leo would be his first priority now, he said, and he wanted very much to meet him as soon as possible.

So we made a date for a visit.

A few days later I drove to the Skukuza airport. As I stood outside the terminal building, watching the two-engine turbo-prop plane come in, I wondered if I would be able to identify Gareth. I had never met him in person.

Among the thirty-odd passengers who disembarked, there was a young man whose shoulder-length blond hair resembled a lion's mane. He had the easy, graceful gait of one who spends most of his life walking. And while most of the other passengers were looking straight in front of them as they approached the terminal building, the blond-maned young man was gazing out over the surrounding bush. He was dressed in a loose T-shirt, shorts and sandals. His only luggage was a tiny battered suitcase.

I stepped up to him and said, 'Gareth?'

Turning towards me, he smiled hesitantly and asked, 'Leo's mother?'

I nodded and smiled back at him, noting his Anglo-Saxon features and accent.

'How did you recognize me?' he asked.

'How can one not recognize you?' I said.

On the drive back we talked about a thousand things, and by the time we arrived home we were old friends.

As we got out of the car, Wolfie came to meet us. But Leo saw that I was not alone, so he kept his distance.

Gareth nodded a respectful greeting to Wolfie. Naturally Wolfie was impressed with this well-bred young man who had the good grace not to be familiar with him and pat him on the head.

Leo was sitting in a flowerbed at the side of the fishpond (flattening Aaron's violets) and quietly watching us.

'He's very handsome,' Gareth murmured to me.

Apart from giving Leo a brief glance-over, Gareth avoided eye contact with him and paid him no further attention, signifying his respect for Leo's right as a lion to decide the distance between himself and a stranger.

Hettie and Karin, who were both home for the weekend, made us sandwiches and tea, and we carried them out into the garden. Leo came over and flopped down on the grass a little distance from us. Gareth still ignored him. Though Leo pretended he wasn't interested in Gareth either, he was quietly studying him, and probably wondering about this strange human who somehow appeared so familiar.

Later, the four of us, together with Leo and Wolfie, went for a walk down into the valley. As we walked and chatted, I noticed that Gareth habitually studied signs on the ground. When we came across fresh elephant spoor, his gaze automatically went out over the surrounding bush. It was nice to have a visitor who reacted to the bush in the same way that we did.

After we'd walked about a kilometre or so, Leo, who was a few paces ahead of us, suddenly stopped, turned and looked at Gareth. Gareth also stopped and looked at Leo. As Leo approached him, Gareth held out his arm to Leo. Leo inspected and sniffed the outstretched arm. Then he gave it a few friendly licks. Afterwards he briefly rubbed his body against Gareth's legs. It was a formal but warm greeting, and a demonstration of acceptance.

Kobus came home in the late afternoon, and after supper we all took our coffee out into the garden and spent the evening discussing future plans for Leo.

Gareth told us that his initial idea had been to propose introducing Leo into the Tuli bushlands, but he had since decided against it. Apart from the ever-increasing poaching activities in the area, farmers along the boundaries were baiting and hunting lions. So instead of the Tuli, Gareth suggested the Save Valley Conservancy in south-eastern Zimbabwe.

The Save Valley, a vast private conservancy of half a million hectares, was established by a group of local landowners who wanted to re-introduce into the area the whole spectrum of former wild animal species, including lions. One method of lion reintroduction involved removing wild lions from stable populations and releasing them into unfamiliar new territory. This method created stressful conditions for the lions. Gareth had proved that the establishment of lions in reserves could be achieved in a different way: hand-reared orphans and other disadvantaged lions could make the successful transition to independent 'wild' status through processes of rehabilitation.

The Save Valley seemed an ideal area for a project such as this, and so Gareth proposed asking the permission of the landowners' committee to introduce a 'man-made pride' into the conservancy. This pride would consist of Leo and two or three other orphaned, hand-reared lions. If granted permission for the project, Gareth would spend approximately two years with the lions, teaching them to hunt and to survive in the wilderness. As soon as they became self-sufficient and people-disfamiliarized, Gareth would gradually withdraw and disappear from the scene. The man-made pride could then constitute the core pride for future generations of lions in the conservancy.

Gareth's proposal sounded good to us. The fact that the Save Valley had no other lion populations as yet meant that Leo and his orphan pride would not have to compete with other lions for a hunting territory.

We spent the rest of the evening talking about a myriad of shared interests. Gareth was thoughtful, eloquent and well read. His stories about his work and his life in Africa were full of pathos, drama and humour, portraying his deep love for the wilderness and his utter dedication to the conservation of wildlife.

Early the following morning, I found Gareth and Wolfie sharing a seat on the garden bench. Gareth was making notes in a book, while Wolfie just sat there watching over his domain and keeping his new-found friend company.

I was amazed. My serious, aloof dog had actually befriended a stranger!

Leo came over and flopped down on the grass a little distance from Gareth. Gareth made a grunting noise like a lion's greeting call. Leo lifted his head and looked at Gareth with an expression that seemed to say, 'Ah! You talk Lionese, do you? How nice.'

I drove Gareth back to the airport later that day, and was sorry that he couldn't stay with us longer. He promised to keep in touch and let us know as soon as he had news for us from the Save Valley Conservancy.

A MEMORABLE AUTUMN

OUR CHILDREN CAME HOME FOR THEIR AUTUMN BREAK AND WE spent our favourite season doing all the things that one should do when the bush is so bright and beautiful.

First, we all accompanied Kobus on a patrol trip along the Nwaswitshaka Creek. I sat in the cab with Kobus while the rest of the family – Hettie, Paul, Sandra, Karin, Leo and Wolfie – rode on the back of the pick-up.

It was a perfect day with soft blue skies and pastel-coloured landscapes. Even the wild animals looked soft and pastel-coloured.

The Nwaswitshaka snakes its way through woodlands, marshlands and savannahs, covering a distance of more than fifty kilometres before it reaches the Sabie River. It is essentially a seasonal creek but has many perennial pools, so animal traffic in the area is usually heavy. On that perfect autumn day we spotted just about everything – from rare birds to black rhinos.

Actually I'm not too crazy about spotting black rhinos. I prefer white rhinos. They're dim-witted and friendly. Black rhinos are dim-witted and aggressive. The moment a black rhino catches sight of anything that appears alien to him he gets hopping mad. As he hops about, you have no idea whether he is going to charge you or not – he gives no indication of his intentions. Probably the rhino himself has no idea of his intentions either, being so dim-witted. The main problem with a black

rhino charge is that it's impossible to decide which way to flee. Once the rhino starts charging, he's all over the place. He's very myopic, so he rushes blindly in every direction, relying on speed, agility and his ability to change direction every few seconds until he has more or less covered the whole landscape and wiped out everything that needed wiping out.

The best thing to do if ever you should come across a black rhino is make sure he doesn't see you. If he does and gets mad, then press down on the accelerator and get out of the landscape.

But there's no need to panic, really. You should be able to get a head start on him because he takes a while to decipher his intentions.

Fortunately the park has relatively few black rhinos. Unfortunately most of them reside in the Pretorius Kop area.

You needn't worry about white rhinos though. They're so dim-witted and friendly that you can almost pat them on the head as you drive past.

But maybe you shouldn't do that. Because if you mistake a black rhino for a white one, you'll be in *big* trouble.

The difference between a black and a white rhino does not lie in their colouring – they are both greyish. It's mainly their feeding habits and the shape of their mouths. The black rhino is a browser and has an elongated upper lip that overlaps the lower, giving the impression of a pout. The white rhino is a grazer and has a broad, square upper lip that gives the impression of a smile. He got his name by mistake. Originally he was called the 'wide-lipped rhino'. But people got confused and called him a 'white-lipped rhino' – and finally just a 'white rhino'. So when a second kind of rhino was discovered, he got named the 'black rhino'.

He's not black, just a darker shade of grey than the other one. The black rhino is also smaller than the white one. He weighs up to 2000 kilograms, while the white one weighs about 3500 kilograms. But if you're not used to estimating weight at a distance, I guess this infor-mation is not very helpful to you in avoiding black rhinos.

Perhaps you would do better to concentrate on the shape of the mouth – although that may be a bit of a problem if the rhino is facing away from you. Or if it's a white rhino that's pouting instead of smiling.

Or a black rhino that's grimacing instead of pouting. (A black rhino never smiles – if that's of any help to you.)

Anyway, when we spotted the black rhinos on that nice autumn day, I knew they were black rhinos because they were hopping mad. There were three of them, and after hopping about for a while they came charging at us like runaway steamrollers. About halfway towards us they got confused and lost their bearings. So they did an acrobatic about-turn and charged some distance in another direction. But a few moments later they were coming back at us again at full speed – which, for a rhino, is about forty-five kilometres per hour. Kobus had to do some clever manoeuvring with the truck to get out of their way. For a while they stupidly ran alongside us and eventually overtook us. So we slowed down. After a minute or so it dawned on them that they were charging directly away from their target instead of towards it. So they did another about-turn, and as they bore down on us, Kobus had to make another quick swerve to avoid a collision. They charged right past and lost sight of us altogether.

I was very relieved that they didn't come back again. But the rest of my idiotic family thought it had been a lot of fun and hoped that we would encounter more black rhinos along the way.

Fortunately we didn't.

But unfortunately we had a most terrifying experience a short while later that scared not only me almost to death, but the rest of my family as well.

We were driving down the bank of a steep donga. I noticed that the track had partly caved in at the bottom of the donga, and I pointed it out to Kobus. But he told me not to worry. He knew about the washaway and he would manoeuvre the truck around it.

We were halfway down the slope when a herd of elephant appeared from nowhere at the top of the opposite bank and started crossing the track.

I didn't like that at all. There were hundreds of them. Or maybe fifty or so. (Elephants tend to look more than they are.)

'Can't we turn back?' I asked Kobus.

'No,' he said. 'But don't worry. They won't bother us.'

As we reached the bed of the donga, the remaining part of the track caved in, leaving my side of the truck hanging over the edge of the washaway.

For no obvious reason, two elephant cows came tearing down the opposite bank, screaming with fury and heading straight for us.

For the first time in my life I found myself in a dangerous situation where I had absolutely no idea what to do. And there was very little time to do it in. I had no idea what to tell my children to do either. If I told them to jump off the truck and run, the elephants might decide to go for them instead of the truck. If I told them to stay put, they'd be in danger anyway.

Kobus had grabbed his rifle, yanked his door open and jumped out of the cab (in uphill-style as the wheels on his side were suspended in the air). It was too late to load the gun and shoot, so he yelled at the elephants – in a voice so loud that the bush seemed to shudder. My eyes remained fixed on the massive faces of the two cows as they bore down on us. The expression of determination in their eyes terrified me. Masses of adrenaline surged through my system, commanding me to do *something . . .* anything! But what?

The girls were lying flat on their stomachs on the back of the truck, their arms covering their heads. Karin was whimpering with fright – something I had never heard her do in her whole sixteen years of life. Sandra was comforting her younger sister, murmuring, 'It's OK, Karin, it's OK.' Paul was reaching into the cab through the open back window, snatching up the bullet-belt and handing it to Kobus.

All this was happening simultaneously.

My gaze was still fixed on the faces of the two elephants, and Kobus was still yelling at them. They were perhaps fifteen metres from us – about three seconds away from impact – when I saw the expressions in their eyes change from determination to hesitation. They came to a sudden halt. Kobus continued shouting at them at the top of his voice.

After a few moments of indecision the cows turned away from us and headed back up the bank. Kobus quickly checked his rifle's magazine and reached for the bullets that Paul was holding out to him. But before he even had the chance to load, the two elephants had turned around and were coming back at us, ears flat against their skulls, trunks tucked under their chests, silent and with deadly determination. Kobus began to yell at them again.

I could no longer bear to look at their faces. I bent over, putting my head on my knees and folding my arms over my head – the posture for impact. And I was surprised and ashamed to hear myself whimpering. But I was really thinking only of my children.

About eight seconds after I had put my head down I knew that the moment of impact was overdue, so I looked up – straight into the eyes of two elephants whose faces filled my whole field of vision. They had come to a halt. I could see in their eyes that Kobus's thundering voice was unnerving them. They backed off a little and stood contemplating us for a few moments. Kobus, still shouting at them, finally had the chance to load and cock his rifle. Fortunately it wasn't necessary for him to fire. The two cows turned and headed back up the bank to rejoin the rest of the herd. There was something wrong up there – the whole herd was milling about.

But there was no time to wonder about that. Kobus was ordering us to get away from the truck and to flee up the bank behind us. I was unable to get out on my side as it was hanging over the edge of the washaway. So I clambered uphill over Kobus's seat to get out. The children jumped off the back and we all sprinted up the bank. The elephants were screaming and screeching now, but we didn't stop to look back until we'd reached the top of the bank.

It was only then, when we'd reached the relative safety of the crest, that I thought of Wolfie and Leo. When survival is the point at issue, the mind allows no other thoughts to distract it. Perhaps I had known sub-consciously that the dog and the lion would look after themselves, and so my mind had blotted out all thoughts of them.

I saw with relief that Wolfie was with us.

But not Leo.

The idiot was on the far bank, teasing the elephant herd. No wonder they were milling about and screeching with irritation.

The children told us that Leo had jumped off the truck as soon as the two cows had come charging down the bank, but they had no idea what he had done afterwards. Wolfie had apparently jumped off the truck the moment he saw Kobus getting out, and he had remained valiantly at Kobus's side throughout the whole nightmare.

We were all talking and laughing a lot now – we were, of course, drunk on adrenaline.

Actually I was the only one not laughing.

I was too busy sulking.

And I was preparing a speech.

My husband was in for a long lecture.

I noticed that his voice had gone quite hoarse from all the shouting. But that was not going to let him off the hook. As soon as we were alone, he would get his lecture.

Eventually the elephants moved on and our naughty lion came running back to us. He looked at us with an expression that seemed to say, 'I had such a good time. Why didn't you all come over and join in the fun?'

'You're quite mad,' I told him.

After the elephants had left we returned to our bogged-down truck, and everyone pitched in to help lift it back onto terra firma – everyone except me. I was working on my speech.

As soon as we were back on the road again, it was lecture time.

I started off with a reminder that I had warned about the washaway at the bottom of the donga, as well as about the elephants on the far bank, and that my warnings had gone unheeded. Then I talked about parental responsibilities, arguing that, being the mother of all those children and animals in the back, I had the right to be taken seriously if I pointed out a dangerous situation. I added that, regrettably, men in general tended to disregard women's judgements of what constituted danger, and that it was a recognized fact that females possessed a stronger instinct for survival than males. I stressed that if men would trust female intuition more often, they would have a better chance of surviving longer.

I could see that my speech so far had made some impression, and although I hadn't finished it yet, I decided to leave the rest out and to replace it with a long, cold silence.

But a while later we came across a gorgeous honey badger digging furiously for something under a tree stump, and he was so cute that I forgot my vow of silence.

I noticed, however, that my irresponsible husband had a chastened look on his face, so I decided to forgive him.

And a while later I even told him that I was grateful that he possessed such a powerful elephant-deterrent voice.

We spent the rest of the autumn vacation exploring the bushlands and climbing to the tops of all the koppies in the area. Though the koppies were all over the place, they were far apart, so that each of them stood in a beautiful landscape of its own with unrestricted views in all directions. We agreed that sitting on the top of a koppie was the sort of elevating experience that changed one's whole outlook on life.

Kobus and the children would explore the world below with binoculars, counting up their sightings of wild animals and getting competitive about it.

Wolfie, being his usual conscientious self, would go about his duties of patrolling the area and checking out all the signs on the ground.

But Leo and I had an entirely different agenda, one that was in a class of its own. We would sit side by side and do nothing at all – but dream and watch the world go by.

One day near the end of the vacation, Kobus told us about a koppie named Matupa that he'd seen from the air while doing an aerial census. There was something about the koppie, he told us, that fascinated him, and so he wanted to go and explore it from the ground.

Paul, Sandra and Karin were eager to go along, but Hettie had a term paper to finish and as her classes would be starting soon, she decided to stay home and catch up on her work. I also had some work to do, so I opted to stay home with Hettie.

Kobus decided that Wolfie and Leo should stay home as well. The koppie, he explained, consisted of enormous boulders and sheer cliffs, and he didn't think that any animals other than primates would be able to climb to the top.

I warned them all to be careful, and they promised they would.

But they forgot their promise as soon as they arrived at the koppie.

Perhaps, in defence of their forgetfulness, I should mention that Matupa is a strange kind of place. It makes you forget lots of things. The moment you set eyes on it, it commands your attention and absorbs your thoughts. There's something about Matupa that doesn't quite fit in with the normal shape of things in this part of the world. Perhaps Matupa was designed for some other landscape, maybe even for another planet, and got misplaced. But it's not only its design that's peculiar, it has an alien aura as well. It looks sort of wrapped up in its own lost world.

It also looks haunted.

Legend has it that the ghost of a Watusi warrior dwells in Matupa's caves. What a Watusi warrior might have been doing out here in this part of Africa I have no idea, since the Watusi people live about three thousand kilometres to the north of Matupa on a hilly plateau in Burundi. I don't think the warrior ended up here because he got lost. Nobody can get *that* lost. He must have had some mission. Perhaps he came out here in search of the misplaced koppie.

Anyway, they say that when the Watusi ghost plays his drums at night, the reverberating sounds echo upward out of the caves and roll out over the landscape. And on full-moon nights, they say, you can see the lonely warrior standing on Matupa's summit, clutching his spears and staring out over the world below.

Matupa is a collection of several gigantic boulders stacked carelessly together, some of the larger ones balancing precariously on top of smaller ones. A few of the smaller boulders have already cracked under the weight, leaving all kinds of crevices and caves that will one day cause the whole structure to collapse. The west side of Matupa is mostly a vertical granite wall, about sixty or seventy metres high. This wall is in fact the side of a single large boulder. The boulder has a wide, flat summit – and it is on this summit, they say, that the ghost of the Watusi warrior appears on moonlit nights.

The reason I'm describing Matupa to you is to give you some background for the frightful encounter that awaited Kobus and the children on that autumn day when they first went to explore the strange koppie.

Their main agenda, of course, was to find a way to get to the top. Having walked all the way round the koppie searching for climbable boulders, they concluded that the only way up was from the east side. If you climbed carefully up the stacked boulders, watching your step across cracks and crevices, you could reach a ledge that slanted upwards and around the north side of Matupa until, about sixty metres above the ground on the west side of the koppie, the ledge broadened into a small terrace, roughly six metres wide and eight metres long. An oval-shaped rock – probably a broken-off piece of the main boulder – rested on the terrace, near its eastern edge. Directly behind this rock, obscured by tangles of vegetation, was the entrance to a small cave.

Naturally Kobus and the children did not know about the cave at the time.

They reached the terrace from the east side. Paul was in front, carrying the rifle. Sandra and Karin came directly behind him. Kobus was a few metres behind them all – he had stopped to tie a bootlace that had come undone. Paul and the girls stopped at the oval rock and decided to split up and walk around either side of it to see if there were any other ledges above or behind it that could help them get higher up the main boulder.

As Sandra and Karin started moving around the west side of the oval rock, Paul started moving around its east side – and bumbled into a lioness who was lying up in the tangled vegetation at the entrance to the cave where, of course, she was hiding her cubs.

She must have heard the party approaching but probably decided to keep a low profile, hoping that the intruders would move on or go away without discovering her and her cubs' hiding place. But when Paul almost fell on top of her, she changed her mind.

With an angry roar that echoed all over Matupa she charged at Paul. He hastily backed off a few paces – which was as far as he could retreat without falling off the cliff. There was no time to cock the rifle, but Paul aimed it at her anyway, pretending it was cocked. Fortunately the lioness believed him – or perhaps it was Paul's body language that saved him.

Meanwhile Kobus had leaped forward, grazing his leg from knee to ankle against a sharp rock, although he didn't notice it at the time. Reaching Paul in one second flat, he took the rifle from him and ordered him out of the way.

Just before the lioness had growled, the two girls had been studying a rock fig that clutched the boulder wall in front of them. Its uppermost branches reached all the way to the summit – about four metres above them. But the boulder wall curved outwards, and the upper branches of the rock fig slanted slightly away from its convex surface so that anyone climbing up it to the top would have to lean over backwards – a rather hazardous thing to do. So the girls had concluded that it wouldn't be a good idea to try to reach the summit by climbing the rock fig. But the shocking sound of a lion roaring directly into their ears changed their opinion in a flash. Three seconds later they were in the top branches of the rock fig and scrambling onto the summit. Kobus ordered Paul to climb up after the girls.

Then Kobus talked calmly to the lioness, explaining that he and his family meant her cubs no harm. He asked her nicely to keep a respectful distance. The terrace wasn't too spacious, and there was no way down except the way they had come.

But the lioness refused to believe him and warned him with an earth-shaking roar that she wanted all humans out of her territory *immediately*.

Kobus tried telling her that they would all dearly love to leave, but that she was blocking the exit.

Meanwhile Paul and the girls were studying the features of the main boulder, hoping to discover some other way to get down Matupa, but they found none. The only way down was the way they had come up – past the cave entrance that the lioness was guarding.

Kobus continued to explain this to the lioness, but she was in no mood for discussions. As far as she was concerned they could find themselves another way down. She wasn't letting *anyone* near her cave nursery. To make her point quite clear, she mock-charged Kobus. As her angry growl thundered out over the landscape, Kobus wondered what to do. Shooting the lioness was not an option. She had her cubs to think of. He glanced over his shoulder and contemplated the sheer drop behind him. No good. It was totally out of the question.

The lioness did a second mock-charge, stopping awfully close to Kobus, and he glanced over his shoulder again. The cliff wasn't so totally out of the question after all.

In fact the drop was shrinking every second.

After the third mock-charge, Kobus saw a way to get down the cliff.

After the fourth mock-charge, the way down looked easy.

On the west side of the cliff, near its bottom, the vertical drop was broken by a ridge that sloped at a climbable angle towards the earth. A tall jackalberry tree grew high up on the ridge, its uppermost branches reaching all the way up to a tiny ledge that jutted out from the cliff face – about four metres or so below the western edge of the terrace.

If they could reach that ledge, Kobus thought, they could try to get into the branches of the jackalberry tree. Reaching the ledge was the tricky part. The only way to reach it would be to jump – but if you missed it you would fall another fifty metres or so.

Kobus asked Paul if he thought he could make it to the ledge, and then into the branches of the tree. If he could manage that, then Kobus wanted him to go down and find anything that could be used as a makeshift ladder and bring it back up to the ledge above the jackalberry tree. Kobus would stay with the girls to protect them from the lioness in case she decided to go up the rock fig after them.

Paul climbed down the rock fig and hurried over to the western edge of the terrace. Studying the cliff face below he spotted the ledge and lowered himself carefully in its direction. He let go and dropped to the narrow shelf below, mercifully making a safe landing. After that he managed to reach the jackalberry tree and he climbed down to the bottom in record time.

Spurred on by the echoing growls of the lioness many metres above, where his young wife and her family were trapped, he hurriedly searched around for a makeshift ladder and found a climbable-looking log about three metres long. Somehow he managed to carry it as he climbed all the way to the top of the jackalberry tree and onto the ledge above it.

Kobus was relieved when he heard Paul calling out to them that he'd found a ladder. The lioness was at the end of her patience and getting really furious.

The girls scrambled down the rock fig and across the terrace. As the lioness thundered a final warning, they lowered themselves, one after the other, over the edge and onto the makeshift ladder that Paul was holding in place against the cliff face.

Fortunately all went well, and after reaching the ledge they managed to get into the treetop. As soon as the girls were safely away, it was Kobus's turn. He said goodbye to the lioness, and it was obvious that she was as glad to see him go as he was to be leaving. Paul held the log steady for Kobus, and moments later they were all climbing down the tall, god-sent jackalberry tree to safety.

They spent a few minutes at the bottom of the cliff, relaxing and getting their adrenaline levels back to normal again. Karin and Sandra took quite a while to get their shakes under control. But they both agreed that their trembling was not the result of shock – lions didn't really shock them any more – but merely of adrenaline overdrive. (Adrenaline overdrive, according to my daughters, happens when your instincts command you to flee but you are unable to do so because the circumstances prevent it.)

On their way back home, Kobus remembered the elephant encounter of two weeks before – and the lecture that he got from his wife afterwards. Worried that he was in for another lecture, he suggested to the children that there was no need to tell their mother the exact details of the lioness encounter.

So when my family got home and I asked how their day had been, all they said was: 'Oh, it was very nice, thank you.'

'What is the koppie like?' I asked.

'Very nice,' Sandra answered.

'Very nice,' Karin agreed.

I was about to ask for a more eloquent description but suddenly noticed the fresh scar on Kobus's leg. 'Oh, look! You've hurt yourself,' I exclaimed. 'What happened?'

He studied his leg with a puzzled frown.

Karin said, 'A lioness growled at us. She probably gave him a fright. So he grazed his leg.'

'A lioness?' I said, surprised. 'On the koppie? She must be hiding cubs there. Did she charge you?'

'Oh, yes,' Sandra replied casually. 'It was quite exciting.'

'How nice,' I said. 'I'm sorry I missed all the fun. So what else happened today?'

'Oh, nothing really,' they replied.

Kobus, who had been holding his breath throughout the conversation, couldn't believe his ears, and he wondered to what he owed his luck. Had his wife missed out on the meaning of the word 'lioness' or what?

I hadn't, of course. It was just that the semantics of the word no longer scared me. Being a lion-mother myself, I knew that lions were only dangerous if you didn't understand them. And of course my family understood lions.

We were a lion-family.

*

A few months later, Kobus took me to see Matupa for the first time and showed me the cave where the lioness had hidden her cubs. It was only then that the full dramatic nature of my family's encounter with the lioness on that autumn day struck home. And when I looked over the cliff edge to the tiny ledge below and the earth another fifty-odd metres down, I was deeply shocked, but at the same time filled with admiration for my family's ingenuity and perseverance in finding a way down rather than shooting the lioness.

On the last Friday of the autumn vacation, Hettie and Leo played a boisterous game of catch, and one of Leo's canines inadvertently cut into her left thigh, leaving a neat but very deep puncture wound.

I mixed one part household bleach with nine parts boiled, cooled water. Then I filled a sterile syringe with it and squirted the solution into the wound. We repeated the procedure every few hours. By Sunday evening I felt confident that the wound was clean and that there were no signs of sepsis. I nevertheless urged Hettie to consult her university doctor as soon as she arrived back in Johannesburg, just to make doubly sure that the wound was clean and also to have it stitched up. But Hettie said no, she knew the wound was clean as there was no pain. And she didn't want stitches. Band-aid would do. And anyway, she couldn't see herself explaining to the university doctor that she'd been bitten by a lion. He wouldn't understand.

On the last day of the autumn vacation we packed a picnic lunch and climbed to the top of Shabeni, one of our favourite koppies.

We had a lovely, uneventful day.

And so the memorable vacation ended on a safe note. Thank heavens.

BITTERSWEET TIMES

GARETH CAME TO VISIT AGAIN TOWARDS THE END OF THE AUTUMN, bringing us the news that the landowners' committee of the Save Valley had granted permission for the introduction of a man-made lion pride into the conservancy. He'd also applied for an import permit for Leo from the Zimbabwe National Parks and Wildlife Department.

Gareth stayed three days, spending most of his time with Leo, getting to know him and winning his trust.

Kobus and I decided that, when the time came for Leo to go to his new home, the two of us, together with Wolfie, would accompany him and stay with him and Gareth for a few weeks to help make the transition easier.

After Gareth's second visit to us, the reality of launching Leo into his own adult world began to strike home, and there were days when I could hardly bear to think about it. I wished desperately that we could postpone the project for another year or so. But our park warden and his directors were getting impatient with us. We'd already received a second official letter from them in April, reminding us that it was against the park's policy for any member of staff to keep a lion and that they could not allow us to keep Leo any longer. If anyone got injured, they warned, the blame would be placed not only on us but on them as well.

Their fears were not entirely unreasonable, of course. Other hand-reared lions had been responsible for fatal accidents in the past. One of George Adamson's lions, Boy, had injured a young child, and some years later killed a member of his staff. In South Africa alone, five cases had been recorded during the previous two years of people who had been fatally injured by either hand-reared or semi-tame lions.

I wrote back to the park warden, explaining that we were in the process of making arrangements to take Leo to Zimbabwe and that we would be leaving no later than the beginning of June. I promised him that, until that time, I would take full responsibility for the safety of anyone who entered our premises.

Leo was a huge and powerful animal now, capable of inflicting serious injury. But he was also a gentle lion, and I did not believe that he would ever hurt anyone. Yet I could not guarantee my beliefs. And if anything happened to prove me wrong, I would not be able to live with the burden of that guilt.

Since adopting Leo I had not really been away from home. And now that he was so big, I knew that I would not be able to go away for as long as he was with us. Kobus often worked away from home for days or weeks at a stretch, and so the responsibility for our visitors' safety was mine most of the time. On the few occasions when I went to Nelspruit or Hazyview to do some urgent shopping, I would post a game guard at our gate with strict instructions not to allow anyone to enter our premises during my absence.

Even-tempered and well behaved though he was, Leo still loved to stalk and startle people. He would catch them gently, clasping them around the waist and pulling them down for a playful wrestle. But a playful wrestle with a lion could end in an accident, especially for small children or older people.

In the days and weeks following Gareth's second visit, I found myself spending most of my free time with Leo, playing with him, hugging him and talking to him, explaining to him that he was a big boy now and that it was time to think of his future. I told him that our wish for him was that he should have a very happy adulthood with a real lion family of his own.

But I wasn't being entirely honest with him, of course. What I really wanted was for him to remain with us for as long as he lived. For I believed that, with us, he would always be happy and safe.

So I would wake up at night, feeling sad and restless. Leo loved us and needed us. How could we even think of abandoning him? I paced the house, trying to think of other solutions. We could all move away to some remote wild place where no other people ever came, and live there happily ever after with our lion.

But how would we live?

We could establish Leo in some remote corner of the Kruger Park – where no-one would know about him – and we would visit him as frequently as possible, often spending days camping with him in the bush.

But how would *he* live – unable to hunt and unable to fend for himself? Unlike the Save Valley that had as yet no lion population, Kruger Park had lions all over the place – wild lions who would defend their territories against interlopers like Leo.

It seemed strange to me that the lion, powerful as he was, should be the most vulnerable of hand-reared orphans when reintroduced to the wild.

During those long sleepless nights I would often think back to the day that Hettie had first gone off to university. We still lived at Mahlangeni then, more than six hundred kilometres from Johannesburg. We took her to the airport at Phalaborwa, and as her aeroplane started taxiing across the runway for take-off, I wanted to run after it, shouting for it to stop and bring back my child. I wanted to explain to the pilot – and everyone else – that it was all a mistake. She wasn't ready for the outside world yet. She was just a child of the wilderness, unprepared for city life . . . she would feel so bewildered, so lonely, so lost.

But who would listen? Who would understand?

After she left, I couldn't sleep or eat properly for many days.

And then, when Sandra's turn came the following year, I thought I was better prepared for it, having already been through the whole trauma once before. But harsh experiences don't make you stronger. They make you more vulnerable.

I decided that the only way I could prepare myself for the eventual parting with Leo was to rely on my belief that happy memories made the future bearable. And so I set about collecting good moments with Leo to add to my memory's repertoire. I also checked my diaries to make sure I had recorded all the good memories of the past.

Here are a few of my favourite ones for the months preceding the parting:

In March of that year, Kobus went to Namibia to deliver a number of rhinos to the Waterberg National Park. He was gone for about ten days, and Leo missed him very much. He waited at the front gate every evening, calling to Kobus. On the day Kobus finally returned, Leo pounced on him and forced him to the ground. Clutching Kobus's head between his huge front paws, he licked his face all over, almost drowning him with lion kisses.

Hettie arrived home for Easter carrying a huge pink teddy bear. Leo took one look at the teddy bear and fell in love with it. As Hettie walked from the car to the house, Leo ran alongside her, begging her to let him have the bear, please.

But Hettie said, 'No, Leo. I'm sorry. It was a birthday gift from a special friend.' She carried the teddy bear into her bedroom and sat it down on her bed. Leo spent the next hour at her bedroom window, his nose pressed to the gauze screen, staring longingly at the pink bear.

I decided to make him his own teddy bear. I searched my sewing trunk for bits of leftover fabric and stuffing until I'd collected enough to make a huge bear. Actually I didn't know how to make a bear, so I made a life-size rag doll instead. When I'd finished it, I carried it outside to show Leo.

'How do you like it?' I asked him as I held the rag doll up for him to inspect.

His eyes said, 'I love it! I love it! I wish it were mine!'

'It's yours,' I told him. 'Come and take it!'

He looked at me with an expression of total surprise, followed by one of sheer delight. Then he pounced on the doll, clutched it to him, rolled on it, sat on it, tossed it in the air, caught it again, and ran off with it. He spent the rest of the day running all over the garden, parading his rag doll to the family, to Wolfie, to Aaron and to anyone who happened to come along. He was so proud of his doll that everyone thought he'd gone a little mad. He even clutched the doll to him when he slept. And he spent the following few days carrying it in his jaws wherever he went.

One afternoon, as we went for a walk down into the valley, Leo kept tripping on the doll as he dragged it along, and eventually he found it too difficult to keep up with us. So he set the doll down and stood glaring at it. He seemed to be saying to the doll, 'Can't you walk by yourself? I'm tired of carrying you.'

'Come on, Leo!' we called to him. 'Leave your doll there. You can pick it up on the way back.'

But Leo looked at us with a pleading expression.

'OK,' Kobus sighed. 'Here, I'll carry it for you.'

As we continued on our walk, I found it rather touching to see a fierce game ranger carrying his lion's rag doll for him.

One day Karin tied a three-metre-long red ribbon to a stick and invited Leo to a game of catch. Racing all over the garden she trailed the ribbon behind her while Leo gave chase, trying to catch the ribbon. But it kept slipping from his grip, so eventually he got fed up with the game and decided to catch Karin instead. Having done so, he sat down on top of her.

Flat on her back with Leo on top of her, Karin was unable to get out from under him, partly because she was laughing too much and partly because Leo refused to move. She still had the red ribbon in her hands, so she resorted to flossing his teeth with it. Leo pulled a funny face. He wasn't too crazy about the flossing exercise. So he moved a bit, giving Karin the chance to wriggle out from underneath him.

At the age of about eighteen months, Leo had a cute-looking tuft of mane on the top of his head. One day Karin tied a pink ribbon around the tuft of hair to make Leo look pretty, and she was so pleased with the effect that she called the whole family to come and admire Leo's new look. Poor Leo had the silliest expression on his face. He seemed to know that the pink ribbon in his hair had changed him from a noble lion into a dumb teddy bear. I took several photographs of him as a teddy bear. But I never showed him the photos. I was afraid they might give him an inferiority complex.

*

One day during the autumn holidays, as we were all sitting on top of Shabeni watching a beautiful sunset, Wolfie was running about as usual, checking out the signs on the ground, followed closely by Leo whose only desire was to trip up the dog. Eventually Wolfie got fed up with Leo's antics. Spinning around he issued a furious warning: 'Do that one more time, and I'll bite you!'

Leo immediately backed off. Running straight to us, he threw his paws around Paul's shoulders and, pressing his face to Paul's head, gave him a long and passionate hug that seemed to say: 'I don't love that dog any more. I love only you.'

WHERE MAY A LION LIVE?

GARETH PHONED US FROM THE SAVE VALLEY CONSERVANCY IN MAY. He'd met with the conservator as well as with the landowner who had offered his section of the conservancy for the lion rehabilitation project. All other arrangements were going well. Lisa Hywood, who ran an animal rehabilitation centre in Zimbabwe, had offered to locate other orphan lions to make up the pride.

Kobus and I set about getting our passports in order, as well as applying for a CITES permit to transport Leo. (CITES is the acronym for the Convention on International Trade in Endangered Species.) We also applied for a visitor's permit for Wolfie from the Zimbabwe authorities.

The vet came over from Skukuza to give Leo and Wolfie the required injections together with the necessary certificates to prove that they were free of disease.

The CITES permit for Leo's transport stipulated that he would have to travel in a cage. (I could hardly bear the idea.) Kobus arranged that a steel and fencing company called MEPS would build us a cage. MEPS graciously did it free of charge. We needed a vehicle that could carry the cage, and so we contacted the Nissan Company in Johannesburg. They kindly offered to lend us a Nissan 4 × 4 patrol truck – free of charge. We were touched by the support and sympathy that our project received from people such as these. Without their help, the costs of transporting Leo to Zimbabwe would have put us in debt for a long time.

The steel cage arrived and we put it on our front patio, leaving its gate open in the hope that Leo would get curious and inspect it, maybe even go inside it. If he could get used to the cage, then we would not need to drug him in order to get him into it on the day of departure. We asked Wolfie to go inside the cage, which the good dog promptly did. Then we tried to persuade Leo to follow Wolfie. But Leo refused. I tried luring him in with a nice chunk of meat, but that didn't work either. He didn't trust the cage one bit. (And needless to say, I didn't blame him.)

One day near the end of May, a phone call from Gareth made things even harder for us. The Zimbabwe Parks Department had refused an import permit for Leo. The reason they gave was that their new policy no longer allowed for hand-reared lions to be released into their parks. They believed that hand-reared lions posed a threat to field staff as well as to visitors. Gareth had faxed them a reply, explaining that part of his rehabilitation programme was to train his lions to become people-disfamiliarized. During their two-year transition period he would allow his lions no contact with humans other than himself – he would in fact teach them to flee from humans, as he had taught his lions in the Tuli to do.

The Zimbabwe Parks Department considered the issue once more, but regretted that they were unable to revise their policy.

What to do now? Gareth was as distressed as we were. But he promised to help find another solution.

I spent the following two weeks making telephone calls to every conservation area in South Africa, only to learn that no provincial park would take a hand-reared lion. A few private parks were eager to take him, but Gareth knew about them and warned me that those were the 'canned-lion' establishments – hunting farms that kept and bred lions for trophy hunting. I could hardly believe such places existed. And the very idea of humans actually shooting lions for the fun of it made my heart ache so I couldn't sleep for several nights.

Gareth made about as many phone calls as I did, only to reach the same conclusion: the status of the lion in southern Africa was such that a hand-reared orphan was doomed to be homeless.

Early in June our park warden sent us a final reminder that we were not allowed to keep Leo any longer. I was in tears when I received a call from a lovely lady, Rita Miljo, founder of CARE (the Centre for Animal Rehabilitation and Education) at Phalaborwa. She told me that she'd learned of a place called the Lion and Cheetah Park in the north of Zimbabwe near Harare. The owner's name, she said, was Vivian Bristow. He kept lions, cheetahs and various other animals for tourism and filming purposes. The lions and cheetahs in his park were mostly hand-reared orphans and their offspring. Although the animals were strictly speaking in captivity, they were actually as free as could be, living together in family groups in large bushveld camps. According to her sources, Rita said, Vivian Bristow and his family took good care of the animals. Rita believed that obtaining a permit for Leo to go there would be no problem as the Bristows were in good standing with the Zimbabwe Parks Department.

After talking to Rita, I dialled the number in Zimbabwe that she had given me.

Vivian Bristow answered my call and said he would be delighted to have Leo. He offered to send a truck to fetch him. I quickly explained that my family and I wished to accompany Leo to his new home, and so we would prefer to bring him ourselves. Vivian graciously offered us the hospitality of his home for whatever period we wished to stay with Leo. He also asked how much we wanted for him.

I was baffled. 'How much? How much of what?' I asked.

'What would you like to sell him for?' he said.

I was taken aback. We didn't own Leo, of course. He was born free. So I replied: 'He's not for sale. We only want a safe home for him.'

I discussed the idea with Kobus that evening, and he agreed that it seemed the only option left to us.

So we called the Tuli Lodge in Botswana, leaving a message for Gareth to contact us. He called us a few days later and I told him of the

Bristows' park. Gareth was sad that his own plans for Leo had failed, but he was relieved to know that we had finally found a safe refuge for him.

Vivian Bristow's wife, Carol, called us two days later to say that an import permit had been granted for Leo and that she would fax us a copy to Skukuza.

Kobus and I spent the next few days making all the final arrangements to leave for Zimbabwe. We were in a hurry to get away since Kobus had to be back before the end of June to attend an international wildlife-management congress at Skukuza.

We wished we could take all the children along, but Paul, Sandra and Karin would be writing their half-year exams. Fortunately Hettie finished early – on 11 June. So after some family discussions it was decided that we would leave on 13 June, returning on the 27th. Hettie would accompany us, while the other children would all visit Leo at a later stage.

At least that was one good thing about Leo's new home – it would not be necessary for him to become people-disfamiliarized, and so he would always be allowed visitors.

I arranged for neighbours to give Karin a lift to her school bus on the morning of the 13th. She was still attending the Nelspruit boarding school and she caught the school bus at Hazyview, a small village twenty-five kilometres from us, early on Monday mornings.

Sandra and Paul came home for the weekend before we left to say goodbye to Leo. And when Sandra hugged Leo to her and told him that she would be looking forward to seeing him again and to meeting his lion-family, I was grateful that parting with Leo was proving to be less traumatic now that we all knew we would see him again.

PAMUZINDA

IN THE DARK, EARLY HOURS OF MONDAY 13 JUNE, THE VET, DR COBUS Raath, arrived and put Leo to sleep with a ketamine injection. The steel cage was in place on the back of the truck. We had covered the floor of the cage with sand and spread the two animals' sleeping mats over the sand. It was midwinter now, so Kobus had covered the whole cage with a tarpaulin, leaving it open only at the back.

As soon as Leo was asleep, Kobus, the vet and two game guards gently rolled him onto a canvas sheet and lifted him into the cage. Wolfie immediately jumped into the cage after Leo to keep a watchful eye on his sleeping friend.

Karin, dressed for school and waiting for her lift to the bus, stroked Leo's head in final greeting, then hugged Wolfie goodbye and told him to take good care of her lion. She was smiling bravely but I knew she was hurting, and my heart ached for her. I promised her I would phone from Zimbabwe to let her know how things were going.

After Kobus, Hettie and I had said goodbye to Karin and wished her luck with her exams, we got into the truck and left.

Leo was still asleep.

But he woke up a few kilometres from home and was extremely upset at finding himself in a cage. So we stopped and tried to calm and comfort him. But every few kilometres or so, Leo became so agitated that Wolfie would howl to let us know it was time we stopped the truck and talked reassuringly with our lion again.

We had a long journey ahead of us, about twelve hundred kilometres, and we realized that we would be on the road for ever if we were to stop every few kilometres to comfort Leo. So Kobus decided to give him a Valium injection. Fortunately that settled him and he remained fairly calm and sleepy for the rest of the journey.

We arrived at the Beit Bridge border post by mid-afternoon and, after a delay of several hours at the customs office, finally crossed the Limpopo River into Zimbabwe. Surprisingly, there was no immediate change in the scenery, as I'd half expected there would be. Baobab trees still dominated the quiet bushveld landscapes that seemed to stretch for ever.

When the sun began to set we stopped at the Bubye River and fed our animals the food that I'd packed for them. We didn't stop long as we had about another five hundred kilometres ahead of us.

Then darkness came and it started getting cold. And the colder it got, the more worried we became about our two animals on the back of the truck. Kobus had tied the tarpaulin in such a way that a small opening remained at the front of the cage directly opposite the back window of the cab, enabling us to peek in and check on the animals when necessary. Every half hour or so, Kobus would ask me how the animals were doing, and I'd stick my torch through the back window and shine it into the cage. Kobus said that if I saw them curling themselves up tightly against the cold, then we shouldn't continue the journey. Fortunately I never saw them doing that. Though they were huddled close together most of the time, their muscles didn't appear abnormally taut.

By the time we reached the midlands, it was really cold. Kobus stopped the truck and got out to check on the animals himself. Their noses were cold to the touch, but otherwise they seemed fine. Kobus checked the tarpaulin on all sides of the truck to make sure it was wind-proof. He discovered a spot where the edge of the canvas didn't quite meet the side of the truck, leaving a gap large enough to let in a lot of cold air. So Kobus took off his lumber jacket and, bundling it up tightly, pressed it into the gap, which it filled adequately. Satisfied that the animals would be better protected now, we continued our journey.

About twenty minutes or so later, Hettie shone the torch through the back window and exclaimed that the jacket was no longer there. Thinking that the wind had probably blown it away, Kobus turned the truck round. As we drove slowly back to the spot where we'd first stopped to check on the animals, we searched for the jacket on and alongside the road, but found nothing. This worried me quite a bit as it was Kobus's only jacket and I was sure that he was going to need it in the cold days ahead.

Eventually we gave up the search, but before turning back again Kobus got out to check on the animals once more.

He found Leo hugging the jacket to him.

Kobus asked Leo to let him have his jacket back so that it could be used to block the gap again. But Leo said, 'Nope. It's mine now.'

We reached Harare around midnight and turned west. Twenty-four kilometres outside Harare we found the turn-off to the Lion and Cheetah Park, and a few minutes later we turned into the driveway leading to the Bristows' house.

Carol Bristow had been waiting up for us and she came out of the house to meet us. We apologized for arriving so late, but she said she knew that travelling with a lion was a difficult business and she was just so pleased that we'd arrived safely. She offered to get us something to eat and drink, but we declined. We were tired and wanted only to sleep.

I asked her if we might open the cage to let our animals out, but she said no, unfortunately not. She had no place to put them up for the night. She had her dogs in the garden and there was no telling how Leo would treat them.

I was rather disappointed as I had hoped we could unload our animals right away. They were as exhausted as we were from the long journey.

Carol explained that Leo's new home would not be at the Lion and

Cheetah Park but at their other park, Pamuzinda, about sixty kilometres further to the west. Her husband and son were waiting there for
us, she said, and she would drive out to Pamuzinda with us first thing
in the morning.

I had not known that. I thought we had reached our destination.

Carol explained that they had decided to establish a pioneer lion
pride in the Pamuzinda Park. The place had no resident lions as yet and
it seemed a good idea to start a lion family there. The pioneer pride
would consist of Leo and two lionesses named Happie and Fat Cat.

Carol showed us to our rooms, and we hurried to bed to catch a few
hours' sleep.

Early the next morning, Carol's cook woke us with coffee. We
quickly got up and prepared for the last leg of our journey.

As soon as I was dressed, I rushed outside to the truck to see how Leo
and Wolfie were.

Carol's two dogs were patrolling the truck and attempting to intimidate my animals. Wolfie paid them no attention, but Leo was
threatening them through the bars of the cage, hissing and snarling at
them. I had never seen Leo threaten other animals before, and was
impressed with his performance. Though Leo and Wolfie were relieved
to see me, it was obvious that they'd had enough of the cage, and it broke
my heart that I couldn't let them out yet. I talked comfortingly to them,
promising them that they would be out of their cage in less than an hour.

After a hurried breakfast with Carol we were on our way.

Zimbabwe is a beautiful country. We'd seen very little of it the
previous day as we'd done most of our travelling through it at night.
Now, on our way to Pamuzinda, we were able to appreciate the scenery
by daylight.

But my heart was not in it. No matter how hard I tried to concentrate
on the landscape, all I could think of was how stressed my two animals
were feeling after more than twenty-four hours in the cage, and how
apprehensive I myself was feeling about whatever lay ahead for Leo
and us.

We reached Pamuzinda's entrance gate after a forty-minute drive. A uniformed guard opened the gate, saluting smartly. We followed a dirt track that wound its way through scenic bushlands. After a few kilometres we reached the site where the new lion camp was being built.

Vivian Bristow, his son Graeme and an assistant park manager, Andy Cader, were waiting for us at the site. They had just finished building a temporary camp for Leo. It was right next to the main lion camp into which Leo would eventually go with his new lion family. At that time there were three lions staying in the main camp. The fifteen-acre camp was not yet fully completed, so the lions were being kept in a temporarily fenced-in section.

Carol parked outside Leo's camp. Someone opened the gate and we drove in and parked inside. Then we hurried to open the cage and release our tired animals. They needed no invitation and leaped out. Leo was so happy to be out of his cage that he bounded all over the place for a while. Then he suddenly realized that everything smelled very strange and he stopped in his tracks, looked about for Wolfie and hurried over to his bodyguard.

The other three lions strolled over to the fence of their camp and studied Leo and Wolfie with keen curiosity.

Wolfie wisely ignored them. For a while Leo remained quite unaware of them. When he finally saw them, he fell down flat in the tall grass and pretended he wasn't there. Kobus went over to him and crouched beside him, encouraging him to take a look at the other lions. With Kobus at his side Leo felt a little braver and lifted his head to peer at them over the tall grass.

The three Bristows and Andy Cader were studying Leo from outside his camp, remarking on how handsome he was and how even-tempered and good-natured he seemed. It also intrigued them that he appeared to be such good friends with the dog.

After a while Vivian Bristow said that he, Graeme and Andy would have to be on their way as they were busy with a film crew from the UK who were using some of their lions. The filming location was only a few kilometres away, and Vivian invited us to join them there whenever we wished to. Carol also left, driving back to their house at the Lion and Cheetah Park where we would see her again in the evening, as we would continue to spend our nights there for the duration of our visit.

I could hardly bear the idea of the house being such a long drive from Pamuzinda, for it meant that my two animals would be alone and very far from us in their camp at night. I wished the Bristows would let my family and me camp out at Pamuzinda with Leo and Wolfie. I asked Kobus about it but he said no; we hadn't brought a tent or even sleeping bags, and it would be ungracious to ask the Bristows to change the arrangements they'd made for us.

After the others had left we made ourselves comfortable in Leo's camp. It was not very large, only about half an acre or so, but adequate for temporary occupation. It was covered with tall yellow grass and a few acacia trees, and in one corner there was a small cement pond filled with water.

As I sat down in the grass Leo came over and sat down almost on top of me. I moved over a little and put my arm around him. He moaned softly, and I knew he was feeling nervous and insecure.

After a while Kobus and Hettie decided to go for a walk to explore the park. I wanted to stay with Leo. So Leo, Wolfie and I sort of huddled together in a corner of the strange camp and tried to feel at home.

One of the other lions suddenly let out an enormous roar, and we all jumped. I hugged Leo closer to me and told him that one day soon he would be able to roar just as loudly.

A young blond-haired girl emerged from the woods beyond the camp and came up to the fence. I got up and went to meet her. She introduced herself as Julie Bristow, Graeme's wife. Pointing in the direction she had come from, she told me their house was less than a kilometre away, and she described how to get there, adding that we should feel free to come up to the house whenever we needed anything

– the bathroom, a cup of tea, whatever. She also invited us to come up to the house at one o'clock and have lunch with her and the rest of the Bristow clan.

I thanked her for her hospitality, and we chatted for a while. She asked a lot of questions about Leo as she studied him through the fence. I found myself telling her how hard it was for us to part with Leo. It wasn't my style to discuss personal agonies with strangers, but I wanted Julie and all the people of Pamuzinda to know that Leo was going to miss us, and that he would need comforting and special attention when we left.

Kobus and Hettie returned from their walk and we shared a flask of tea while I told them about Julie's visit. Afterwards Kobus decided he would go over to the film set and see what they were doing. Hettie opted to stay with me and the animals.

Leo was asleep under the acacia tree. I'd been sitting with him for a long time, and as I got up to stretch my legs he immediately woke up, lifting his head to see where I was going. But as Hettie lay down on the grass beside him, he relaxed again, putting one front paw on her shoulder and letting it rest there.

Looking at Hettie and Leo resting so peacefully together in the grass I was suddenly overcome by an intense nostalgia. I wanted nothing more than to protect these two fragile souls for ever from the harsh realities of an indifferent world. They were both so trusting, so loving, so vulnerable – the sweet, tender-hearted girl, forever a wilderness child, confused by the complexities of life at a city university; and the gentle, affectionate lion, abandoned as a cub, soon to be abandoned by his human family in a strange land far away from his childhood home.

Life certainly didn't seem fair, and tears stung my eyes.

Wolfie sat up, ears pricked, his gaze following a movement in the woods beyond the camp. Turning, I saw another young woman approaching us along the winding footpath. I went to the fence to meet her.

She was Maria Cader, wife of the assistant park manager, Andy

Cader. An attractive woman in her early thirties, she had short curly hair and gentle brown eyes. She told me that Andy's and her house was right next to Graeme's and Julie's, and she also offered help and hospitality. Her gaze went to Leo and she asked if she could come into the camp. I was delighted that she'd asked and rushed to open the gate for her. Leo was in a very docile mood, so I felt confident that he would not even look at Maria, let alone bother her.

Maria said a casual hello to Wolfie and Leo, then sat down in the grass with Hettie and me. I admired her for being the first person at Pamuzinda who'd been brave enough to come into Leo's camp, and told her so. She admitted that she was scared of Leo, but said that she had no intention of letting him know this.

Maria spent over an hour chatting to Hettie and me, and we found her company utterly delightful. When I confided to her how hard it was for us to part with Leo, she was sympathetic, assuring me that her husband Andy was extremely fond of lions and that he would spend a lot of time with Leo as soon as his work with the film crew was over. She explained that Andy's job on the film set was to take care of the lions that were being used in the film.

I asked Maria about the three lions in the main camp. She said the female was Happie, one of Leo's future wives. The other two were males. One of them was very old, twenty-four years old in fact, and his name was Trade. He'd been brought over from the Lion and Cheetah Park to retire at Pamuzinda. The other, younger male was Samson. He was a temporary visitor, an understudy for the film. As soon as filming was completed Samson would return to his family at the Lion and Cheetah Park. Fat Cat, Leo's other future wife, was at the film set. She was one of the stars of the movie.

It had been awfully nice talking to Maria and I was grateful that she had come to visit. She promised she would come again the following day.

At midday Kobus and the others returned from the film set, and we all went up to Julie's house for lunch. I wished that I didn't have to go.

I really only wanted to stay with Leo. But I didn't want to seem ungracious.

In the end I was glad that I'd gone. Julie's lunch was very good and I felt much better afterwards.

Leo and Wolfie had obviously been waiting anxiously for our return, and they were very relieved to see us again.

Andy Cader brought over a chunk of wildebeest meat for Leo's lunch, and it pleased me that Andy came right into the camp to put the meat down for him. Leo ignored the meat and remained lying down, pretending that he wasn't aware of Andy either.

Andy stayed and chatted to us for a while, and it was evident that he was as lovely a person as his wife Maria was. He also seemed genuinely fond of lions. He even talked to Leo. But Leo didn't understand a word. I had to explain to Andy that Leo wasn't bilingual like us – he understood only Afrikaans.

'No problem,' Andy reassured me. 'Leo and I will soon find a common language.' He stepped up to Leo to give him a friendly pat on the rump, but Wolfie immediately parked himself firmly between Leo and Andy, fixing Andy with a toothy glare that said: 'Don't you dare touch my lion!'

I hastily told Wolfie that it was OK, Andy was a friend. Andy said not to worry, he would remember first to ask Wolfie's permission the next time he wanted to give Leo a pat.

Andy left us to go back to the filming location, and Kobus and Hettie decided to go with him for a while.

I stayed with my animals.

I picked up the chunk of meat that Andy had brought and carried it over to Leo. But Leo only sniffed at it and wouldn't eat. Perhaps he felt too nervous to eat, or maybe it was the strange smell of the meat that put him off – he'd never had wildebeest before. Poor Leo. Everything was so different: the language, the country, even the food.

An African man turned up in the late afternoon and poured fresh water into Leo's drinking pond through the fence with a watering can.

I started to greet him in Tsonga then suddenly remembered that Zimbabweans didn't speak it. Their native tongues, Shona and Sindebele, were quite foreign to me. Fortunately the man understood English, so we talked for a while. He told me that he'd never seen a dog in a lion's company before and he wanted to know why the lion didn't eat the dog. I explained that the dog was the lion's friend. He told me that if he were the dog, he would not trust the lion one bit. He added that if he were I, he wouldn't trust the lion either, and he suggested that, in my own interests, I got out of the camp while I was still alive. I said that I was the lion's mother and that lions didn't eat their mothers.

He shrugged and said, 'OK. You do what you want. But remember I warned you. So don't blame me if the lion eats you.'

I thanked him for his concern and promised that I would remember not to blame him if the lion ate me.

From time to time throughout the day, the lions in the other camp would stroll up to their fence and study us with curiosity. Wolfie decided it was best to ignore them altogether, but Leo remained very frightened of them and tried to hide in the tall grass whenever he saw them looking at us. I tried to show him that I wasn't scared of the lions, but he wouldn't believe me.

So I left Leo's camp and walked over to the main camp. I stood at the fence and chatted to the strange lions – just to show Leo that it was no big deal. The lions contemplated me with mild curiosity. After a while the female, Happie, came right up to the fence and, pressing one side of her body against the wire, rubbed her head and shoulder against it, inviting me to a feline greeting. I was delighted. I stepped up to the wire and, pressing myself against it, stooped to rub shoulders with her, enjoying the moment immensely.

When Wolfie saw me rubbing shoulders with the strange lioness, he gave her a warning bark – just to let her know that he was watching her and that she'd better not try any tricks. The lions all made strange grumbling noises when Wolfie barked. They were obviously not used to dogs and didn't trust Wolfie at all.

All three lions looked extremely healthy and in good shape, even twenty-four-year-old Trade. It was only his shaky movements that gave away his age.

I went back to Leo and asked him if he'd noticed how friendly Happie had been. But he looked at me with a forlorn expression that seemed to say: 'Yes. But can't we all go home now?'

I put my arms around him and wept.

At dusk Kobus, Hettie and the others returned from the film set, and Graeme Bristow invited us to his house for a drink. I declined. We would soon have to leave Leo and Wolfie alone in their camp for the night, and I wanted to stay with them as long as possible. Hettie offered to stay with me, but I persuaded her to go with the others and enjoy the company.

So I sat in the tall grass between Wolfie and Leo. And together we watched the sun set. Dusk came, and we listened to the sounds of the bush. Then it got dark – pitch-black, inky dark. We huddled closer together.

One of the lions in the main camp started roaring. It sounded like Samson. Then another joined in, probably old Trade. The two of them were having a competition to see who could roar the loudest. Their thundering voices rolled over the landscape like an earthquake, silencing all other night sounds, and my two animals and I felt very vulnerable. I put my arms around them and told them not to worry: there were fences between the lions and us. What unnerved me, though, was that I could no longer see the fences. What if they had dissolved? Anything was possible on a dark moonless night in a foreign country.

Kobus and Hettie arrived in the truck to fetch me, and I asked them if we could stay with Leo and Wolfie a while longer. So Kobus and Hettie joined us in the long grass. Kobus told me that he'd met Leo's other future wife, Fat Cat, at the film set that day. He said she wasn't quite as young and attractive as Happie, she was middle-aged and very fat, but altogether a delightful old girl, extremely friendly and affectionate. I was very pleased to hear that. Perhaps Fat Cat would be kind to Leo, in a motherly sort of way.

Eventually Kobus said we had better get going as Carol Bristow would be expecting us for dinner.

I really hated leaving my two animals out there alone in the strange camp. I fetched their sleeping mats from the truck and spread them close together in the patch of grass where we had been sitting. Wolfie seemed to understand that this meant they were to spend the night in the camp without us. I explained to him that we had to go back to the house but would return again early the next morning, and I asked him to take good care of Leo. He walked to the gate with us, followed by Leo, and the two of them looked very forlorn when we closed the gate behind us and got into the truck without them.

My heart felt so heavy at the sight of my two animals standing at the gate, watching us drive off.

Later that evening, after dinner, Kobus mentioned to me that Vivian Bristow was concerned about my spending so much time alone with Leo in his camp.

'Why?' I asked, surprised.

'He worries about your safety,' Kobus replied.

The idea exasperated me. Did no-one see the bond between Leo and me?

We drove back to Pamuzinda early the next morning and found Leo and Wolfie sitting close together on their sleeping mats, their ears pricked as they listened for the sound of our truck. As soon as they saw us approaching they leaped up and bounded over to the gate to welcome us.

And so we spent another day in more or less the same way as the previous one. Kobus and Hettie visited the film set at intervals or went for walks in the park, and I stayed with Leo and Wolfie.

Whenever Kobus was in the camp with us, he would sit in the grass near the fence facing the main camp and persuade Leo to join him. Leo would hesitantly go over to Kobus and sit down next to him. The other lions, noticing that they were being watched, would stroll up to their fence and study Kobus and Leo with curiosity. In an attempt to bolster Leo's confidence, Kobus would discuss the lions with him in a cheerful and encouraging tone of voice. Occasionally Trade or Samson, or both of them, would let out a few magnificent roars, and poor Leo would crouch low in the grass beside Kobus.

Kobus would say to him: 'Come on, Leo, you're a big boy too! Roar back at them – I know you can do it!'

But Leo would look at Kobus with an expression that seemed to say, 'I don't know. Those are real lions. I'm just a dog.'

We had lunch at Julie's house again, and afterwards Andy came back with us to visit Leo for a while. Though Wolfie allowed Andy to sit near Leo, he kept a very watchful eye on him. I asked Andy how long the film crew would be working at Pamuzinda, and he said a few more weeks. My heart sank. I wanted the film crew to leave so that Andy and Leo could spend more time together and start bonding. I asked Andy if it would be possible for Leo to go into the main camp with Happie and Fat Cat before we went back home. But Andy said no, that it usually took a hand-reared lion a while to realize that he was a lion. And as long as Leo didn't know he was a lion, it would be cruel to put him in the main camp with the other lions. He'd spend all his time trying to hide from them.

I felt close to tears, but tried to hide my disappointment. I had so hoped that we would see Leo happily established with his new family before we left.

Andy noticed that Leo still hadn't touched his wildebeest meat, so he promised to bring Leo a chunk of fresh meat as soon as he returned from the film set in the late afternoon.

The third day with Leo followed much the same pattern as the previous two days. Leo was still feeling nervous and insecure, and he spent most of his time resting and doing little else except snuggling up close to me or Kobus or Hettie. He would try to sit on our laps, but it was no longer possible. He was about ten times too big for that. Poor Leo. He was obviously trying to tell us that he was still just a baby and wanted to go home.

Later in the day I went over to the main camp again, and Happie came to greet me, rubbing shoulders with me through the wire. I stuck my arm in through the fence and stroked her head. She liked that and made happy grunting noises.

On the fourth day, Hettie accompanied Carol Bristow on a shopping trip to Harare, while Kobus and I spent the day following what had become our routine: I stayed in the camp with Leo and Wolfie while Kobus divided his time between me and the animals and visits to the filming location. So the fourth day would have been very much the same as the third, except that a terrible thing happened to me about halfway through the day.

I went over to the main camp again, and after rubbing shoulders with Happie I stuck my arm through the fence and stroked her head. She made happy grunting noises. I turned to see if Leo was watching – I wanted him to take note that Happie was just a friendly, harmless lion like him.

At that moment Happie's mood suddenly changed and, with an angry snarl, she grabbed my hand. I yanked it away, but my thumb caught in her jaws, gripped tightly between the upper and lower incisors. I tried not to panic and relaxed my hand, thinking that perhaps she'd let go. But I could feel her teeth going through the bone. I called to Kobus who was in Leo's camp.

'Get away from her!' he yelled to me. He was already running to the gate at the bottom of Leo's camp.

Happie was raising one paw, and I realized she was going to hook her claws into my arm.

'Get *away* from her!' Kobus yelled again as he raced towards me.

I yanked as hard as I could. The top half of my thumb came off at the joint as I fell over backwards. Kobus reached me and helped me to my feet.

'My thumb is off,' I told him. I didn't want to see the wound. So I looked away as I showed Kobus my right hand.

Kobus said: 'Let's get into the truck.'

I kept my right hand covered with my left hand to make sure I wouldn't see it. In the truck I found a towel and wrapped it around my injured hand, looking the other way as I did so.

I felt no pain. Only shock. And I believed firmly that as long as I didn't look at my thumb (or what was left of it) I would not feel any pain. It worked.

Kobus drove me to Julie's house.

He asked her for disinfectant and sterile bandages. Julie immediately ran to Maria's house to fetch her. Kobus told me to sit down. I sat down at Julie's kitchen table.

Maria arrived with some first-aid stuff.

Kobus filled a bowl with disinfectant and dipped my hand in it.

Julie handed me a cup of sweet tea. I said, 'No thanks.' I was shaking uncontrollably. I wouldn't be able to hold the cup.

'You must drink it,' Maria said. 'For the shock.'

Julie helped me hold the cup and I swallowed the sweet tea. It helped. A few minutes later I stopped shaking.

Kobus bandaged my hand and asked Maria and Julie which hospital in Harare he should take me to. Maria offered to come with us. She knew Harare well and would be able to direct us to the hospital she had in mind.

I didn't want to go to hospital. I wanted to stay with Leo. We had only a few days left with him. But there was the problem of sepsis, of course. I would lose more than just my thumb if I didn't get proper treatment.

I apologized to Julie for leaving her kitchen full of blood-soaked things.

Kobus, Maria and I got into the truck and set out for Harare, about ninety kilometres away.

I hoped I wouldn't have to stay in hospital long. Poor Wolfie and Leo, left all alone in their camp with no idea where we'd gone to or why we'd departed so suddenly.

Maria suggested that we stop at the Bristows' house at the Lion and Cheetah Park and that I collect any of my stuff that I might need at the hospital.

We did this, and while I changed out of my bloodstained clothes into some clean things, Maria quickly wrote a note to Carol and Hettie, explaining where we'd gone. She gave the note to the cook, asking him to make sure that Carol and Hettie got it as soon as they returned from Harare. Maria also asked Kobus how much money we had with us. We had a few hundred Zimbabwe dollars. Maria said the hospital would require a deposit of about six thousand dollars (the equivalent of almost £700).

We were stunned.

'Can't we send them the money as soon as we get back to South Africa?' Kobus asked.

Maria said no, they would refuse to admit me unless the deposit was paid. But she told us not to worry. She rushed off and found one of Vivian Bristow's assistants. He kept Vivian's chequebook and there were several signed cheques in it. He handed us one of the signed cheques. Maria said she would explain to Vivian about the cheque that evening, and that Kobus could arrange with Vivian to repay him at a later stage.

Maria was an angel. She thought of everything and took care of everything, allowing me to relax and think of nothing.

Once we were on the road again, she regaled us with amusing stories about life at Pamuzinda.

And I laughed a lot.

But I felt so sad.

Losing my thumb wasn't so bad really.

Losing Leo was.

IN A HOSPITAL IN HARARE

MARIA DIRECTED US TO THE AVENUES CLINIC IN HARARE. THE deposit required was Zim$6250. Maria filled out the cheque and, in her haste, made an error.

The hospital would not accept the cheque.

Maria told us not to worry. She had friends living in Harare. She asked if she could take the truck to get to their house. Kobus offered to drive her there.

I waited for them in the hospital waiting room.

There were several other people in the room – Shona-speaking people. Their strange language made me feel ignorant and insecure. Then I overheard a mother saying something to her sick child in a language that sounded familiar. Sindebele. It sounded almost like Zulu. The mother started singing to the child. The words of the lullaby were easy to understand. The mother looked up and found me staring at her. I hadn't meant to stare. I was concentrating on the words of her song. I smiled apologetically. She smiled back at me. And life didn't seem so altogether awful any more.

Kobus and Maria returned, bringing with them a signed cheque from Maria's friends.

I wondered if her friends were saints or something. How could they not mind lending such a huge amount of money to total strangers – and foreigners at that?

Maria said not to worry. Her friends had obviously liked Kobus's face and decided he was trustworthy.

I was admitted to the casualty ward and handed over to Dr Gwatidzo.

Worried for a moment about whether we would have a language in common I started searching my Zulu vocabulary to explain that a lion had bitten me, hoping that Zulu would prove to be close enough to Sindebele for him to understand. But Dr Gwatidzo spoke fluent English, as did most of the other hospital staff.

I looked the other way as the doctor removed the bandages from my hand.

He asked if I wanted an injection for the pain. I said no thank you. As long as I didn't look at the wound, it didn't hurt. He asked what about my index finger.

'What about it?' I asked.

'The skin has been grazed along one side,' he said. 'Did the lion do that too?'

I had no idea. Perhaps a canine had grazed it. Or maybe the wire of the fence.

The doctor poured the contents of a bottle of disinfectant over both my thumb and index finger. Then he bound up my hand and told someone to contact the surgeon and to book a theatre for me.

Someone replied that the theatres were fully booked for the afternoon.

The doctor said: 'So book one for the evening.'

Kobus and Maria accompanied me to my room, and as soon as I was settled in I urged them to go back to Pamuzinda. I wanted Kobus to spend what was left of the day with Leo and Wolfie.

After they'd left, I lay wondering about Happie. Why had she suddenly wanted to attack me? What did I do wrong?

I thought and thought about it. And eventually the answer came to me.

Just before I had gone over to the main camp to socialize with

Happie, I had been stroking Wolfie's back. And so my hand must have smelled of Wolfie. At first Happie didn't notice the smell. I was stroking the top of her head and her neck. Then, as I turned to see if Leo was watching, my hand touched her cheek. At that moment she probably caught a whiff of the dog smell on my hand and decided I was a traitor – a dog disguised as a human.

Leo was used to Wolfie's smell, but those other lions weren't. And they obviously didn't like dogs.

I was relieved at having found the answer to Happie's sudden change of mood. I wondered, though, how I was going to convince her that I wasn't a dog. But I decided I would worry about that later.

I shared a room with three other patients, all of them white, female, English-speaking Zimbabweans. They asked what had happened to my hand. I told them a lion had bitten half my thumb off.

First they gasped. Then they laughed. Then they apologized for laughing.

It was an interesting reaction.

There was one white nurse in our ward. She had reacted in exactly the same way – gasp, laugh, apologize. But all the other nurses were African women. And not one of them had laughed. Their reactions had been only of shock and sympathy.

(Later, when I got home and was admitted to the Nelspruit hospital for further treatment, I encountered exactly the same responses. Every white nurse or patient who asked about my hand would gasp and then laugh at my answer. And then apologize for laughing. But the African nurses and the African patients who shared my ward were totally horrified, and would express their deepest sympathy.)

Strange, this difference in sentiments.

I thought about it. And it occurred to me that the idea of a lion biting off a person's thumb was, in fact, funny. I guess that proves that white people have a morbid sense of humour.

Later in the afternoon a nurse brought me a form to sign: patient's consent for surgery.

How would I sign it – minus a thumb and with my right hand all bandaged up? I decided my left hand would have to do the job.

I reached into my handbag for my reading glasses. They weren't there. The nurse searched for them in my bedside cabinet. They weren't there either. So I had to ask the nurse to please point me to the place on the form where my signature was required. She did. And I discovered that my left hand was unconnected to my brain. It couldn't even hold a pen, let alone sign my name.

'I give up,' I told the nurse. 'This hand can't write.'

'Don't worry,' she said. 'But you must sign the form. A cross will do.'

'Draw a cross,' I said to my left hand. It drew a shaky-looking four-legged spider.

'Not there,' the nurse said. 'Here.'

I'd missed the signature space by about half a page. But where was it exactly?

'Please show me again,' I asked the nurse. She did, and I eventually managed to produce an insecure-looking squiggle in almost the right place.

'Good girl!' said the nurse.

I was shaken. I had become illiterate.

I spent the rest of the afternoon feeling illiterate, insecure and sad. Mostly sad.

A nurse came to take my pulse. 'You're not smiling any more,' she said. 'What's the matter?'

She wouldn't understand about Leo. So I told her I'd lost my glasses.

'Where?' she asked, alarmed. 'When?' She took out a file from the holder at the foot of my bed and wrote everything down. Patient lost her glasses. Possibly in casualty ward. Approximate time: twelve fifteen.

'Please don't worry,' she begged me. 'And please don't feel so sad. We'll find your glasses for you right away!' She rushed off.

I was startled. I certainly hadn't meant to cause an uproar over my glasses.

After that, a nurse appeared at my bedside every ten minutes or so to report that everyone in the hospital was looking for my glasses. The casualty ward had been checked, as well as the reception desk and all the lifts. But I mustn't worry, they kept assuring me. The glasses would be found.

I felt awfully guilty. And I tried to explain to every nurse who talked to me that I hadn't meant to cause them all so much trouble. But no-one listened. They were convinced that my heart was breaking because I had lost my glasses.

I fixed a smile on my face.

No-one was going to catch me looking sad again.

Finally the staff nurse herself appeared at my bedside and told me she had good news for me: a patient in Ward B said she had been admitted to the hospital at the same time as a patient with an injured hand.

'That would be you,' said the staff nurse, pointing at me. 'And the patient in Ward B says that before you went into casualty you handed your glasses to a lady in a green tracksuit.'

'Ah, yes!' I said. 'That's Maria. She and my husband brought me in.'

'Would you like us to call her on the phone for you?' the good staff nurse offered.

I said no thanks. I knew Maria would take care of my glasses and return them to me.

Everyone smiled and looked happy. I thanked the staff nurse and everyone else for their trouble, and I also asked them to thank the observant patient in Ward B.

After an hour or so I got tired of lying in bed with a perpetual smile on my face. So I decided to get up and take a walk.

It was then that I saw the notice attached to the rail at the foot of my bed. The lettering was large, so I was able to read it without my glasses. It read: 'Patient: Mrs K. Kruger. Attending surgeon: Mr G. A. Vera.'

Mister Vera? Why *mister* instead of doctor? Surely my condition required a doctor!

I panicked. How could a surgeon not be a doctor? Did they have a shortage of properly trained surgeons in Harare or what? Goodness.

What would a mister know about stopping septicaemia? What if he resorted to some primitive method – like amputation?

I decided the only thing to do was to make sure Mr Vera knew his job. And the only way to do that would be to remain wide awake in theatre. I would refuse anaesthesia.

So I went off and found the ward sister. I told her that I'd forgotten to mention to her that I was allergic to general anaesthesia. She looked concerned and came back to my room with me to record the information in my file.

Mr Vera came to see me at seven thirty that evening and spent a while chatting to me. He seemed a pleasant person. His accent sounded slightly different from that of the other hospital staff. I wondered if he was originally from some other African country. Tanzania perhaps. Or Kenya. I didn't ask him about his training, of course. That would have been impolite. And ungracious.

He asked me about my allergic reactions to anaesthesia and I stammered something about anaphylactic shock. I'm not sure he believed me. But he said it was OK. If I didn't want general anaesthesia then he would anaesthetize only my hand.

That was good. I could remain awake and make sure that no-one chopped off the rest of my thumb.

Eventually I was wheeled down to the theatre floor. A nurse appeared and informed Mr Vera that there had not been time to clean any of the theatres, so none was available. She suggested that he use one of the pre-op waiting rooms. Mr Vera refused, telling the nurse that he wanted a sterile theatre and that he would wait for one if it took all night. The nurse hastily assured him that a sterile theatre would be ready for him within two hours.

So I was wheeled back to my room again. I didn't mind. I was relieved that Mr Vera had insisted on operating in a sterile theatre.

At nine thirty that evening I was finally wheeled into a sterile theatre.

Mr Vera unwrapped my bandages and anaesthetized my hand with four injections, which he warned me would hurt. But they didn't.

Perhaps my hand was still in shock. It was resting on a sterile steel table next to the bed. I thoroughly avoided looking at it.

After a while Mr Vera brought over a tray of instruments and took a pair of forceps from it. I asked him what he was going to do with them. He explained that the tendons in the thumb had drawn back and had to be pulled back into place. I could actually feel the tendons being pulled back up. A strange sensation. Then he took a pair of scissors from the tray.

'What are you going to do now?' I asked him.

He explained that, in order to inhibit sepsis, he needed to cut away the severed ends of the tendons as well as other damaged tissue.

I started getting the impression that Mr Vera knew his job.

Eventually he scrubbed the wound, and then reached for a surgical needle, explaining that he would sew a flap of skin over the severed bone to keep it covered. That would also help prevent sepsis, he said.

I asked if he didn't think it necessary to remove some of the damaged bone as well.

He replied that ordinarily he would prefer to do that. But the thumb was an important digit, he explained. So he would choose to save as much of the bone as possible and rely on antibiotic treatment to prevent possible bone sepsis. If it didn't work, then further debridement would be necessary, of course. But he believed that for the time being it was a risk worth taking.

'Will you be treating me with gram-positive as well as gram-negative antibiotics?' I asked.

'Yes,' he said. And glancing up he added, 'You seem to know a lot about the treatment of lion bites?'

'So do you,' I said. 'Where did you do your training?'

'Oxford and Edinburgh,' he replied.

'But then you're a doctor!' I exclaimed. 'A real surgeon, I mean!'

He grinned and said that yes, in fact, he was.

'So why are you called "mister" and not "doctor"?' I asked.

He explained to me that the British convention was to call a surgeon 'mister'.

'But why?' I asked.

'I suppose it's a kind of inverted snobbishness,' he replied.

'But that's silly,' I said. 'You study for many years to become a doctor. Then you study several years more only to end up as a mister again. It seems unfair, doesn't it?'

By way of reply, he told me the following story. Back in the Middle Ages the medical practitioners had a dim view of surgeons. The surgeons were the people who stole corpses for their research and to practise their operating skills. So they were regarded as the black sheep of the profession – the 'butchers'. And the practitioners refused to call them 'doctors'.

I liked Mr Vera.

And he certainly wasn't a butcher.

Kobus and Hettie came to visit me early the next morning, bringing me chocolates, magazines and my reading glasses. I was so happy to see them.

Kobus told me that he'd borrowed a cheque from Vivian Bristow to repay Maria's friends. He would repay Vivian as soon as we got back to South Africa.

I was relieved to know that those trusting strangers had been repaid.

I asked how Leo and Wolfie were.

Kobus said they were fine. Andy had brought over a young lioness named Sheila to Leo's camp the previous afternoon. She was one of the stars of the film, about a year old and very tame. Andy reasoned that since she was so much smaller than Leo, he would not be as scared of her as he was of the other lions. Unfortunately Sheila had refused to go into Leo's camp because of Wolfie, so Andy stood with her at the fence and called to Leo. At first Leo pretended not to see her, but after a while he gave in to curiosity and went closer, sitting down near the fence and stealing occasional glances at the young lioness, and sometimes hissing at her, just in case she had dubious designs on him. Still, Andy felt the visit had gone well and said he would bring Sheila over to Leo's camp every afternoon for a visit.

I was so pleased at the news.

In the late afternoon, further examination and X-rays revealed that my hand was still free from sepsis. I asked Mr Vera if I could be discharged. He said he would prefer to keep me there for another day or two. So I explained to him about Leo, adding that I had only a few days left with him. Mr Vera understood and agreed to discharge me that evening, on condition that I contacted him the moment I suspected any indications of sepsis. He asked also that I make an appointment to see him again in three days' time.

ONWARD, LEO

L EO WAS SO RELIEVED AND HAPPY TO SEE ME THE NEXT MORNING
that I thought my heart would break. How could I possibly leave
him in only a few days' time?

He kept rubbing his face against mine and uttering sorrowful groans
that seemed to mean: 'Where were you yesterday and the day before? I
missed you so much!'

'I missed you too,' I told him, and hugged him to me for a long time.

Later Maria and Julie came to ask how my hand was, and they spent
a while chatting to us.

After lunch Andy came to visit Leo again, and I noticed that Leo was
looking a lot more relaxed with Andy now, allowing him to stroke his
fur.

Kobus mentioned to Andy that Leo loved riding on the back of a
pick-up, and he asked if it would be OK if we took Leo for a drive
through the park. Andy said we were most welcome to do so, and he
promised that he too would take Leo on sightseeing drives once his
work with the film crew was finished.

As soon as Andy left us, Kobus told Leo and Wolfie to get onto the
back of the truck. Wolfie jumped up eagerly and Leo followed, a little
hesitantly. He wasn't sure if he wanted to explore this alien land yet. So
he huddled close to Wolfie. But after a while he started to relax a little
more and take an interest in his surroundings.

Pamuzinda is a beautiful park with both lowveld- and highveld-type vegetation.

We came across kudu, eland, buffalo and herds of sable antelope. Later we stopped at a creek and walked along its banks for some distance. Leo stayed close to us, and although he remained wary he enjoyed the walk.

When we arrived back at Leo's camp, Hettie went up to Julie's house for a drink of water and came back carrying a leg of impala – a gift to Leo from Julie. Leo was delighted with the familiar fare and got right down to devouring it. I was so pleased to see him eating well again. He'd hardly touched the wildebeest meat that had been delivered to his camp every day.

At dusk, Andy turned up with the young lioness Sheila on the back of his truck and let her into Leo's camp, saying she could spend the night. Leo eyed her warily and flopped down onto the grass, the way lions do when they're not sure what to do next. Sheila was scared of Wolfie and sought refuge in a far corner of the camp, even though Wolfie was behaving very nicely and keeping his distance. Andy suggested that we take Wolfie with us to Carol's house for the night.

I knew Leo would feel very insecure in his camp without Wolfie. But I very much wanted him to make friends with Sheila. Perhaps if he did, he would start to realize that he was a lion and not a dog. So we agreed to take Wolfie back with us for the night.

Leo looked extremely upset when he saw Wolfie getting onto the truck. Hettie asked her father to wait a while. Getting out of the truck, she went over to Sheila and sat down on the grass near her, talking calmly to her, winning her trust, until Sheila allowed Hettie to reach out and stroke her head. Then Hettie turned and called softly to Leo, pleading with him to come over and make Sheila's acquaintance. Leo got up and went a little closer, but after a few steps his courage failed him and he again flopped down onto the grass. He was still lying there when we left, and I hoped with all my heart that Sheila would go over to him and try to befriend him.

I lay awake half the night, wondering what Leo was doing.

On our return the next morning, Sheila had already left with Andy, and Leo was very relieved to see Wolfie and us again. He followed Wolfie about, moaning and complaining to him, obviously wanting to know why his friend had abandoned him the previous night. I asked Leo whether he and Sheila had at least spoken to each other. But he ignored my question. He wanted only to talk to the dog.

Andy arrived at midday with the news that the film crew had decided to take the afternoon off. So he was free for the rest of the day, and he thought it would be a good time to accompany us on a drive with Leo.

We drove some distance, then walked. Leo enjoyed the outing but stayed near us all the time, watching us closely.

Occasionally Andy would sit down and call Leo to him. Leo would turn and look to me for guidance.

'Go to Andy,' I would tell him in Afrikaans.

Leo would understand and go to Andy, obediently sitting down beside him. And Andy would stroke Leo's fur and say encouraging things to him. It gave me a lot of comfort to see how seriously Andy intended to win Leo's trust and friendship.

Andy remarked to us that he'd never before met a lion as even-tempered and well-behaved as Leo.

I told him that Leo wasn't always so docile – he could be quite mischievous sometimes, but that he was extremely sensitive to a harsh tone of voice, and actually a very gentle lion.

In the late afternoon we drove back to Leo's camp. As soon as we parked inside the camp, we saw a change in Leo's behaviour: he seemed both relieved and happy to be back in the familiar camp, and he even got quite playful, stalking us and inviting us to play wrestling games with him.

It was so good to see Leo showing some spirit again.

In the evening Andy brought Sheila to Leo's camp again, so we took

Wolfie with us, once again leaving Leo alone with Sheila for the night.

The following day was our second last day with Leo. Kobus, Hettie and I spent the whole day with him, taking him for drives and walks, resting with him in his camp, hugging him a lot and talking to him.

Leo was starting to show more interest in his surroundings now, as well as in the other lions. Whenever they weren't looking his way, he studied them quietly, peering intently at them over the tall grass, nose to the wind, and a frown on his face. He still avoided looking at them when they roared, but he no longer tried so hard to become invisible.

On our last day I had my appointment with the surgeon. Kobus drove me to Harare while Hettie stayed with Leo.

Mr Vera was satisfied that my hand showed no signs of sepsis, and he wrote me a report to give to a surgeon in my own country.

Afterwards Kobus and I stopped at a supermarket and bought a chicken as a farewell present for Leo.

We returned to Pamuzinda and spent the rest of the afternoon with Leo, staying with him until long after dark.

Then we stopped by Andy's house to tell him that we would be leaving early the next morning, as soon as we'd said goodbye to Leo. And we asked Andy if he would please, if possible, visit Leo soon after we left and stay with him a while to comfort him.

Andy promised that he would. Maria also offered to go over to Leo's camp the following morning and talk to him. She suggested to me that I leave Leo something with my smell on it – a blouse or a jacket perhaps. She said it would give him comfort in my absence.

I thought about Maria's suggestion that night. And I decided I would leave Leo my pillow. I had a favourite pillow that travelled with me wherever I went. It was a soft, thick, down-filled pillow, and it had belonged to me ever since I was a child. I knew Leo would love it. He loved soft things.

Early the next morning we drove back to Leo's camp for the last time.

We couldn't bring ourselves to tell Leo that we were leaving him. So we just hugged him a lot and stroked his fur.

Eventually we gave him his chicken. He was surprised and delighted at the sight of his favourite fare – but only for a moment. He knew something was wrong. He sensed our mood, and his eyes were full of questions.

'We have to go now,' Kobus said finally. He gave Leo a last firm hug, patted him on the back and then walked to the truck and got in.

Hettie hugged Leo wordlessly, spilling tears onto the top of his head. Then she too got into the truck.

I fetched my pillow from the truck and gave it to Leo. He slumped to a crouching position, clutching the pillow to his chest. And when he looked at me, there was comprehension in his eyes. He knew then that we were leaving.

It was the hardest moment of my life.

I wanted to give him a final hug but I was afraid that he would sense my anguish. So I merely patted his head. Then I got into the truck and we drove off.

I couldn't look back.

Kobus and Hettie didn't look back either.

It was only Wolfie who looked back.

He stared at his friend until he could no longer see him.

TEARS AND CONSOLATION

WE DIDN'T TALK MUCH ON THE LONG DRIVE HOME.
But we tried.

We remarked on the scenery. And we stopped from time to time for tea, or to give Wolfie a drink of water. And then we commented on the scenery once more.

We arrived home in the early hours of the following morning. After a few hours' sleep, Kobus drove me to the hospital in Nelspruit. My hand was sore and slightly swollen.

The surgeon did further debridement.

Two days later when I was home again, my trouble-sharing friend Annette came to visit me. It was so good to see her again.

She said she was sorry about my thumb. I told her it hardly worried me.

She said, 'OK. So talk to me about Leo. Tell me everything.'

I did. And, in a way, it helped me to get things into better perspective.

Afterwards I said, 'I miss him a lot. But I can cope with that. What I can't cope with is the idea of how much he misses us.'

'I know what you mean,' Annette said. She looked so sad.

We poured ourselves some more coffee.

After a while Annette said, 'You must try to take comfort in the fact that Leo is still young. Young people have a lot of emotional resilience, you know.'

I nodded.

'Well, I know Leo's not a person,' she added. 'He's a lion. But what's the difference? Anyway, I also believe that a happy childhood provides a good foundation for a happy adulthood.'

I thought about that. And it gave me some comfort.

Hettie went back to university. Paul and Sandra came home. Sandra shopped, cooked and cleaned the house for me. I was touched. She need not have done it. My hand wasn't sore any more. But I guess she knew it wasn't my hand that was hurting.

Friends and family called. They were sorry for me because of my thumb. This baffled me at times. What's so tragic about losing half a thumb?

After a few days I decided it was time to get on with the business of living again.

So I worked hard and talked and laughed and did all kinds of normal things.

I even managed quite well without my thumb.

Except that I dropped a lot of things.

In fact, I dropped so many plates and dishes that my kitchen cupboards began to look alarmingly empty.

But I didn't care.

It was nice to see things hit the floor and break into tiny pieces.

Insomnia was my main problem.

What kept me awake at night was the expression I had seen in Leo's eyes when I gave him my pillow. He'd known then that I was saying goodbye. And he'd accepted it – quietly and stoically. No complaints. But his eyes had been so full of sorrow.

Wolfie missed his friend too. He would look at me with a big question mark in his eyes. And I would explain to him, over and over, why we had had to leave Leo in Zimbabwe. Eventually he seemed to understand that there were valid reasons, so he accepted it with a sigh that seemed to mean, 'Yes. I see. But I kind of miss the brat.'

I promised Wolfie that we would get him a new friend – a real dog, one who would look up to him and have respect for him.

I went back to hospital again for cosmetic surgery. The surgeon made slits along each side of my thumb, cutting right into the subcutaneous tissue. Then he lifted the sections of loosened skin and tissue, stretching them to cover the piece of exposed bone that was sticking out where the knuckle used to be.

When I woke up after the surgery, my thumb hurt so much that I could hardly talk. I felt rather cheated. I thought there had been an agreement between my thumb and me that it wouldn't hurt as long as I didn't look at it.

For a few days my whole hand seemed to ache. Then the pain finally went away, and I removed the bandages to look at my thumb for the first time since Happie had eaten half of it.

It was much too short. And there were so many stitches sticking out in all directions that it looked like a miniature hedgehog. So I bound it up again and decided to keep it covered until the stitches came out. But when the stitches were finally out, my thumb still failed to look pretty. So I bandaged it up again.

'You can't wear bandages the rest of your life,' Kobus told me.

'I can,' I told him.

But eventually I got tired of bothering with bandages. So I threw them away and decided to ignore my thumb.

'Your thumb is not so ugly,' Kobus told me.

'It is,' I told him.

'Well, don't worry,' he said. 'I still love you.'

'You have no choice,' I reminded him. 'Your scarred leg isn't too pretty either.'

Karin said, 'Oh heavens, I have such disgusting parents – both of them chomped up by lions!'

Her gay laugh always lifted my spirits. I knew she missed Leo very much too. But she kept her sorrow under wraps and never allowed it to spill over into her everyday life.

Gareth phoned near the end of July to ask how Leo was doing. It was good to talk to him again. He understood all about the anguish of parting with a lion.

He was on his way to the UK for the promotion of his new book, *The Last of the Free*. I wished him luck and invited him to visit us as soon as he got back to tell us all about it.

He promised he would.

Karin taught me an alternative way of holding a pen, and so I was soon able to write again.

My main problem was typing. It took my brain a surprisingly long time to realize that it could no longer send messages to the missing half of my right thumb. 'Hit the space bar,' it would command my right thumb. And my poor half thumb would respond immediately but miss the space bar and hit the desk instead.

I decided that in future my left thumb should take over the responsibility of striking the space bar.

But as soon as my brain sent out the message to my left thumb to hit the space bar, my right thumb would respond instead and hit the desk.

'No, not you!' I'd reprimand my right thumb. And looking hard at my left thumb I'd tell it, 'You! Hit the space bar!'

But my left thumb's response was always the same: 'Who, me? What space bar?'

Eventually my right index finger got impatient with my left thumb for being so slow and opted to take over the job itself. The result is that my right index finger operates in constant overdrive – darting every which way to strike its own quota of keys as well as the space bar – while my idiotic left thumb just hangs there above the keyboard, doing nothing at all.

It's a pity Happie hadn't eaten my left thumb instead. It would have served it right for being so useless.

Every Sunday, week after week and month after month, I'd make a phone call to Pamuzinda. It didn't help much. Often the connection was so bad that I would have to shout down the line.

Occasionally I would be able to hear a voice at the other end – Graeme's or Julie's – and it would tell me that Leo was just fine.

I wanted desperately to know more. What was he doing? How was he looking? I thought once that I heard Julie telling me that Leo had made friends with Sheila. But I wasn't sure. The connection was so bad. On the few occasions that I got a good connection the family weren't home, only the cook, and he didn't really know how Leo was.

I was seldom able to speak to Andy as he didn't have a phone in his house, and he wasn't always within calling distance of Graeme's and Julie's house. But on the few occasions that I did manage to talk to him, he assured me that he and Leo were getting along well and that Leo was fine. Those few calls lifted my spirits a bit. But I wished Andy would tell me more. Perhaps there wasn't much more to tell. Or maybe Andy didn't want to tell me on the phone how much Leo still missed us.

Our telephone bills were staggering. And the frustrating nature of the calls meant they weren't really worth it.

Then one day at the beginning of October something good happened. I answered a telephone call and heard Andy's voice at the other end.

'Andy!' I called out in surprise. 'Is that really you? You sound so close!'

'That's because I am,' he replied. 'I'm at Skukuza.' He explained that Vivian Bristow had sent him to buy elephants from the Kruger Park for Pamuzinda.

'How long will you be staying?' I asked anxiously.

'One night,' he said.

'Please come over and spend the night with us!' I begged him.

'That's why I'm calling,' he said. 'To ask if you can put me up.'

I was elated. 'Please hurry up and get here as soon as you can,' I told him.

I called Kobus on the VHF radio to share the news with him and he answered that he'd be home within an hour or so.

Kobus and Andy arrived more or less at the same time.

'How's Leo?' were my first words to Andy. Then I realized I was being ungracious. So I hugged Andy and backtracked: 'Hi, Andy! How are you? I'm so pleased to see you. Please come right inside and tell us all about Leo.' That didn't sound too gracious either, and I felt ashamed of myself.

But Andy grinned and said, 'Leo is fine. If you wish, I'll talk non-stop about him for the rest of the evening.'

I rushed to the kitchen to get our evening meal ready, and then – at last – I sat down to listen to news of my lion.

Andy told us everything, leaving nothing out.

Some parts of the story made me very sad. But I appreciated Andy's honesty.

He told us that initially Leo had missed us very much. He'd spent most of his days clutching my pillow to him and listening for the sound of our truck. For about two weeks he wouldn't eat and he lost a lot of weight. Then, gradually, he started eating again and taking an interest in his surroundings. Andy regularly took him for walks and drives all over Pamuzinda, and the two of them became good friends. Leo also became playful again. He would steal Andy's cap and run off with it, or stalk Andy and challenge him to a wrestling game. He also made friends with a buffalo who often came to graze near his camp. He would stalk it quietly, creeping right up to the fence of his camp, and then leap up and startle the buffalo. The buffalo would run off for some distance, then turn round and come charging back at full speed. Leo would flee and hide in the tall grass. Then the game would start all over again.

Andy had let the young lioness Sheila share Leo's camp nightly for about two weeks, until the filming was completed and Sheila had to be returned to her own family at the Lion and Cheetah Park. Although Leo had seemed to enjoy Sheila's company, he'd remained wary of her, as Sheila tended to be moody – affectionate and playful one moment, short-tempered and snappish the next. And since Leo didn't altogether trust lions yet, it unnerved him when Sheila got quarrelsome, even though she was much smaller than him.

Meanwhile, the main lion camp had been completed, and old Trade together with Happie and Fat Cat had taken up permanent residence in their new quarters. Leo no longer tried to hide in the tall grass when he saw the other lions looking at him, but would merely turn his head and respectfully look the other way. Whenever they weren't looking at him, he enjoyed watching and studying them. He found old Trade especially fascinating. Trade still marked his territory every day and broadcast his dominion over it. And whenever Trade started roaring, Leo would gape in pure admiration. Leo's instincts were evidently telling him that Trade was the king – as well as his role model. Occasionally Leo would try to imitate Trade's roaring. But his voice wasn't quite up to it yet. It tended to break. And so his attempts at roaring sounded a bit like yodelling.

All in all, Andy concluded, Leo was beginning to settle down. He'd gained weight again, and he was looking well. And the fact that he idolized Trade seemed a sure indication that he was beginning to catch on to the idea that he himself was a lion.

I asked Andy if we could visit Leo in December. Andy said he didn't think we should come so soon. Leo would certainly be overjoyed to see us again, and then the inevitable parting would only be heartbreaking for all of us all over again. Lions had very long memories, Andy reminded us. Leo would never forget us. But it would be best for him, as well as for us, if we postponed our first visit to him until he was happily settled in the main camp with the other lions.

I asked Andy how long it would be before Leo could go into the main camp.

Andy said he wasn't sure. Time would tell. As long as Leo remained scared of the other lions, it would not be safe for either him or them to share a camp. If Leo felt threatened, he might react with aggression. And then the other lions would also feel threatened and they might attack him.

'How will you know when he's ready?' I asked.

Andy smiled and said, 'Well, for one thing, when he stops hugging your pillow to him.'

'He still does that?' I asked, surprised.

'Yes,' Andy said. 'He does. It's his security blanket. It reminds him of you.'

I tried to smile, but the lump in my throat got too big. So I said: 'Let me get us some fresh coffee.' I hurried into the kitchen, closed the door behind me and wept into the dish-towel.

Then I made us some good strong coffee and carried it into the lounge.

As we sat sipping our coffee, Andy told us to remember that Leo was still a young lion, just entering adulthood, with a long and happy life ahead of him. He would always have a lion family of his own, as well as human friends. He would always be protected, well fed and looked after. All in all, Andy assured us, Leo's life would be easier than that of a wild lion.

Dear, good Andy – he'd brought us a lot of comfort.

After Andy's visit to us I asked Kobus if he believed, as Andy did, that Leo's life would eventually be easier than that of a wild lion. Kobus said yes, he did. As much as he'd wished for Leo to be a free lion, he found that he could now take comfort from the knowledge that Leo would never get caught in a poacher's snare or die from a hunter's bullet, never go hungry or suffer sickness or injuries.

In the wild, Kobus told me, the average life expectancy of a male lion was about twelve years.

Trade was twenty-four years old.

I hoped that Trade's story was an indication of what Leo's life would be like.

Trade had been the king at the Lion and Cheetah Park for most of his life and he'd enjoyed the love and admiration of his wives and off-spring for many years. When he got too old to fulfil his role as king, Vivian Bristow moved him to Pamuzinda, together with two of his granddaughters (Happie and Fat Cat), so that he might retire there in peace.

I thought this was a rather nice story for a lion.

And I liked the idea of Leo becoming king of the Pamuzinda pride one day. I also liked the name 'Pamuzinda'. Translated from the Shona language, it means 'Meeting Place of the Royals'.

Perhaps, one day, people will think the name referred to the meeting of two lion kings: Trade and Leo.

DOMINATED BY A GENET CAT

ONE DAY IN OCTOBER, SHORTLY AFTER ANDY'S VISIT TO US, A TEAM of maintenance workers came to rethatch the roof of Kobus's office. While removing some of the damaged straw, they surprised a family of genets that had been nesting in the thatch. The genets fled, leaving one of their kittens behind. The workers put the abandoned kitten in a box and left it inside the office, but forgot to tell Kobus or me about it.

Kobus found the kitten in his office the following morning. After the thatchers had explained the story to him, Kobus came to tell me about the kitten, asking what we should do about it.

The idea of being a foster mother all over again frightened me. So I decided that if the kitten's mother didn't come back for it, I would give it to Annette. She would make a good foster mother. And she would understand that the timing was wrong for me. I still missed Leo too much.

I followed Kobus outside to his office to have a look at the kitten. It was still in the box. Kobus opened the box and I peered inside. A small grey bundle greeted me with a furious hiss. As I reached into the box, it lashed out at me with sharp little claws. I lifted the frightened creature out and hugged it to me, willing it to relax. It fixed me with a bold gaze and tried to look fierce, but the defiant glare failed to hide the look of sheer misery on its little face.

I carried it back to the house and, after wrapping it in a warm shawl, tried to persuade it to take milk from a medicine dropper. Fortunately the hungry kitten soon got the hang of it, gulping the milk as fast as it could. Afterwards I stroked its fur until it fell asleep in my lap.

Kobus judged the kitten to be about six weeks old – young enough to be tamed, but old enough to sense that it had lost its real mother and to miss her very much.

Poor little thing.

And so I became a genet-mother.

That's how these things always happen to me.

I did try, however, to give the kitten back to its real parents. For several nights I stayed up late, listening to every sound in the garden, hoping that I'd hear the parents calling to their lost kitten. But no genet called. Perhaps the parents couldn't count too well and didn't realize that one of their children was missing.

One morning, a few days after we'd adopted the kitten, Wolfie knocked at the front door, asking to meet the new member of the family. I invited him inside.

The kitten was asleep on my bed. Wolfie approached it carefully. Sticking out his nose, he sniffed gently at it. The kitten woke up and promptly gave Wolfie a furious slap on the nose. Wolfie spun round and, facing me, let out a bark of surprise. The bark was not aimed at me, of course, nor was it intended for the kitten – it was a purely involuntary bark. Dear Wolfie would never dream of barking at a defenceless kitten.

When Karin arrived home on the Friday she was delighted to find that our family had once again acquired a new member. She named him Kitzi and spent most of the weekend cuddling him – spoiling him beyond redemption.

On Monday morning Karin went back to school, and I was left alone with a kitten that demanded constant cuddling. Whenever he woke up he called to me with a loud plaintive 'wheep' that never failed to send me rushing to him. He soon learned that the more soul-stirring his call sounded, the faster I would come running.

After a week or so Kitzi became playful, which was nice but exhausting since he refused to play alone. I provided him with all kinds of toys to keep him occupied, but he had better ideas. Possessed of a wild imagination, he preferred games of the make-believe kind, such as pretending that he was a man-eating tiger. He would lie quietly in wait on top of a bookcase or a curtain rail, a door or a cupboard, until I came within pouncing distance. I acquired the habit of checking out all possible hiding places and dashing through rooms at top speed. But the tiger would launch himself at me from nowhere, usually landing on my head.

Another game was to pretend that he was a mad ape. Swinging from the curtains and dashing crazily through the house at top speed, he would leap like lightning from bookcase to couch to table – to me. If I tried to get out of the way, he gave chase and, catching up with me, ran straight up me as if I were a tree.

I was grateful that the kitten still spent a good number of hours sleeping during the day, or I might have gone crazy. Unfortunately he didn't sleep a lot at night, and he didn't want me to sleep a lot at night either. If I refused to wake up he licked my eyelashes or chewed my hair. And if that didn't persuade me to wake up and play, he would get under the bed covers and bite my toes.

Fostering a cheeky genet was an exhausting business. Even so, I liked the brat – especially when he curled up in my lap and licked my arms with his rough little tongue, purring with contentment.

I was surprised that he could purr. I thought only members of the feline family purred. Genets belong to the *Viverridae* family. Other members of this family are the civets and mongooses. Mongooses don't purr, and I don't think civets do either.

The genet looks like a cross between a domestic cat and a mongoose. Its movements are graceful and catlike but it has the elongated body and shorter legs of the mongoose. It has a long tail which it carries straight out when on the move. The short, soft and dense coat is a light brownish-grey on the upper parts, buffy-white on the lower parts, and

heavily spotted all over. Being both terrestrial and arboreal, the genet can run up a tree faster and better than most members of the cat family.

My genet kitten ran straight up bookcases and wooden doors, as well as straight up me, of course. I spent most of my days as a genet-mother covered in claw marks.

When in a calmer mood, Kitzi loved to ride on my shoulder. Wherever I moved inside the house, he would ride along, observing my activities. If I bent down to pick something up, he would dig his claws into my shoulder and hang on. There was no way that I could get him off my shoulder if he didn't want to get off. He especially enjoyed perching on my shoulder to watch me wash my hair. Apparently the foaming shampoo fascinated him. On a few occasions he got carried away with fascination, lost his grip and fell into the washbasin.

Although Kitzi felt very much at home in the house, he remained frightened of the outdoors for several months. So as soon as he was old enough to start eating solids, I had to go out hunting every day to find his food for him. His favourite fare was grasshoppers, crickets, beetles and the like.

I'm not a hunter at heart. In fact, I find hunting most distressing. But that's motherhood for you. I carried an old shoebox on my hunting expeditions and put everything that I caught inside. Then I brought the box back into the house and, removing the lid, allowed everything to escape – giving all a fair chance. If the genet caught and ate them, then at least I didn't need to feel too directly responsible for their fate. It was also a good way of teaching him to hunt for himself. He would soon require larger prey such as frogs, lizards and other reptile fauna, and I had no intention of catching those for him.

When Kitzi was about three months old I insisted that he started hunting for his own food in the garden. Being a nocturnal animal he refused to leave the house in the daytime, but at night he was willing to accompany me out of doors, if somewhat wary. At first he would run straight up me at the slightest noise or movement in the dark. But as time went by he became braver and learned to enjoy our nightly expeditions.

The children came home for the Christmas holidays, and Paul and Sandra brought us a beautiful border-collie pup named Jasper.

Wolfie, his usual aloof self, pretended that playing with a pup was rather beneath him. He would be the pup's mentor and role model, nothing else. But he didn't fool me. Often, when he didn't know I was watching through a window, he would be playing madly with the pup, allowing it to chase him round and round a tree, or to pounce on him and bully him while he lay on his back, paws in the air, with an idiotic grin of happiness on his face.

I had never seen Wolfie behave so foolishly in his entire life. No wonder he chose to play with the pup only when he thought no-one was looking.

Although Jasper enjoyed playing outside with Wolfie and the children during the day, at night he wanted to be near me. (He was, after all, just a three-month-old pup who still needed a mother when it got dark.) So he slept under our bed. The genet didn't like that at all. The house belonged to him, and so did I.

At first Kitzi was a little scared of Jasper, so he did nothing much except threaten the dog from the top of a tall bookcase, and then sulk the rest of the night to let me know how offended he was at having to share his domain with a dog.

Jasper got very excited the first time he saw the cat and he wanted very much to sort him out. So I had to have a serious talk to Jasper, explaining to him that the house did in fact belong to the genet, and that dogs weren't allowed to bark at a genet in its own house.

Being an intelligent dog, Jasper understood and accepted the situation.

But on Jasper's fourth night with us, Kitzi decided he'd had enough, and he attacked the pup under the bed in the middle of the night. Jasper, however, wasn't having any. He barked the genet right out of the room and chased him all over the house.

A little while later Jasper returned. Getting back under the bed he flopped down to continue his peaceful dreams.

Before long the angry genet came back and attempted to rough up the dog again. So I had to get out of bed and give them both a serious lecture.

This went on for several nights until Kobus got really mad and said that if the nightly riots didn't stop, then either my brood and I would have to sleep outside or he would.

So the following evening I made a bed for Jasper in the garden shed where Wolfie slept, explaining to him that the only reason I was changing the sleeping arrangements was because the warfare between him and the genet wasn't too good for my marriage.

The older the genet got, the more possessive he became of me, and the more jealous he was of anything that occupied my thoughts outside of himself.

His daily routine started with attacking me in my bed at the dreadful hour of about five in the morning to tell me he needed attention. I'd throw him out of the room and shut the door. But he'd scream and scratch at the door until I could sleep no longer. As soon as I was up and about, he'd either ride along on my shoulder or play ambush games with me.

At about ten in the morning, he'd eat his breakfast of minced meat mixed with egg and calcium powder. Afterwards he visited his sandbox and then went off to find himself a place to sleep, usually in a wardrobe, and I was able to enjoy some peace until about four in the afternoon.

As soon as he woke up he would come looking for me to tell me he was ready for fun and games again. If I was busy he would try his best to drive me crazy. The madder I got with him, the more he enjoyed the game. He'd leap onto my head, slide down my hair and disappear like lightning if I tried to smack him, then be back again in a flash for more fun.

In the evenings he enjoyed pestering the rest of the family if they were home. But he was never as bold and cheeky with them as he was with me.

After our evening meal it would be hunting time. Depending on how long it took us to find enough prey in the dark garden to fill his stomach, a hunting session could last from half an hour to two hours. After that, he'd be calmer and would content himself with resting in my lap while I read or listened to music.

I was pleased when, at the age of about six months, he started spending time outdoors on his own at night. I always left a window open for him on the veranda, and whenever he came in – sometimes at midnight, sometimes in the early morning hours – he'd rush straight to me and wake me up to tell me all about his nocturnal adventures.

As he got older and bolder, he started out on his nightly expeditions much earlier in the evening and entirely on his own. I was very proud of him.

Kitzi was about nine months old when I woke up late one night to the sound of a genet screaming for help. I ran outside with my torch. Following the sound of the calls I aimed the beam into a tree wistaria.

And there was Kitzi, high up in the branches, with another genet. Frightened by my presence the strange genet fled. And so I believed that I'd saved Kitzi from a territorial fight with another male genet. I called to him to come down to me. But he gave me a disdainful look and proceeded to lick his paws in the complacent way of cats.

'OK,' I told him. 'You fight your own battles then!'

I went back to bed.

But before long the screaming of genet cats woke me again.

Rushing outside with my torch, I again found the two of them in the top of the tree wistaria. They didn't really seem to be fighting. My presence unnerved the other genet, and it fled once more.

'What was all that screaming about?' I asked Kitzi. He refused to answer me.

The answer came to me the next evening when the screaming started again.

A territorial fight it was not. It was a courting serenade. The other genet was a female.

When Kitzi came in later that evening I was still reading. Jumping onto my lap he stretched himself out and started washing himself all over, purring contentedly.

'So you've found yourself a girlfriend?' I said. 'Aren't you a bit young for that?'

I had no idea at what age genets started dating. I checked my book on small mammals, but found no answer.

The courting continued over a period of several days, and some nights my genet didn't come in at all.

Eventually he stayed out for four days. Presumably he'd gone off and got married. After the honeymoon he came back, bringing his wife along, intent on persuading her to move into his house with him.

Jumping onto the sill of the open veranda window, he sat there and called to her. She climbed up the tree wistaria and refused to come any closer to the house. So Kitzi sat at the open window, calling, 'Please,

please come and see my house – you'll love it! There are always snacks available, as well as free rides on shoulders!'

But his wife answered from the tree wistaria with a plaintive wail, telling him that if he didn't stop being idiotic she would file for divorce.

Night after night Kitzi tried to persuade his wife to move into his house, but to no avail. Eventually it dawned on him that he would have to choose between his wife and his mother's house. The wife won. And so he moved into her house – a comfortable den among the large and densely packed fronds of a palm tree in a far corner of the garden. He also shared her hunting territory, which comprised our whole garden as well as the gardens of the two trail rangers across the road.

Although I missed the domineering brat, I was very pleased to know that he was happily married.

And whenever I heard him and his wife singing to each other in our garden at night, I would think back to that first night in our new home when I'd been welcomed by a genet serenade. Those genets must have been Kitzi's parents.

Little had I known then that I would one day be obliged to raise one of their kids for them.

NEWS OF LEO

ON A SUNDAY MORNING IN THE SAME MONTH THAT KITZI GOT married, which was May, I tried to make a phone call to Graeme's and Julie's house at Pamuzinda but the lines were out of order. So I called Vivian's and Carol's home at the Lion and Cheetah Park. I hadn't had any news of Leo for more than a month, and I longed desperately to know how he was. It was now almost eleven months since we'd last seen him.

Carol Bristow answered my call, and fortunately we got a very clear line so we didn't need to shout at each other. She told me that Leo had been moved into the main camp in April, and that he was now living happily with the other lions. He was still a little wary of Fat Cat, but very much in love with Happie.

When I put the receiver down, it occurred to me that I was the happiest person in the whole world.

For the next few weeks Leo was constantly on my mind, and the longing to see him again became almost unbearable.

Kobus was working hard and was seldom home. But every time I saw him, I asked him: 'When can we go and visit Leo?'

His answer was always the same: 'Soon now. As soon as I've finished this job.'

There appeared to be no end to the urgent jobs scheduled for him in May and June. Apart from the normally busy winter programmes, a large number of elephants had to be relocated to parks elsewhere in southern Africa to prevent the depletion of overstocked pastures in Kruger.

Finally one day at the beginning of July, Kobus looked at his calendar and said, 'I can take ten days' leave – from 17 July. You can start making arrangements for us to visit Leo.'

I was so excited that I could think of nothing else in the days that followed.

Karin would be home for her winter vacation and so she would be able to accompany us. I made reservations for the three of us at Pamuzinda Safari Lodge – a recently completed establishment on the Pamuzinda estate. Unfortunately dogs weren't allowed at the lodge so we arranged for game guard Andries Tshabalala to look after Wolfie and Jasper in our absence.

Apart from feeling guilty about leaving my dogs at home, and regretting that Hettie, Sandra and Paul were busy with exams and unable to accompany us, I looked forward to our Zimbabwe trip more than anything else in the world.

I was finally going to see my lion again.

Perhaps if I returned home with happy memories, they would lay to rest the one incredibly sad memory that was still haunting me – of that last morning with Leo when I had given him my pillow.

A VISIT TO THE KING

Dawn was just a hint of mauve in the eastern sky when we left home on 17 July. The sun rose over the acacia bushlands near Skukuza, revealing a bright and beautiful winter's day.

We travelled at a leisurely pace, stopping to admire animals and scenery along the way and enjoying our eight-hour journey through the park as much as any tourist would. Or perhaps even more.

We arrived at Punda Maria – the northernmost camp – in the late afternoon, and spent the night there.

Leaving at dawn the following morning, we saw the sun rise over the Luvuvhu River, and about an hour later we left the park through Pafuri Gate, travelling west towards the Beit Bridge border post. From there we tackled the six-hundred-kilometre journey north to Harare. It was nice to be able to enjoy the vast and quiet bushland landscapes of southern Zimbabwe without feeling weighed down by the sadness that had accompanied us on our journey to and from Pamuzinda the previous year.

We reached Harare in the late afternoon and turned west towards Pamuzinda, arriving at the entrance gate at dusk. The gate guard informed us that Graeme Bristow was expecting us and that we were to drive to his house before going on to the Safari Lodge.

We duly followed these instructions – and were surprised to find a whole welcoming party awaiting us. Graeme, Julie and Andy were there, as well as the senior Bristows, Vivian and Carol, who had driven all the way from their home at the Lion and Cheetah Park. (Only Maria was absent. She was visiting her parents in South Africa.)

Another member of the welcoming party was a young girl named Fiona Nelson. Half Scottish, half English and with a degree in Zoology, she had worked for Iain Douglas-Hamilton (the renowned elephant expert, ecologist and writer) at Naivasha in Kenya before coming to work for the Bristows. Although Karin, at the age of seventeen, was a few years younger than Fiona, the two of them struck up an immediate friendship and spent the evening sharing their views on life, which, judging from their laughter, appeared to be of an upbeat nature.

We thoroughly enjoyed the evening and the company.

First we talked about Leo, of course. And Andy gave us the following account of Leo's introduction into the main camp.

On D-Day, Andy moved old Trade out of the main camp to Leo's former camp, and he also locked up the two lionesses in an enclosure in one corner of the main camp. Then he fetched Leo, who had been waiting on the back of his pick-up, and persuaded him to accompany him into the now lion-deserted camp. Leo bravely set foot in the alien territory, looked around for a while and, after some encouragement from Andy, started exploring the place.

Sniffing at the bushes that Trade had marked, Leo set about re-marking them in his own name. And for the better part of the day, Leo and Andy patrolled the camp while Leo checked and marked the boundaries of his new domain. In the late afternoon, when Leo was finally satisfied that the land had been adequately transferred into his own name, he sat down in a patch of tall grass not far from the lionesses' enclosure. And so he spent the last hours of the day contemplating his new kingdom, while stealing occasional glances at the two females behind the wire.

On the following day Andy opened the gate of the enclosure, letting Happie out into the main camp with Leo. She bounded over to Leo in a playful way. Leo fell flat in the tall grass and tried to make himself invisible. But Happie capered right up to him and begged him with umf-umf noises to say hello to her. Leo insisted on pretending that he wasn't there, so Happie pressed her head close to his and tried to sweet-talk him out of his invisible act. Eventually Leo got a bit braver and lifted his head. Happie uttered a groan of happiness and promptly rubbed heads with him. Leo had never before in his life rubbed heads with a real grown-up lioness, and for a moment it felt rather scary. But then it started to feel awfully right. So he got to his feet and they rubbed heads some more. Next they rubbed shoulders. Then heads again and, as Happie kissed him right on the cheek, it occurred to Leo that Happie was the cutest lioness this side of heaven.

Soon he was bounding after her, and the two of them started courting each other in all manner of ways.

Later, when the sun got hot, they flopped down in a shady spot under some trees and spent the next few hours gazing fondly at each other.

Andy was pleased at the outcome of things between Leo and Happie, and so he went home.

The following morning he found them rubbing heads and grunting sweet nothings to each other.

A few days later, Andy locked Happie up in the enclosure and let Fat Cat out.

Fat Cat approached Leo with an arrogant air.

Andy saw trouble coming, so he hurried over to Leo's side. Leo also saw trouble coming and decided to get out of Fat Cat's way. But he wasn't quick enough. Fat Cat caught up with him and started slapping him around. Andy shouted at Fat Cat to stop, but she wouldn't. So Andy grabbed a stick and, while screaming and shouting at Fat Cat, he whacked her with the stick until she stopped roughing Leo up. Andy chased her off, threatening her with murder if she didn't behave. (Let me explain here that Andy is a gentle person. He is soft-spoken and tender-hearted, tall and lean, and he weighs about three hundred pounds less than an adult lion.) After chasing Fat Cat a good hundred metres or so away, Andy returned to Leo and found him extremely upset and offended. So Andy sat down with Leo for a heart-to-heart talk.

Eventually Leo started feeling a bit better, and he and Andy went for a walk around the camp.

Fat Cat was resting under a tree, minding her own business. Or so it seemed.

As soon as Andy and Leo entered her field of vision, she let out an angry roar and went for Leo again. Leo tried to take evasive action but Fat Cat caught up with him. As Leo turned to beg for mercy, she gave him another vicious slap across the nose. Without waiting for any encouragement from Andy, Leo decided he'd had enough of the fat arrogant cat, and so he slapped her right back. That seemed to put Fat Cat in her place and she immediately became more respectful.

A little while later the two lions were each resting in a shady spot, at a sensible distance from each other.

The stalemate continued for the rest of the afternoon. By the end of the day, Andy felt that Leo would be able to hold his own against Fat Cat, so he decided to leave them to it and go home. At that stage Leo was sitting beside the fence of the enclosure, talking to Happie, no doubt telling her all about his dreadful day with Fat Cat.

On the following day Andy found Leo and Fat Cat still ignoring each other. Leo spent most of his time either patrolling his new kingdom or visiting Happie. The two of them would lie down on either side of the fence, rubbing heads through the wire and grunting softly to each other.

A few days later, when Andy felt confident that Fat Cat no longer had murder on her mind, he opened the gate of the enclosure to let Happie out. Leo and Happie were thoroughly delighted at being properly reunited.

For another week or so, Fat Cat kept her distance. Then she started making friendly overtures to Leo, adding a good measure of female coquetry. So Leo decided to let bygones be bygones. He forgave Fat Cat and they kissed and made up.

Although Happie was evidently Leo's favourite wife, Leo was on good terms with Fat Cat now and he even appeared to have become quite fond of her.

I asked Andy if there were any signs of jealousy between the two lionesses. Andy said no, none at all. They were like sisters. They'd more or less grown up together and they'd also raised their first litters of cubs together. So the bond between them was very strong.

Old Trade was still in good health, Andy told us. But he was very old now. In fact, at twenty-five he was probably the oldest lion alive in Africa. So it had seemed a good idea to move him into his own private camp and allow him the peace and quiet that an old lion needs. He now spent most of his days eating, sleeping and enjoying regular visits from Graeme and Andy, as well as from the senior Bristows who liked to drop in for a chat with old Trade whenever they were in the area.

While we were talking about the lions, two yellowish blurs suddenly dashed through the lounge – in through one door and out the other.

'What was that?' Kobus and I exclaimed simultaneously.

The next moment they were back – another fast dash through the lounge – and we saw they were two cheetah cubs playing a game of tag. They appeared to be about six weeks old.

Meanwhile, Julie Bristow sat on the carpet in a corner of the room, surrounded by her two young children as well as three dogs and two sleepy hyena cubs.

Fascinating.

Karin couldn't keep her eyes off the hyena cubs, so Julie invited her to come over the following day to play with them. Fiona mentioned that she was raising three orphaned cheetah cubs, and invited Karin to come over to her place the following day and meet them as well.

After a most enjoyable evening, we said our goodbyes and drove to the Pamuzinda Safari Lodge.

The agenda for the following morning was that Andy would meet us at the lodge directly after breakfast and escort us to the lion camp.

*

On our arrival at the lodge we were welcomed by the manager Hans Strijdom and other members of the staff. They escorted us to our chalets, carrying our luggage for us and enquiring if there was anything that we needed. We were rather surprised at the royal welcome. We were also surprised by the five-star luxury of our accommodation. Both the architectural design and the decor of the chalets portrayed ethnic royal culture, and the emphasis was on 'royal' comfort.

We hadn't expected such luxury and service, and it occurred to us that our visit was probably going to cost us a fortune. So we worried a little. Well, a lot actually. (Game rangers get paid mostly in sunsets.)

It was a cold night, but our chalets were nice and warm with oil heaters and there were hot-water bottles in our beds.

Karin's chalet was right next to ours, and after I'd been to say good-night to her I returned to find that Kobus was already in bed and half asleep.

'Come and get some sleep,' he murmured. 'Tomorrow is going to be a special day.'

I agreed that sleep was a good idea.

But I found that I was unable to fall asleep.

After a while I got up again, put on some warm clothes and walked out onto the wooden balcony. There were two deckchairs, so I made myself comfortable and spent the following hour or so gazing at the stars and the moon and the silhouettes of the trees that lined the banks of the Serui River below us. When I finally became drowsy and was about to go to bed, something happened that was so unexpectedly dramatic – so overwhelming in its emotional impact – that it seemed to me the whole world would stop and take note.

A lion started roaring, his magnificent voice rolling out over the dark landscape, silencing all other night sounds.

I knew it was Leo.

I listened and listened, mesmerized by the powerful, triumphant voice that soared out into the starry night: the voice of my foundling prince – now king – proclaiming his sovereignty over that strange land.

I was moved beyond imagining.

Leo continued roaring solo for several minutes, then another lion with a huskier voice joined in – Trade.

When the last echoes of the roaring duet finally died, I thought that sleep would never come to me that night.

But eventually it did, and I slept soundly for a few hours.

At dawn someone knocked at the door, bringing us a pot of steaming, aromatic coffee and informing us that breakfast would be served at seven.

Breakfast was an elaborate affair, served on a broad patio at the front of the lodge overlooking the Serui River. The winter morning was crisp and sunny and full of exuberant birdsong. We met our fellow tourists at breakfast and learned that they were from all over the world: the Netherlands, Australia, Canada.

Andy arrived with Fiona and joined us for a quick cup of coffee. After that we all set out for the lion camp in a custom-built safari Land-Rover.

A few minutes later we stopped at the gate of the camp. Andy opened it and we drove inside.

While driving about the camp, searching for the lions, Andy called out to Leo. After a while we spotted Fat Cat lying in the long grass under a sprawling acacia tree. As she lifted her head to peer at us over the grass, I was shocked at her size – she was enormous! Or had I simply forgotten again how big lions really were?

Kobus and Andy called out to Leo again, and then suddenly Karin exclaimed: 'There he is!'

He appeared from between the trees to our right and came running towards us. My heart caught in my throat – he was so *big*, bigger even than Fat Cat, but his eyes and features were the same, and so unbearably familiar . . .

We all called his name, and he stopped in his tracks to stare at us, an expression of extreme puzzlement in his eyes. He recognized Andy, but he was unable to comprehend who the rest of us were.

Kobus got out of the Land-Rover and walked towards Leo, softly calling his name.

Leo turned his puzzled gaze towards Kobus. And then, all of a sudden, as if he had been struck by an immense revelation, his eyes came alive with a surge of recognition, of overwhelming surprise and of joy. With a deep shuddering groan, Leo rushed forward, throwing himself at Kobus while at the same time turning his body sideways to lessen the force of the impact. Kobus bent forward and, with both arms, hugged Leo's enormous head to him. They rubbed cheeks, heads and shoulders – over and over – talking non-stop to each other.

I was shaking like a leaf.

The moment was too big for me.

The moment was probably too big for Leo as well, for he was so overcome with joy at seeing Kobus again that he didn't even notice Karin and me.

So we got out of the Land-Rover and walked towards him, calling his name. Leo lifted his head to look at me, and there was that same surge of recognition, surprise and joy in his eyes all over again. As he rushed towards me, I was struck once more by his size – the top of his head would be on a level with my chin – and I feared that I would get hurt if he greeted me too boisterously. So I held my hands out in front of me, saying, 'No, Leo!' He stopped close to me, looking me in the eyes, his face crumpled up with emotion, asking me for a clue as to how he should greet me. I held out my arm to him and he clasped it between his jaws in a gentle, loving embrace. Then I threw my arms around his neck and hugged his enormous face to mine for a long time, my tears spilling onto his fur.

Finally I stepped back so that he could see Karin.

She stepped forward, saying his name, and once again he uttered that deep, shuddering groan. As she reached out to touch him he clasped her outstretched arm briefly between his jaws, as he'd done with mine. Then Karin hugged him to her and they cried to each other for a long while.

Afterwards Leo turned round to see where Kobus was, but as he rushed towards Kobus for another greeting, something strange and frightening happened. Leo suddenly stopped in his tracks, spun round and charged at the Land-Rover. Both Fiona and Andy were sitting in it. Throwing the upper part of his body into the vehicle, Leo snarled at Andy and Fiona in a threatening way. Andy was totally taken by surprise. Leo had never behaved even remotely aggressively towards him – why was he so angry with him now? Andy tried to talk with Leo about it, asking him, 'Hey, Leo, what's the matter? What have I done wrong?'

Leo only got angrier and his snarls became more threatening.

Andy shouted at Leo to stop. Kobus called loudly to Leo in order to get him away from the vehicle. Fortunately Leo turned and rushed back to Kobus for another fond greeting.

At that moment, Fat Cat – who was still lying in the grass under the acacia tree, less than ten metres from us – started calling to Leo.

It occurred to me that she might be jealous of Karin and me. Hand-reared lions, as well as lions who live in close association with people, do not always draw a clear distinction in their minds between humans and lions, and so they tend to become jealous of human members of the same sex who pay too much attention to their spouses.

Andy suggested that Karin and I get back into the Land-Rover just in case Fat Cat wasn't too happy with us.

Leo ignored Fat Cat's calls and continued to rub heads with Kobus, grunting and groaning with joy. Then, suddenly, Leo spun round and charged the Land-Rover again, roaring with anger. At that moment I realized what the reason for his behaviour was. He wanted the Land-Rover with Andy and Fiona out of his camp; he wanted to be left alone with his family from the past.

As he threw the top part of his body into the vehicle once more, snarling with fury, Andy reached for his rifle. It was a very frightening moment. Fiona clambered to the back of the Land-Rover to be out of Leo's reach. Andy shouted at Leo, cocking his rifle in case he needed to fire a shot into the air. Karin and I were also in the Land-Rover now, planting ourselves firmly between Leo and the ashen-faced Fiona. As Leo continued to snarl and growl at us, his jaws wide open, his face crumpled up with confused emotions, I knew that not only was he commanding Andy and Fiona to leave, he was also begging Karin and me to get out of the Land-Rover and stay with him and Kobus.

Poor Leo. He was so scared that Andy and the Land-Rover would take us all away from him again.

Kobus finally managed to get Leo away from the Land-Rover and to keep him occupied long enough for the rest of us to have a quick conference on the situation. It was obvious that, if Andy and Fiona didn't leave, Leo would continue to threaten them. Karin suggested that she and I get out again and stay with Kobus and Leo, allowing Andy and Fiona to leave. But Andy said no. He was responsible for our safety and couldn't leave Karin and me in the camp without protection against the two lionesses. It seemed the only solution was for all of us to leave, and then continue our visit with Leo from behind the safety of the fence. The idea broke my heart, but I didn't want things to go wrong. Leo was obviously overwhelmed and he needed to calm down a bit.

So, after Leo had charged the Land-Rover a third time, it was agreed that we should leave.

Andy started the Land-Rover and drove slowly towards Kobus and Leo, allowing Kobus to get onto the moving vehicle before Leo could decide to do the same. As we drove back towards the gate, Leo ran alongside us, begging us not to leave him. Kobus tried, with a reassuring tone of voice, to explain that we weren't leaving.

Meanwhile Graeme and Julie had arrived to witness our reunion with Leo, and their truck was parked at the gate. When they saw us approaching, they hurriedly opened the gate, closing it again behind us. Andy parked outside the gate. Kobus, Karin and I got out and hurried over to Leo who was standing at the fence, calling to us.

We took turns rubbing heads and shoulders with him through the wire, over and over, and we stuck our arms through the fence to touch his face and stroke his head. And all the while he uttered an endless stream of grunts and groans, as if he were trying to tell us a thousand things. Occasionally Fat Cat would call out to him. But Leo ignored her. He wanted only to be with us.

After a while we began to feel emotionally exhausted – the way one feels when joy and sorrow get all mixed up and out of control. We needed a break from it all. And so did Leo, I thought.

So we said goodbye, and Andy drove us back to the lodge.

After lunch, Kobus decided to go back to Leo. He wanted to visit him in his camp again, and Andy offered to escort him. Kobus suggested that they go in our car rather than in the open Land-Rover. Perhaps Leo would object less to Andy's presence if he waited in a closed car.

I decided to stay at the lodge. I needed to be alone for a while in order to decipher my mixed-up emotions.

Fiona invited Karin to go home with her to meet the three cheetah cubs she was raising. Karin was very excited at the prospect, and I was pleased that Fiona had asked her.

After everyone had left, I retired to the balcony of my chalet. The quiet beauty of the Serui River landscape put me in a calmer mood, so I set about sorting out my discordant feelings.

First, I played a rerun of the morning's rendezvous in my mind, and I tried to tell myself that it had been a very happy occasion.

But a huge lump settled in my throat.

Why did it make me sad that Leo had been so overwhelmed with joy at seeing us again? Naturally I had hoped that he would be happy to see us. But the intensity of his joy had somehow caught me unprepared.

I thought about it.

And a phrase came to mind: 'Your joy is your sorrow unmasked' – the words of the Lebanese poet Kahlil Gibran.

The idea only deepened my sadness.

But then I remembered the very first expression in Leo's eyes when he recognized us. It had been an expression of surprise. And it occurred to me that, for Leo, the surprise must have been more than over-whelming. He hadn't seen us for a whole year. And he'd had no way of knowing that we were coming. We had simply appeared from nowhere, unexpected, unannounced.

So perhaps it was his surprise at seeing us again that had been so extreme, and not his joy.

I hoped that was the case.

But I wasn't sure.

Kobus returned an hour or so later and told me that the visit had gone well. At first Leo had once again overreacted at the sight of him, but after a while he had calmed down. Andy had remained inside the car, and although Leo had initially tried to chew the car up a bit, he'd finally lost interest in it and decided to sit down and enjoy Kobus's visit.

Kobus suggested that Karin and I go back to visit Leo on our own. He believed that Leo would be better able to cope with his emotions if we didn't all visit him at the same time.

So we drove to Fiona's house to fetch Karin. But there was nobody home. We drove over to Julie's and Graeme's house. There was nobody home there either. Kobus and I spent a while playing with the hyena cubs. They were the cutest, craziest young animals I'd ever met.

Eventually we returned to Fiona's house and found that she and Karin had just come back from a visit to Leo. Karin explained that, after she and Fiona had bathed and fed the cheetah cubs, she had wanted to go to Leo, and so Fiona had walked with her to the lion camp. Fiona had waited at a distance while Karin had gone up to the fence and called to Leo. He came to her immediately, and the two of them spent a wonderful hour together.

I was happy for her.

Kobus and Karin drove with me to Leo's camp, and Kobus parked some distance away to allow me to visit Leo on my own.

I went up to the fence, calling his name. He didn't come. I walked some distance along the wire but couldn't find him. He was obviously in another part of the camp. So I went back to the car and we drove halfway round the camp.

Again I walked along the fence for some distance, and then I spotted the three lions lying together under some shady trees. Leo lifted his head in my direction and pricked up his ears. And the next moment he was rushing towards me, answering my call with loud grunts. As he reached the fence I pressed my head and shoulders to the wire. He put his enormous face against mine, groaning in that deep, shuddering way of his. Then we sat down on either side of the fence. I stuck my arm through the wire and stroked his head and face. We talked of a thousand things, and it felt so good. Leo was in a much calmer mood now, and so was I.

While Leo and I talked, I noticed that both Fat Cat and Happie were watching us and I wondered what they were thinking.

Karin and Kobus got out of the car and came over to join me. As Leo saw them approaching, he leaped up and called to them. He greeted them joyfully, and we all sat down to a very happy family reunion.

After a while Happie got up and strolled towards us. Focusing her gaze on me, she came right up to the fence and began to rub her head and shoulders seductively against the wire, inviting me to a feline greeting. I felt a little apprehensive about the invitation but decided to humour her. She was, after all, Leo's wife. So I got up and pressed my shoulder to the wire. But Kobus said, 'No, don't! Look at her tail!'

Her tail was straight up in the air, the tuft jerking spasmodically, signifying feline hostility and mischief.

I hastily stepped back from the wire, wondering if Happie was still remembering the day that my hand had smelt of Wolfie.

At dusk we saw an African man carrying a sack up to a far corner of the camp where the lions had their sleeping quarters. The man removed several dead chickens from the sack and deposited them in the camp. Leo and the lionesses rushed over to enjoy their supper. The man then walked over to Trade's camp, which was right opposite the sleeping quarters of the main camp, and dispensed more chickens.

While Leo and the lionesses were eating, we walked over to Trade's camp to say hello to him.

He'd been asleep at the time of the food delivery, and as we reached his camp he was just waking up and staggering to his feet. After a good stretch, he gave us a friendly but very myopic look. We moved closer so that he could see us better. He peered at Kobus and me with a look that seemed to say, 'Ah, yes. I've seen the two of you somewhere before. How are you? Now, if you'll excuse me, I'd like to have my dinner.'

Old Trade sniffed at his chickens and then sat down with a contented grunt to enjoy his meal. Most of his lower teeth were missing, so he ate slowly, but without too much difficulty.

After dinner, Trade tottered down to the bottom of his camp and stood there for a while, contemplating his surroundings. Then he drew in his breath and started roaring. His voice was husky but still very powerful. He continued roaring for several minutes, and when he was finally satisfied that he'd done a good job of broadcasting his sovereignty to the world, he turned round to see what the other lions were doing. Fat Cat was still busy eating, but Leo and Happie were gazing at him with pure admiration. Old Trade walked back to his lair, stretched himself out on the straw and, with a contented sigh, went back to sleep.

We said goodnight to Trade, and then to Leo and the lionesses. Leo invited us with pleading grunts to stay the night. I explained to him that I didn't altogether trust his wife, Happie, but promised that we would be back the next morning.

Andy came over to the lodge early the following morning to have breakfast with us. He was looking very pleased with himself and told us that he had just been to Leo's camp. He'd been feeling very hurt at the way Leo had treated him the previous day, so he'd decided to pay him a private visit to talk things over. As soon as he'd parked inside the camp that morning, Leo came rushing to him and gave him his usual exuberant welcome. I was very pleased for Andy. His story proved my theory that Leo had not really been angry at him the previous day. He'd merely wanted his family from the past all to himself for a while without any interference.

*

We spent the rest of the week visiting Leo, relaxing at the lodge and enjoying the company of Andy, Graeme, Julie and Fiona. I missed Maria, and wished she would come back before we left.

Our host and hostess at the lodge, Hans Strijdom and his wife Diana, treated us as special guests and made our visit most enjoyable. The lodge organized sightseeing safaris for their guests, and although we were often invited to join them, we declined. We wanted to spend as much time as possible with Leo.

Initially Hans, his wife and the two safari guides were the only people at the lodge who knew the real reason for our visit to Pamuzinda. We decided to keep it that way and not to mention anything to the other visitors, as we didn't want to be the centre of conversation at every mealtime.

But Hans had two little dogs (half Maltese and half something else) who changed all this for us. They never barked at any of the other guests – only at us. Every time we arrived back at the lodge after a visit to Leo, the two little brats would bark their heads off.

The reason, of course, was that we smelled of lion.

To make matters worse, they followed us to the dinner table and spent the entire mealtime sniffing our legs under the table, making growling noises.

One of the guests eventually remarked that the dogs appeared to have some special interest in South Africans, and so Hans came out with the truth and explained the real reason for the dogs' behaviour. After that, of course, there was no getting away from it: we became the centre of attention, and every mealtime was dominated by questions about Leo.

All the guests were moved by Leo's story. And although they had all been to the lion camp during one of the sightseeing safaris, every one of them expressed the wish to see the lions again. So the safari guides promised to take them there once more.

One of the guides later told us that Leo was fast becoming the most photographed lion in Africa.

*

One day, while we were having tea on the patio with some of the other guests, Karin decided that she wanted to explore the scenery on the other side of the river. Unaware that guests were not supposed to leave the area around the lodge unescorted, she set off and walked down the river bank. This was the dry season and so the river, a seasonal one, was dry except for a few stream-linked pools.

All conversation on the patio ceased as the guests turned their heads to watch Karin walking off into the dangerous wilderness. Some of them voiced their concern, but Kobus reassured them, explaining that, having grown up in the wilds, Karin was more than capable of looking after herself.

There was a sign nailed to a tree on the river bank bearing the legend: DANGER: DO NOT GO BEYOND THIS POINT. Karin reached the tree and stopped to read the sign. Having done so, she promptly ignored it and disappeared over the far bank of the river. She knew that, apart from crocodiles, no other man-eating carnivores roamed Pamuzinda. Leo and his family were the only big cats on the estate and they, of course, lived in their own camp.

While Karin was gone, four young elephants turned up to drink at the pan. And as we sat watching them from the terrace, the guests got even more agitated. What if the elephants were still there when Karin returned? How would she get safely past them?

The elephants did in fact stay on, spending most of the afternoon grazing on the river bank. But I wasn't worried about Karin. She would see the elephants, of course, and find another route back to the lodge.

Having done just that, Karin returned an hour or so later and reported that she'd come across a lovely variety of animals on her walk.

On the evening of our last day at Pamuzinda, Kobus and I went to Hans's office to settle our account. We were pleasantly surprised to learn that Carol and Vivian Bristow had arranged with Hans to charge us only half the normal price. And even the normal price was not as high as we'd expected it to be. We were even more surprised – and touched – when Hans decided not to charge us anything for our last day at Pamuzinda.

'But why?' we asked.

'Because you're Leo's parents,' he replied.

We appreciated the kind gesture immensely.

Early the following morning, Andy arrived to escort Kobus to the lion camp for a final 'inside-the-camp' visit to Leo. The plan was that we would all visit Leo again after breakfast to say our goodbyes through the fence. But Karin suddenly wanted desperately to go along with Andy and Kobus to visit Leo inside his camp. So I gave my permission, if rather reluctantly, making her promise that she would stay close to the car and watch out for the lionesses at all times.

I longed to go with them as well, but my problem was adrenaline. Every time Happie fixed me with her mischievous gaze, I'd become jittery. And I didn't want to smell of adrenaline while inside the camp with the lionesses.

To an animal, fear and aggression have the same smell: that of adrenaline. So it's not wise to smell of adrenaline in a wild animal's company – your fear might be mistaken for aggression.

I stayed at the lodge and finished our packing.

When Kobus and Karin returned from their visit, I saw that Karin was looking sad. I asked Kobus about it. He said that Leo had been in a boisterous mood. As soon as Karin got out of the car, Leo was all over her, begging her to play with him. Karin was quite willing to play, but Kobus and Andy agreed that a wrestling game with Leo was no longer safe for Karin. Leo weighed more than 200 kilograms now. Moreover, the lionesses had sensed Leo's boisterous mood and it made them restless. So Karin had been ordered back into the car.

I felt so sorry for her. I could well imagine how much she longed to play with Leo again. I had that same longing.

After a quick breakfast, we said goodbye to everyone at the lodge and packed up to leave.

Andy came to the car to see us off.

As Karin opened the back door to get into the car, I was surprised to see a gaping hole in the seat's upholstery. Kobus explained that Leo had done it. That's how boisterous his mood had been that morning.

I wondered if our insurance people would believe the story.

We said goodbye to dear Andy and thanked him for everything. He had done so much for Leo and for us. He promised to keep in touch with us and to let us know as soon as there was any indication that Leo was to become a father.

Kobus, Karin and I arrived at Leo's camp for our final visit.

We found the three lions enjoying the early morning sun in a grassy patch near the south fence of the camp. Leo leaped up and came running to us. After the usual happy greetings, we all sat down and talked.

We talked of many things – of Wolfie, Hettie, Sandra and Paul who had all sent him their love, and of all the good times of the past.

Leo gave us his full attention, his ears pricked, his gaze focused on us with warmth and affection.

It was altogether a very lovely visit.

Eventually Fat Cat called to Leo. He answered her with a grunt. Then he looked at us with an expression that seemed to say, 'Excuse me, I have to go now. The wife is calling.' He got up and walked back to the lionesses, flopping down in the grass next to them but keeping his gaze focused fondly on us.

I wanted some photographs of Leo and the lionesses, but they were too far from the fence for nice close-ups. So Kobus offered to go into the camp and take the photos for me.

As Kobus walked up to them, I watched the lionesses closely but they seemed unperturbed by his presence.

While Kobus was taking the pictures, I thought of the photos we had taken of Leo at Pamuzinda the previous year: there had been a lot of tension in his eyes and in the lines on his face then, and for many months afterwards I had been unable to look at those photographs without feeling incredibly sad.

Now, as he posed for photographs with his wives, he looked regal and handsome, and the expression on his face was of contentment and well-being. I looked forward to having my new photos of Leo, and to placing them in my photo album right next to the sad ones of the previous year. They would provide my photo album as well as my memory album of Leo with a happy ending.

Eventually we called Leo back to us to say our goodbyes.

We rubbed heads and pressed our faces to his in farewell, and when my turn came I sat down and talked to him for a while, explaining to him that we had to go home now but that we would be back for another visit some day soon. I told him how good it had been to see him again, and how precious my memories of him would always be to me.

All through my speech he paid close attention to the tone of my voice, and when I had finished, he tilted his head to one side – in the same way that a human does when smiling at a loved one – and his rust-coloured eyes were warm with love and trust.

I knew then that Leo was happy: happy to be a lion, and to be among lions, and happy that we had visited him and shown him that we had not forgotten him.

Fat Cat called to him again. She was evidently getting to be a rather possessive wife. Leo got up and walked back to the lionesses.

As we drove off, we leaned out through the windows, waving and calling goodbye to Leo and his family.

And so I buried my heart at Pamuzinda.

ALL THINGS WILD AND WONDERFUL

SHORTLY AFTER OUR RETURN FROM ZIMBABWE, A ROGUE ELEPHANT bull got into the habit of vandalizing our neighbours' gardens at night. I knew our garden would soon get its turn, but hoped it wouldn't happen before Kobus got home. (He was attending a meeting in the north of the park.)

But, of course, my luck didn't hold. I was woken late one night by the resounding clanging of a steel fence in trouble. Jumping out of bed I rushed outside, calling to the dogs for assistance.

They obligingly barked at the elephant as loudly as they could, while I shouted at him at the top of my voice. Finally the elephant got the message and turned away, but by then he'd already broken a fence post, pulled part of the wire down and demolished half a tree.

He came back again the following night, bringing a friend with him. Fortunately Kobus had returned home, so I woke him up.

'Please go and talk to the elephants,' I asked him. 'You have a better elephant-deterrent voice than I have.'

Kobus jumped out of bed, pulled on a pair of shorts and rushed outside, calling to me to bring him an egg.

An egg? I thought. Now what does the man want with an egg?

But I didn't argue: I took him the egg.

He threw it at one of the elephants, hitting it square on the shoulder. The elephant lifted its trunk and pressed it to its shoulder, sniffing at the spot where the egg had splattered.

'*Aargh!*' he screamed and fled into the night, followed closely by his friend.

They never returned.

I liked what I'd learned.

Next time, instead of yelling my lungs out, I would simply hurl a couple of eggs at the intruders.

A few nights later we were woken by lions roaring so close to us that the whole house trembled. Kobus leaped out of bed like a bolt of lightning.

'Where are you going?' I asked in alarm.

'I forgot to close the gate,' he replied.

I thought of our dogs and our horses, and I jumped out of bed.

Kobus was in such a hurry to get outside to close the gate that he didn't waste time putting on a pair of shorts first. (He doesn't own pyjamas. Excuse me for mentioning this, but it's relevant to the story.)

'Shall I bring some eggs?' I called after him.

But he didn't hear me. He was already outside and heading towards the gate at top speed.

It occurred to me that a naked human might look very edible to a hungry lion, so I ran after Kobus. The roaring started up again, and I felt as if I were running straight towards an earthquake.

As soon as I rounded the bend at the fishpond, I saw two enormous lions standing right at the open gate.

Stopping dead in my tracks I screamed at Kobus to come back.

I needn't have bothered. The lions took one look at Kobus and fled. And they didn't utter another sound all night. Evidently they'd never seen a naked human before, and they were shocked speechless.

I supposed there was something to learn from this episode as well, but I decided I'd rather stick to the egg trick.

*

It was late winter now, and the grass cover in the veld was getting sparse. A herd of impala and a few bushbuck took to grazing in our garden. Naturally we were delighted to have them. They became so tame that one could walk right up to them and have a chat. Wolfie and Jasper left them in peace.

The nice thing about herding dogs is that they are so tolerant of wild animals. Though they have a tendency to herd them, they will not harass them.

Even from an early age, Jasper's herding instincts were so strong that he used to get into our fishpond to herd the fish. At first he tried to herd everything that moved, but Wolfie, acting as his role model, taught him that antelope and other small animals were not to be disturbed. Only baboons and monkeys, if found in the garden, were to be herded out at top speed.

One afternoon in late winter, when Karin took the dogs for a walk down into the valley, a herd of impala came fleeing out of the bush, crossing the track right in front of her. Karin and the two dogs stopped, waiting to see what the impala were fleeing from. A pack of wild dogs came charging out of the bush, also crossing the track right in front of them, but slamming on their brakes to stop and stare curiously at Karin and her two companions.

Karin commanded Wolfie and Jasper to stay with her and be quiet, which the good dogs promptly did. Wolfie stood protectively between Karin and the wild dogs, keeping a very watchful eye on them. Jasper, who had never met wild dogs before, tried to look invisible behind Karin's legs.

The wild dogs studied Karin and her companions for a while, then the leader of the pack started edging towards them, his eyes full of curiosity. Wolfie wasn't too happy about this. So he took a few steps forward with hair bristling and upper lip lifted in a warning that said, 'Don't you dare come any closer to Karin.'

Karin, enjoying the unique encounter, knew that the wild dogs were only curious and that they intended her no harm. Unfortunately, as soon

as Wolfie started moving towards the leader, the whole pack suddenly became restless.

Sensing the change in the pack's mood Karin knew that she would be unable to protect her two dogs if the pack came for them. Disappointed that the meeting had to end this way, she flung her arms into the air and shouted at the wild dogs to go away. They turned and fled.

The spring rains came early, and a funny thing happened right after the first rains. In the evening, as I was feeding the fish, a little terrapin climbed out of the fishpond and studied my foot.

Not believing what I was seeing, I bent down to have a closer look. He lifted his funny little face and looked me straight in the eyes.

Perhaps I was being over-fanciful, but it seemed to me that the expression on his face said: 'Are you my mommy?'

'No,' I told him hastily. 'I'm not. I'm a primate, see? A mammal. We're not even distantly related.'

He looked down at my foot again, and took an experimental taste of my toe.

'Oh, you're hungry?' I said. 'OK, I'll get you something to eat.

But that still doesn't make me your mommy, understand?'

I fetched him a few slivers of chicken from the fridge. To my surprise, he ate it right out of my hand.

After that, every evening when I went to feed the fish, he got out of the pond and demanded that I feed him as well. I kept telling him that I was not his mommy, just the lady from the Welfare Society. But the silly little creature appeared to have bonded with me. If I tried to introduce him to Kobus or the children, he got shy and ducked into the water.

Why would he allow only me to feed him?

I knew that a terrapin had a lifespan of a few hundred years, which probably meant that it had a very long childhood – about fifty years or so.

I didn't want to be a terrapin-mother for the rest of my life.

Annette said my problem was that I had an aura about me that transmitted a message to all strays and orphans that I was their mother.

I don't think she was right. I think animals are just extraordinarily good at spotting humans like me who can't say no to them.

Believe me, animals are far cleverer than we think they are. They sense things that we don't even know about.

Which reminds me of something that happened back in 1994.

A few weeks after we'd returned from our first visit to Zimbabwe – the one when we'd taken Leo to Pamuzinda – I drove to Hazyview one day to buy some groceries, and I forgot to stop at a four-way intersection. At that very moment another motorist also forgot to stop at the intersection, and so we collided right in the middle of the crossing. Fortunately no-one was injured, but both our cars were badly smashed up and had to be towed away.

I felt so awful. I'd never before been involved in a car accident. And I knew that the only reason I'd had the accident was because I'd been thinking of Leo instead of paying attention to my driving.

I spent the rest of the day feeling incredibly sorry for myself. When I got home, I paced the garden – up and down, up and down – wondering why life was treating me so badly.

When I got tired of pacing, I sat down on the grass and stared into the marula woodland. And there stood a waterbuck bull, contemplating me with an expression that seemed to say: 'Lady, what *is* the matter?'

So I told him what the matter was, explaining how I'd lost my lion as well as my thumb and my car.

He just went right on staring at me with wise, soulful eyes.

After a while I asked him, 'Well, aren't you going to say anything?'

He walked off into the bush.

But it didn't matter.

A therapist would have looked at his watch and told me my time was up. And he would have sent me a bill. And he wouldn't have listened to my story with such soulful eyes.

And, anyway, I was feeling much better.

We have a beach cottage in the Eastern Cape, and shortly after our return from our second trip to Pamuzinda it occurred to Kobus and me that we hadn't been to our cottage for almost four years – we'd been too busy raising orphans and getting chomped by lions. We decided to plan a family holiday for the coming summer.

So as soon as all the children had finished their year-end exams, we packed two cars full of people and dogs and set out for Paradise Beach.

Paradise Beach is a stretch of wooded dunes and wide sandy beaches between the Seekoei River and the Krom River in the Eastern Cape. A quiet, out-of-the-way place, it has only a small scattering of privately owned beach houses. Seagulls and many species of waterbirds abound in the area, while small mammals such as bushbuck, genets, monkeys and mongooses inhabit the wooded dunes. Dolphins and whales are often seen playing in the sparkling coastal waters.

We had a truly splendid vacation.

Clever Wolfie, who always knows what life is all about, spent most of his days sitting on the beach – on a beach towel under a beach umbrella, contemplating the sea. (All he needed was a pair of sunglasses to complete the picture.) Jasper worked very hard, charging up and down the dunes, across the beach and into the surf, battling to get the seagulls to stay together in a herd. The children swam and surfed, went fishing and snorkelling and supplied us with all kinds of delicious seafood.

One day, as Kobus and I were walking along the beach we saw a school of dolphins swimming round and round in a wide circle just beyond the breakers. We went through the surf and swam out towards them. Allowing us to come very close they circled us for a long time. We could hear the mothers calling out to their young. At times they were so near we could have reached out and touched them. But we didn't – in case they didn't want us to. They were taking such care not to touch or bump into us, so perhaps they expected the same courtesy. It was pure magic to be surrounded by animals of such incredible beauty and grace. We spent almost an hour among them.

Afterwards Kobus and I agreed that many of life's most wonderful moments were those shared in friendship with wild animals.

We all need animals. Just think how lonely the world would be without them – as Chief Seathl wrote in his letter to the United States President in 1855: 'If all the beasts were gone from the earth, man would die from great loneliness of spirit.'

We returned from our vacation in the Eastern Cape a few days before Christmas. The bushlands were glowing with the green sheen of generous summer rains. The animals looked fat and healthy. It was good to be back.

On Christmas Eve we all climbed to the top of Shabeni to watch the sun set.

A troop of baboons sat on a clifftop nearby, discussing us and other things among themselves. The sun set lazily, hovering above the horizon in a blaze of reds and purples. From the bushlands below echoed the calls of guinea fowl and francolin. The last rays of sunlight played on stands of silver cluster-leaf trees, turning them into wispy clouds of aquamarine. As the familiar feel of wilderness and solitude settled in my soul, my thoughts wandered to Mahlangeni and lingered there a while.

Part of me still belonged to that wild and lonely Eden, and always would, but I no longer regretted having moved away. The years after had brought us to other Edens, and had filled my heart with new and precious memories.

A booming bark interrupted my reverie. It came from one of the baboons on the nearby clifftop, presumably the leader, who wished to remind us who was boss in the area.

Kobus answered him with a friendly salute.

From the thickets at the foot of the koppie emerged a handsome giraffe couple. Sampling the greenery along the southern slope of Shabeni, they began munching their way higher up the koppie.

We sat so quietly that they didn't see us until they were quite close. Stopping mid-munch, with leaves dangling from their mouths, they fixed us with puzzled gazes.

A martial eagle landed on a rocky ledge nearby. Folding its wings and turning its head towards us, it fixed us with an imperial stare.

The baboons, of course, were also still studying us.

'We are being watched,' I murmured to Kobus.

'Always,' he said. 'The bush is full of eyes.'

It occurred to me that we'd had this conversation before – in fact on many occasions. In the wilds you are never alone. You are known. You are part of nature.

The crimson sun had disappeared over the distant hills, and now only pale gold rimmed the horizons. Soon the smoky-blue veil of dusk settled over the bushlands below until they became hazy and ethereal, like a dream dissolving, and the evening breeze was full of the whisper of ancient memories.

From somewhere between the night and us rose the stirring cry of a jackal.

We said goodbye to the baboons, to the giraffe couple and to the eagle, and started climbing back to earth.

But just before we did, I stood for a moment to absorb the silvery magic of the wilderness twilight.

And a phrase came to mind.

Ici reste mon coeur. Here remains my heart.

POSTSCRIPT

LEO BECAME A FATHER IN JULY 1996 WHEN FAT CAT GAVE BIRTH TO three beautiful female cubs. In November of the same year Happie had a single cub, a little male, called Oscar – the spitting image of his father. In May 1998 Happie again gave birth to a single male cub, a lovely fellow named Freddie. Of all the cubs, Oscar remains the one that most resembles his father in looks and temperament, and he is often called Leo Junior.

ACKNOWLEDGEMENTS

FOR THEIR HELP IN THE PREPARATION OF THIS BOOK I AM DEEPLY INDEBTED to my agent, Carole Blake; my editor, Francesca Liversidge; my copy-editor, Deborah Adams; and Julia Lloyd, Alison Martin, Emma Dowson and all the rest of the wonderful Transworld team.